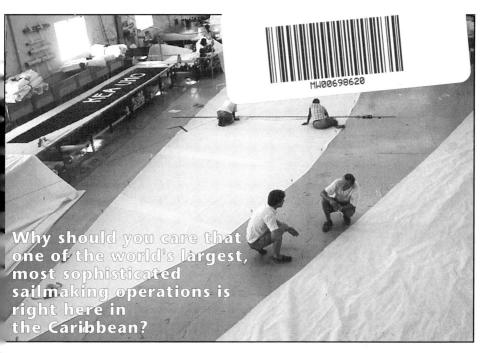

CRUISING GUIDE TO

Text and charts by
Chris Doyle
and
Jeff Fisher
Illustrations
Sally Erdle

Photos by:
Jeff Fisher

Other contributing photographer
Aerial of Bonaire by
Jerry Schnabel

PUBLISHED BY

CHRIS DOYLE PUBLISHING
in association with
CRUISING GUIDE PUBLICATIONS

ISBN 0-944428--38-X

First Published as *Cruising Guide to Trinidad and Tobago, Venezuela and Bonaire* in 1994

This Venezuela and Bonaire edition published 1997

DISTRIBUTION

USA AND WORLDWIDE
Cruising Guide Publications,
P.O. Box 1017
Dunedin, Florida 34697-1017
Tel: 813-733-5322 Fax: 813-734-8179
orders only: 800-330-9542

CARIBBEAN
Jeff Fisher
c/o Tikal, box 51, Young Street,
St. George's, Grenada
Tel:809-440-2310
Tel/Fax:809-440-2556
e-mail: fisher@caribsurf.com

VENEZUELA AND BONAIRE

USING THIS BOOK

In the text and our directory at the back of the book we give the telephone numbers of business establishments and the credit cards they accept. We also give a very rough price guide to the restaurants. This is an idea of what you might spend to eat out and have a drink per person. Our guide runs as follows:

$A is $50 U.S. or over
$B is $25 to $50 U.S.
$C is $12 to $25 U.S.
$D is under $12 U.S.

We use the following abbreviations:

F = Facsimile T = Telephone
cc = Credit card A = American Express, Dn = Diner's Club, Ds = Discover, V = Visa group, including Master Card, Barclaycard and Eurocard.

In our sketch charts the main shoal areas are marked in yellow with major reefs and rocks with crosses. These have been drawn for yachts drawing up to about 6.5 feet of water. Those navigating deeper draft yachts will have to refer to the depths on their charts. On some charts we have also used dotted lines to delineate areas of shallower navigable water from deeper. We have only done this where it seemed helpful to clarify the depths.

Compass roses point to true north, but where we give bearings they are magnetic.

Latitude and longitude, where given, were taken by GPS using a Garmin 50 set on WGS 84 map datum.

In this book we have not included the Venezuelan part of the Gulf of Paria, or approaches to the Orinoco River.

NOTICE

The information in this guide was correct to the best of our knowledge at the time of going to press.

No warranty, expressed or implied, is made by the publishers for any errors or omissions in this publication. The skipper must use this guide together with proper charts and other navigational aids and not place undue credence in the accuracy of this guide. This guide should not be used for navigation.

AUTHOR'S ACKNOWLEDGMENTS

Special thanks to all those who sent us information. These include Gerard van Erp, Manuel at MBS, Marianella, Peter Burch, Gail Borzilleri, Tom Massopust, Olof & Katrin Hansen, Guy and Anita Comeau, Tom & Gerdie van Oudgaarden, Leonard Connely, Coleen Ryan & Brian Savage, Tony Taylor, Sissel & Tor Gransaether, Jean-Pierre Ancot, Peter Fixman and Jan on Mary C. This is by no means a complete list, we have some good reports where the names have become detached. Anyway, thank you, all of you, we appreciated all your help and we did use most of the information in this update.

El Oculto

CRUISING
GUIDE
TO
VENEZUELA
& BONAIRE

Thank you for buying this book. If you find it useful, please encourage others to do the same. We depend on cruising sailors to make this book work. We want to keep this book up-do-date, which means a new edition every two or three years. To do that we need to sell one to just about everyone who goes down there plus a few.

We are happy to accept advertising. It gives extra information and helps keep the price of the book reasonable. If you wish to keep it that way, tell all the restaurateurs, services and shopkeepers "I read about it in the Cruising Guide" it helps us no end.

In this edition we have gone to color sketch charts. We feel that they are much more readable than the old hand-drawn black and white ones. We feel this is particularly important in this guide where these sketch charts are often the only thing available for many anchorages. It has increased our printing cost a little which is reflected in the price of the book. However, with over a hundred sketch charts, loads of information and many aerial photographs, we still think it is a bargain when you consider it is still less than the price of just two charts.

Would you like to be part of an information exchange on this area? This is a rapidly changing area and one in which rumor is often easier to come by than fact. Security is a big issue these days, and it is very hard for us to assess just how things are. Those with bad news tend to shout it loud, but how many people are cruising around in deserted anchorages without a problem? Please let us know of your experiences both bad and good. Business cards from those you have found particularly helpful or difficult would be appreciated. If you are looking for updated information or have specific questions about Venezuela we will do our best to help. Either way contact Jeff Fisher as follows:

Jeff Fisher
P.O. Box 51,
St. George's
Grenada, W.I
Phone and Fax: 809-440-2556
email: fisher@caribsurf.com

Have a wonderful time!
Chris Doyle and Jeff Fisher

Venezuela covers the northeastern part of South America. It is a beautiful country, vast enough to offer all kinds of landscapes and climates. There are rainforests, deserts, idyllic islands and Andean mountains so tall they are capped in snow. There are immense areas of mangroves and savannas with table mountains. Here you find the world's tallest waterfall, Angel Falls.

Venezuelan society has been influenced by Indian civilizations, Spanish conquest and a long hard struggle for independence. Today it is a thriving independent country with a Spanish tradition. Oil is a major resource and Venezuelans are technologically advanced.

Many yachtspeople visit Venezuela to haul out and refit their vessels. One of the big advantages of hauling here is that the coastal area around Puerto la Cruz and Cumaná is extremely dry, excellent for both drying out hulls and getting work done.

Venezuela offers superb cruising. You can get away from it all and find uncrowded and deserted anchorages. There are idyllic beaches and mangrove islands where you can watch parrots and scarlet ibis.

When you run out of time on your immigration card, it is sometimes more fun to sail to Bonaire than to deal with the officials to get an extension. Also for those heading west Bonaire is the gateway to the ABC islands.

Bonaire lies to the west of Venezuela's offshore islands and it is part of the Netherlands Antilles. Bonaire is small; you can drive right round it in a day with time to spare, but it is also delightful, with a sparkling clean town and clear water. It would take weeks to explore Bonaire's dive sites which are so good and plentiful that this diminutive island is a world class diving center. Bonaire produces salt and is also known for the delicate pink flamingos that come from Venezuela to feed on the salt flats.

While many boats visit Venezuela and Bonaire, it is still enough off the beaten track to bring out the adventurer in all of us.

Welcome to Venezuela and Bonaire!

INTRODUCTION

TABLE OF CONTENTS

Page

True Shell Shock.
Edna married a CLAM.
WHAT?
a BIVALVE?!!?
I can't believe it!
well, she always did go for those BIG MUSSELS...
OSIE '87

CRUISING INFORMATION

Cruising Comfort

The water temperature throughout this cruising area is a few degrees colder than in the Eastern Caribbean. It makes for pleasant swimming and a refreshing plunge in the heat of the day. Scuba divers and snorkelers who are sensitive to the cold might find a wet suit jacket helpful.

The wind often dies at night along the coast of Venezuela. This can make it warm for sleeping below, especially in marinas. Windscoops or efficient 12-volt fans are useful luxuries. Those planning to spend long periods in marinas might find a small air conditioning unit worthwhile.

Many interesting anchorages along Venezuela's coast are in mangrove lagoons or very close to shore. Considering this, they are far less buggy than one might expect. However, the odd whining mosquito often manages to find your ear in the middle of the night. Screening the cabins with mosquito netting, while not essential, may save you some aggravation. Screens are not necessary for sitting out in the cockpit. For those that do not have screens, a can of bug repellent and a pack of mosquito coils should suffice for the occasional buggy anchorage.

Fishing

Fishing is excellent throughout this region. The westerly setting equatorial current hits the continental shelf, causing colder nutrient rich water to rise from the sea bed. That old lure and line that has been hanging unsuccessfully over the stern of your yacht for hundreds of miles is likely to jump into action and surprise you.

In Venezuela spear fishing is forbidden in all park areas, which includes most of the best anchorages. In addition, when you are in some park areas, officials are likely to want to hold your speargun till you depart, which can be a hassle. My suggestion is to trade your speargun for a light casting rod. A trip out at daybreak or sunset will often bring in a tasty little barracuda or snapper. If you don't have any luck casting, troll behind the dinghy going close to mangroves and reefs with a small lure. If all else fails, trade or buy from the fishermen.

From our questioning of locals it appears that cigatera poisoning is extremely rare throughout this region. However, to ensure you own safety, avoid really big barracudas and jacks.

Swimming

Water clarity varies a lot with location. In the outer islands visibility can be fantastic, as can the snorkeling. Closer to shore some locations seem clear, others murky. The abundance of Christmas tree and fan worms makes for brightly colored underwater landscapes.

I have heard of no shark attacks or unusual aquatic dangers in Venezuela or Bonaire. Caimans and small crocodiles exist in some areas, but they prefer the muddy backwaters you are unlikely to swim in. Be aware of currents, watch where you put your feet, and enjoy the swimming and snorkeling.

Money Matters

The currency in Venezuela is the Bolívar and in Bonaire they use NA guilders. (Details are given under island sections.)

US dollars are welcome in Bonaire and are becoming more widely accepted in Venezuela.

US dollars can easily be changed into local currencies, but there is always a theft risk if you have too much cash.

Travelers checks are excellent and credit cards work very well. In Venezuela change houses, called cambios, are much quicker than banks. You can change cash and travelers checks in cambios, but you cannot get cash from credit cards except in a bank. Credit cards work well for goods and services throughout the region, though there have been occasional problems in Venezuela because of very high credit card charges.

Language

Spanish is spoken in Venezuela, and English is understood by only a small number of people. If you have a chance to learn some Spanish before you go, so much the better. If not, pack along some Spanish books or tapes and study as you go. It doesn't take much to pick up the basics necessary for shopping, traveling and going to restaurants. The people in Venezuela are generally very patient and kind to those struggling with their language. We have added some Spanish words and phrases in the back of this guide to help you along.

In Bonaire they speak Papiamento and Dutch. Luckily, both English and Spanish are also spoken.

Photography

Photographic supplies are available in the large towns in Venezuela and in Bonaire. Film is usually reasonably priced. First rate facilities are there for developing and printing your print film. Slide film can also be developed fast and well but it has to be the E6 process type (Fujichrome, Ectachrome). Some places are a bit careless with finger prints and hairs when they mount slides. Getting them unmounted avoids this problem and is less expensive. You can store unmounted slides in negative holders and buy reusable mounts to do the rest yourself. When you are leaving a major town to go cruising, buy plenty of film because nothing will be available in smaller towns and villages. For aquatic shots a polarizing filter brings out the water colors.

Medical Care

Medical care in Venezuela is excellent. Many people without insurance visit Venezuela for medical services as the cost is only a fraction of the USA.

It should be appreciated that Venezuela has first rate, up-to-date equipment even for highly specialized procedures. These include advanced eye-surgery both for the removal of growths and cataracts and for correction of lens shape. Venezuela's dentists are also highly trained, modern and reasonably priced.

We have listed some of the most used facilities in our directory section.

Bonaire is too small to have extensive medical facilities, but you can easily fly to neighboring Curacao.

Venezuela has abundant wildlife which includes poisonous snakes like the fer-de-lance, bushmaster and coral snake. There are also scorpions and centipedes. Most of these stay in the wilder regions. They don't present much danger as long as you keep your eyes open and tread carefully. Small ticks and biting insects can be more annoying. The liberal use of repellent or long pants and shoes and socks is advisable when you go exploring in the forest. Insect repellent can also be handy ashore in the evenings.

Drugs

Illegal drugs are taken very seriously by law enforcement officers throughout this area. Anyone getting caught even with one joint can expect confiscation of the yacht, a monster fine and a long jail term.

Vampire Bats

Sooner or later you will hear tales about vampire bats. These make wonderful after-dinner stories as you sit out in the cockpit: The quiet flutter of wings as you sleep; the tiny furry body that cuddles up ever so gently to your toes so as not to wake you; a small incision carefully made with razor sharp teeth and then the bat gently licks away the blood while you sweetly dream. As an actual threat they rank very low. They are unknown in Bonaire. In Venezuela bats have been known to feed on yachtspeople, but this is very rare.

Before 1987, when only a few hundred foreign yachts would cruise these water annually, I didn't hear of any attacks. I suspect the chances of being bitten are so low that there were just not enough yachts to make it likely. Now that two or three thousand yachts visit annually, there have been a handful of reports. I know of five over a six year period and three of these five attacks occurred in Isla Boracha. The others happened on the coastline between Isla Esmerelda and Cabo San Francisco.

Isla Boracha lies a few miles off Puerto La Cruz and there is a small fishing village in the anchorage. Villagers say that a few of them have been bitten by bats. The Venezuelan health authorities believe that there are no vampire bats in this area and that fruit bats are the culprits, perhaps mistaking pink toes for overripe cherries. The chances of getting bitten by a bat are very low unless you anchor in Isla Boracha. If the thought worries you, screens provide effective protection. Medically, a bite from a vampire bat would be trivial, were it not for a chance of contracting rabies. If you are the unlucky one who gets bitten, then a rabies shot is advisable. It is not worth taking chances with rabies.

Hepatitis and Cholera

We have not heard of any yachtsperson getting cholera. We have heard of a few cases of hepatitis. To be on the safe side, wash everything well and do not eat raw oysters or fish.

Security

Bonaire is probably among the safest places you will find in the Caribbean and no special precautions are necessary.

Venezuela appears to have more problems than the eastern Caribbean. One reason more boats are broken into in Venezuela is because yachtspeople behave differently. They sometimes stay for weeks or months anchored in major towns and theft is a problem worldwide in large cities with seaports often topping the list. The more boats there are anchored in a town the worse the theft seems to get.

More worrying are the increase in armed robbery and break-ins in quiet anchorages. This particularly effects yacht

VENEZUELA

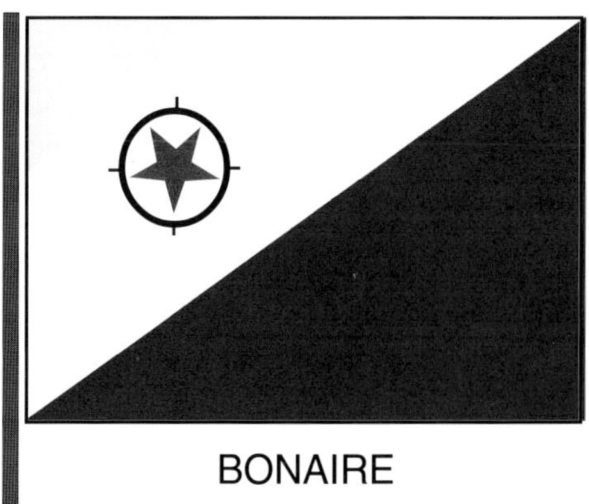
BONAIRE

NATIONAL FLAGS

in lonely spots. To date the main areas affected include Boca del Rio in Margarita, the west coast of the Peninsula de Araya and the Mochima National Park, though Mochima itself seems fine. The outer islands have a better record, and we have not heard of too much happening from Carenero west. Efforts have been made to curb crime in some areas, and some gangs have been caught. I would not let the thought of robbery deter me from cruising but I strongly recommend the following common sense precautions:

The most commonly stolen items are dinghies and outboards. Locking wires are not a sufficient deterrent at night and you should try to arrange some system of hoisting your dinghy and outboard out of the water. If this is not possible, remove your outboard at night and lock it on deck. Then lock your dinghy alongside the boat. Lock your dinghy whenever you leave it by day. If possible cruise to Venezuela with a battered looking solid dinghy and oars or an ancient 2-horse outboard.

Do not leave anything on deck including scuba tanks, snorkeling gear and washing hanging from the lifelines.

Be especially careful in large towns like Puerto La Cruz and Cumaná. Ask other yachts in the area how things are and leave someone on board at all times if necessary or go into a marina that has good security.

When you go ashore in Venezuela be streetwise. It is unwise to wear flashy jewelry. Pickpockets do exist, so stay aware of what is going on around you. Don't set your handbag or brief case down somewhere and move away. Take taxis at night if going through doubtful areas. If you are renting a car, do not leave anything valuable, even in the trunk. It is also advisable to use a wheel locking device if it is supplied. Do not keep large stashes of cash on board; use travellers checks and credit cards.

Before venturing into isolated areas, get local information on whether there have been any recent problems. You can ask other cruisers or request information on one of the "cruisers nets" that sometimes operate on the VHF. Listen also to the Caribbean Weather Net on Saturdays after the 4003 weather and on Sundays after the 8104 weather. Try to get information from people who have recently cruised where you are going. If you decide to anchor in a deserted area that may be risky, then figure a way to lock yourself in for the night. If anyone boards, use the VHF - if you cannot raise anyone, pretend that you have got through and speak loudly. Keep a fog horn handy which has a chance of scaring a prowler away.

Keep in mind most people cruise without having a problem, and those places where others fear to drop anchor are often some of the best.

The weather is generally pleasant, with temperatures of 78-85° Fahrenheit year round. The Venezuelan coast varies from desert regions with very little rain to mountainous rainforests that plunge into the sea. In general the rain falls on the mountains and the interior and conditions get drier towards low lying coastal areas. Smaller offshore islands are almost desert like. Many boatyards are around Puerto la Cruz and Cumaná, which are relatively dry. This makes them excellent for getting work done.

The rainy season is usually from late June through November. In the really dry areas there is almost no rainfall even in the rainy season. Bonaire is very dry.

In some coastal areas in Venezuela thunderstorms build up regularly in the afternoons and subside before dusk.

The offshore islands right through to Bonaire lie in the regular trade wind belt and you usually have a good breeze. The weather close to the coast of Venezuela is different from the islands. Along the coast from Carenero to Cumaná the winds vary in direction, with light breezes coming from the south through west to north. It often blows hard from the east along this coast from about noon to dusk. From Puerto Cabello to Carenero and from Cumaná to the eastern end of Trinidad an easterly wind prevails, but it often blows hard during the day and then calms down at night. Many yachts heading east power overnight. This rule is not cast in stone and it is less likely to be calm at night when the trades are blowing hard.

A very strong northeasterly wind often blows through Coche and Cubagua and the eastern half of the Golfo de Cariaco. In these areas the wind picks up in late morning, howls through the afternoon and drops off at night.

A westerly setting current flows throughout the area. It flows consistently as far west as Margarita, though the strength is variable. Farther west it is more fickle. Sometimes it flows at a brisk one or two knots; at other times there is no current or it can even be reversed. One can usually keep out of the current by staying within a mile or two of the mainland.

This whole area is considered to be south of the hurricane belt, which is why many people visit during the summer. However, there have been one or two during the last few hundred years. Less severe tropical storms, though rare, are not unknown. It is sensible to listen to the weather, not only because of hurricanes, but because easterly waves and other dis-

THE "ARE YOU SURE WE WANTED TO LEAVE TODAY?" DEPT.
those Venezuelan marineros were telling me how to predict the weather by reading the cloud formations...
Oh?
yeah, it's no problem once you recognize the signs!
So...?

turbances can come through with a lot of rain and wind. Throughout the region you can probably get the weather in English on Transworld Radio from Bonaire on 800 kHz am band. They have a weather forecast weekdays at 0715 and after the 0800 news. It is not detailed, but it should give you news of major weather systems. (See also our section on SSB and Ham radio if you have one.) Should a storm threaten, go to a secure harbor. In Venezuela there are endless excellent harbors tucked into mangrove lagoons.

While this area is too far south to be subject to northers, the swells from these systems do affect the area, creating uncomfortable seas and rolly anchorages in harbors that are exposed to the north.

You can visit Venezuela any time of the year. However, the trip back eastwards is going to be tougher in the winter, when the trades are blowing hard. Also, many outer island anchorages like Los Roques are more pleasant in the gentler summer winds.

NAVIGATION

Venezuela is not as well charted as the Eastern Caribbean. For many areas, coastal detail is sparse. Proceed cautiously and keep a good lookout whenever you are close to shore. In this guide we provide sketch charts of many areas where the navigational charts are inadequate. As far as we know, these are the only charts available for quite a few anchorages.

The plus side to this is that you have to be part explorer and this adds to your sense of excitement, discovery and satisfaction.

Lights

Lights throughout this region are unreliable and should be treated with caution. In more remote stations they are solar powered and fully automated. Unfortunately, they are not all checked as often as necessary to keep them in full working order. We have seen a light come on promptly at dusk and die within the hour as the aging battery failed to keep its charge. If you work with the idea that any one light has about a 60 percent chance of working, you will not go too far wrong.

Buoys

The whole area comes under the IALA B system (red right returning). But, buoys are not always in place and there are places where a channel is buoyed in red on both sides of the channel. Treat buoys with caution.

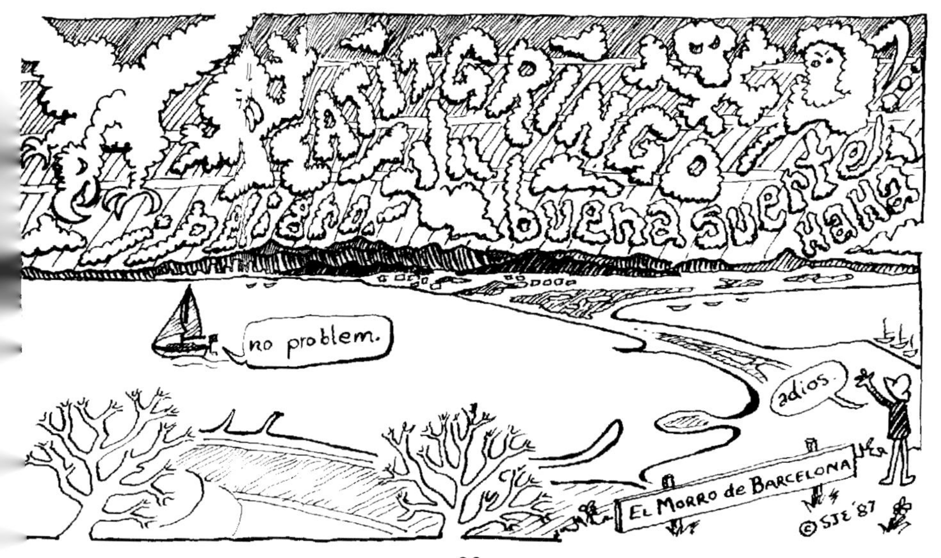

Fishing Boats

Night sailing along the north coast of Venezuela requires great caution. Fishing trawlers sometimes do not carry lights. Stay well clear of fishing boats whenever you can. Large nets of tough plastic are set which could ensnare your yacht. In Venezuela collisions between trawlers and yachts are not unknown. In one case the autopilot on the fishing boat was not working so the crew jammed a chair under the wheel while they went to eat. The chair fell out and the trawler swung hard around and rammed a yacht.

Do not approach Porlamar or Pampatar at night. Many fishing boats set nets in this area.

Oil Rigs

Oil rigs are now uncommon because of the low price of oil. However, if the price goes up, be prepared to watch for floating oil rigs. These have electronically controlled mile-long anchor cables that are best left well alone.

VHF AND SSB RADIO

Around Margarita and Puerto la Cruz there is often an informal VHF net with information on such things as weather and security. This can be very helpful in Venezuela where such news is not always easy to come by. We give more information under the ports concerned.

Those who have SSB radios can get weather on the Antilles Emergency and Weather Net on 3815 kHz LSB at 0635 AST or on 7163 kHz LSB at 0640 AST. The Caribbean weather net is on 4003 kHz at 0815 (local time) or 8104 kHz at 0830. There is also a broadcast on 8107 kHz at 1815, but only when there is a warning. English Harbour radio broadcasts weather on 8297 kHz just after 0900.

With special thanks to Jody Feavearyear of the Strasenburgh Planetarium, Rochester, NY.

STAR

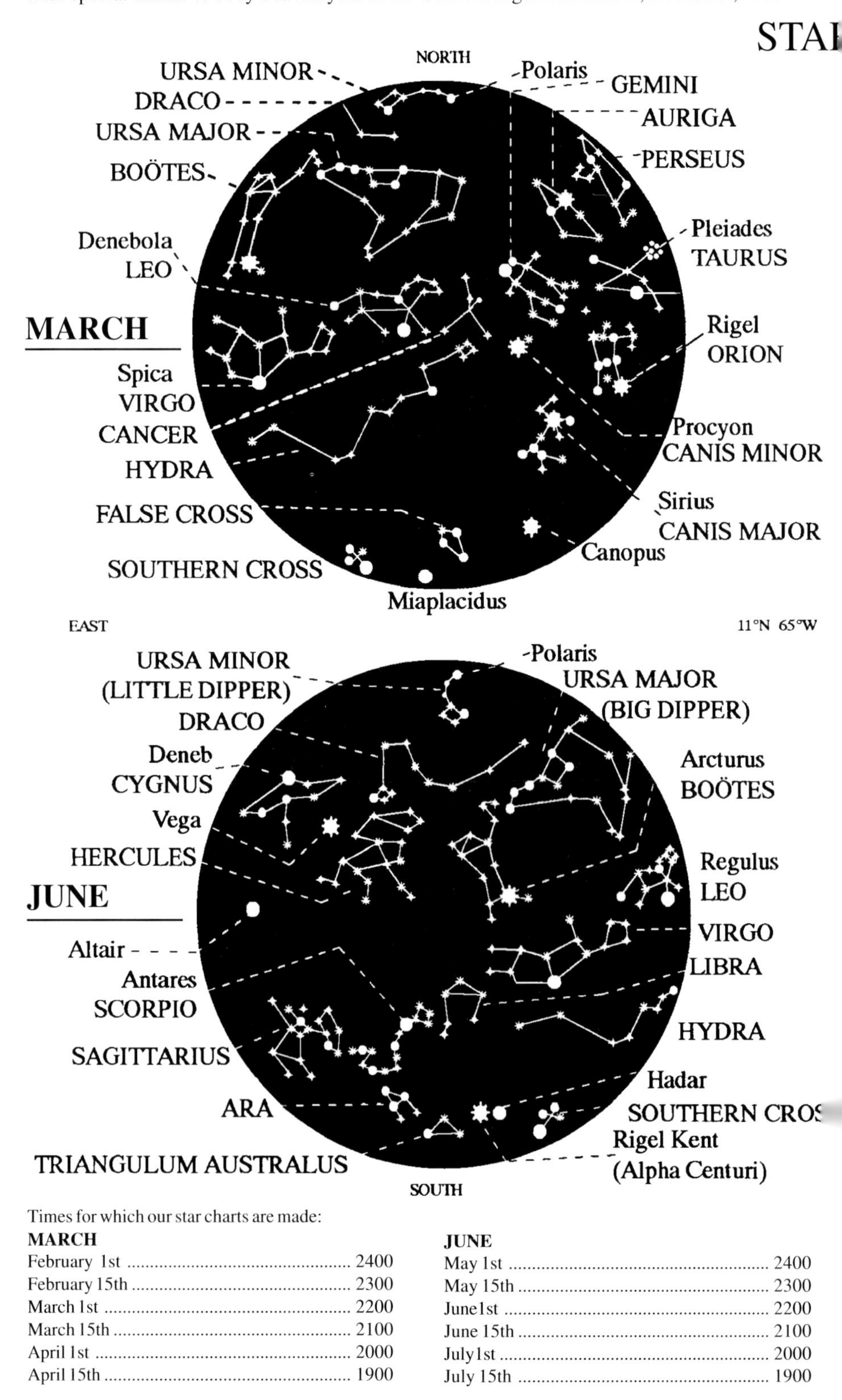

Times for which our star charts are made:

MARCH

February 1st	2400
February 15th	2300
March 1st	2200
March 15th	2100
April 1st	2000
April 15th	1900

JUNE

May 1st	2400
May 15th	2300
June1st	2200
June 15th	2100
July1st	2000
July 15th	1900

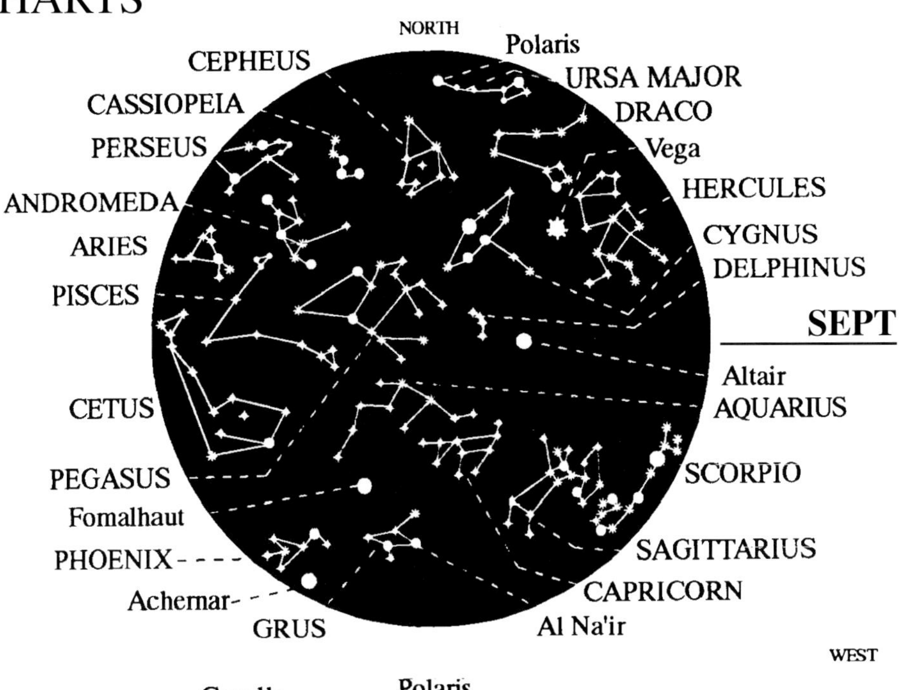

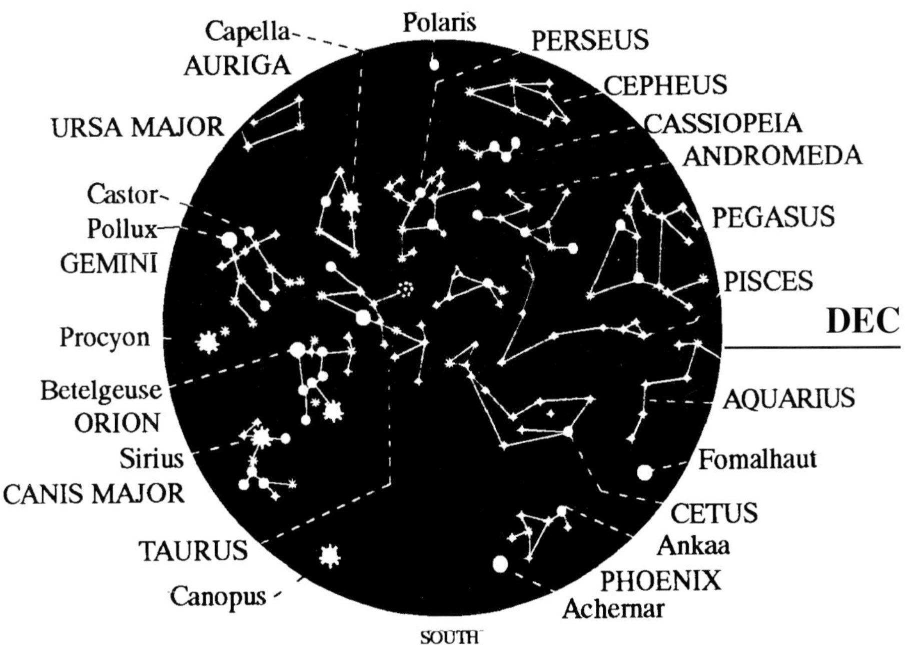

SEPTEMBER	
August 1st	2400
August 15th	2300
September 1st	2200
September 15th	2100
October 1st	2000
October 15th	1900

DECEMBER	
November 1st	2400
November 15th	2300
December 1st	2200
December 15th	2100
January 1st	2000
January 15th	1900

Customs and immigration in Bonaire is simple and easy. Venezuela has a huge bureaucracy and it often seems like the left hand doesn't know what the right is doing. There have been many good changes recently, and I am sure there will be more in the years to come. But changes often go into effect slowly and are sometimes confusing. For example, tourists arriving by plane do not need a visa. Instead they get a tourist card normally issued by the airlines. The government passed a law making this the same for visiting yachts, however, it has not gone into effect as it seems the yacht visa fees are about the only source of income the embassies have. So for the time being anyway, you do still need a visa.

You need to get your visa from the embassy in the country from which you are leaving for Venezuela. The current cost is $38US per person. You will need two passport photos and a passport for each crew member. It is best to get a multiple entry visa for one year. The process will involve at least two or three trips to the embassy and a trip to the embassy's bank.

Allow a few days.

When you get to Venezuela official clearance charges are about $30US, though some port captains and other officials may charge more. We advise using one of our recommended clearing agents

Flamingos in Bonaire

(listed under the relevant anchorages) where possible.

Immigration will check each person in for a maximum of two or three months. You can extend month by month up to six months for a reasonable fee. (These charges keep changing as does the value of the bolivar, so we are not putting them in.) After this you have to leave the country and when you leave you pay a departure tax (again it is not worth putting in how much, as it changes). Once you have left the country you can return again as soon as you like for another two months.

Time Restrictions

Bonaire has a 6-month time restriction on yachts, after which they become liable for duty. However, it is possible to make special arrangements if you want to leave your boat in a marina there for longer periods. Check current details with the marina managers.

In one of the best recent changes Venezuela has made, you can now keep your boat in Venezuela for up to 18 months. This makes it practical to leave your yacht in long-term storage afloat or ashore.

Customs and your Cruise Plan

In Venezuela, customs procedures are complicated, sometimes expensive and extremely cumbersome. Not only do you have to deal with more officials than anywhere else, but you are supposed to clear in and out of every major port you visit. This is mitigated in two ways. In several major ports there are agents who will do it all for you, which makes it wonderfully easy. You just give the agent your ship's papers and a crew list and they do the rest. Make sure you use an agent recommended by us or other reliable people, because there are a few unscrupulous agents. The cost of the transactions and honest agent's fees combined may be as little as $15 or as much as $50, depending on the port. Don't let it put you off. You will save that much and more on your first purchase of diesel, gasoline and engine oil.

There are some loopholes that can save you trouble if you plan your cruise. Each major port has a port captain and he controls an area of the coast around his port. The main ports yachts are likely to visit are; Margarita (Pampatar or Porlamar), Cumaná, Puerto La Cruz, La Guaira, Carúpano and Puerto Cabello. Luckily, you can get a clearance from one end of Venezuela to the other and visit all ports in between. For example, if you clear into Porlamar and then clear out of Porlamar for Puerto Cabello, you can go anywhere between the two. This gives you freedom to cruise all Venezuela's offshore islands and most of the coastline. The only time you will have to clear into an intermediate port is if you visit a marina or main town for more than a night en-route. A similar rule applies if you clear out of the country. You are allowed 24 hours at any number of stops in between. The 24 hours can be flexible if no one checks you. Thus you can clear out from Puerto La Cruz to Grenada and spend a couple of weeks getting there. Regulations change, so ask a good agent to update you when you arrive. When making your plan, keep in mind you now need a cruising permit for Los Roques, which may make a difference. A few people have been to Bonaire without clearing out from Venezuela. So far the Bonaire authorities have not been checking clearances from the last port, though this may change anytime.

PROTECTING THE ENVIRONMENT

Anchoring

Probably the worst damage yachts do to the environment is to destroy coral when anchoring. Always anchor in sand or mud. If you have to anchor in an area with a lot of coral, dive on your anchor to make sure it is not doing any harm. If necessary, use two anchors to stop your rode from chewing up the bottom as the boat swings around.

Garbage

Take your garbage to a proper facility. If you are away from civilization, dump all your food scraps in deep water (over 600 feet). Choose a location where the wind and current will carry them away from reefs. All plastic bags, wax-lined cardboard and tinfoil must be stowed and placed in a proper disposal place. The same goes for aerosol sprays, old paint cans and anything containing potentially harmful chemicals. Plastic bags are particularly bad. Leatherback turtles eat jellyfish and often mistake plastic bags for their prey, with deadly results. If you have a smelly plastic bag from meat or fish, wash it well in sea-water before stowing it.

Store paper and cardboard and empty cans till you get back to a dump. If for some reason you cannot do this, hole your cans, shred your paper and cardboard and dump them in water over 600 feet deep, well away from reefs.

	Tobago (Scarborough)	Trinidad (Boca de Monos)	Trinidad (Pointe-a-Pierre)	Punta Pargo	Carúpano	Testigos	Margarita (Polamar)	Coche	Cumaná	Mochima	Puerto La Cruz	I. de Píritu	Blanquilla	Isla Tortuga (Playa Caldera)	Carenero	Los Roques (Sebastopol)	Caraballeda	Bonaire	Puerto Cabello	Chichiriviche
Grenada (Prickly B.)	83	78	103	80	119	86	139	155	190	192	208	220	170	214	274	288	311	390	381	388
Tobago (Scarborough)		63	88	83	153	141	184	192	231	234	249	272	234	265	321	350	363	456	434	443
Trinidad (Boca de Monos)			25	23	95	94	130	135	175	177	189	212	188	211	261	300	304	405	375	388
Trinidad (Pointe-a-Pierre)				47	118	115	154	151	197	200	214	229	213	236	289	324	330	424	401	412
Punta Pargo					72	74	107	113	150	153	167	182	166	189	242	277	283	375	353	365
Carúpano						43	39	44	80	82	100	122	106	118	172	207	215	314	287	295
Testigos							49	68	97	100	114	135	92	128	188	207	225	316	295	308
Margarita (Polamar)								19	47	49	67	88	78	86	137	175	180	277	252	265
Coche									37	40	54	70	78	76	129	167	174	272	240	253
Cumaná										10	32	55	85	68	113	161	158	266	229	241
Mochima											23	43	88	62	105	156	150	260	223	232
Puerto La Cruz												20	96	57	91	148	136	250	209	217
I. de Píritu													102	52	70	138	118	233	186	198
Blanquilla														64	118	116	150	223	216	220
Isla Tortuga (Playa Caldera)															62	94	101	200	168	179
Carenero																83	55	169	124	138
Los Roques (Sebastopol)																	71	109	112	111
Caraballeda																		127	71	86
Bonaire																			102	74
Puerto Cabello																				30

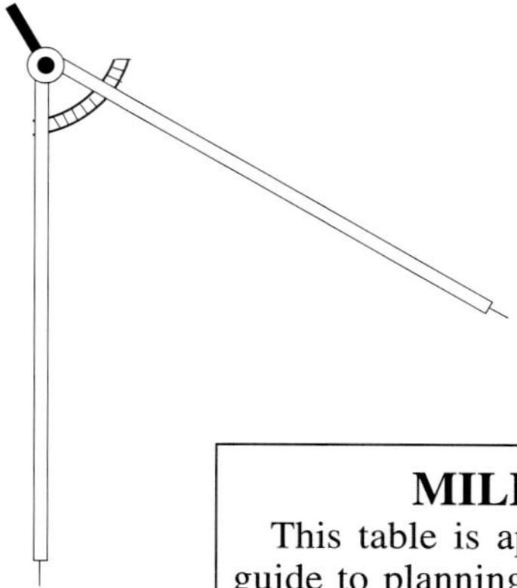

MILEAGE CHART

This table is approximate and is offered as a guide to planning. Distances sailed vary greatly due to wind and current.

We used a Garmin-50 GPS on WGS-84 map datum in our research. Many of the sketch charts in this guide were drawn by plotting a series of GPS readings. The GPS (including its predecessor the Sat Nav) was the first major global advance in navigation systems for yachts since the development of the chronometer. Like most other yachtspeople, we find this instrument invaluable. The major problem seems to be that it so accurate that people sometimes expect it to do more than it can. The US government creates intentional errors in the system which can change your position by over a hundred yards. They plan to stop this soon. We have heard occasional reports of people getting strange errors of a much larger order. It would be extremely unwise to use a GPS to thread your way through rocks or reefs at night. The GPS is a great aid, but it must be used with visual sightings and depth

PLACE	LAT (NORTH)	LONG (WEST)
Venezuela's offshore islands	**deg mins**	**deg mins**
Aves de Barlovento, Isla Oeste	11 57.6	67 28.0
Aves de Barlovento, Isla Sur	11 56.0	67 27.0
Aves de Sotavento, Isla Larga	11 59.6	67 41.0
Aves de Sotavento, northwest of reef	12 04.5	67 41.2
Blanquilla, center, from chart, GPS NA	11 51.0	64 36.0
Coche, buoy off northwest shoal	10 50.1	64 00.9
Coche, El Saco	10 45.6	63 57.7
Cubagua, off northeast point	10 50.7	64 09.5
Los Roques, Carenero	11 53.0	66 50.5
Los Roques, West Cay	11 49.0	66 57.5
Los Roques, Dos Mosquises	11 47.5	66 54.1
Los Roques, northeast of Crasqui	11 54.5	66 45.0
Los Roques, Noronsquies	11 55.0	66 44.5
Los Roques, northeast channel	11 58.0	66 37.8
Los Roques, Sarqui	11 53.5	66 48.4
Los Roques, Sebastopol Channel	11 46.6	66 34.8
Margarita, West Coast	11 01.0	64 24.0
Margarita, Boca del Río	10 57.0	64 10.0
Margarita, Juangriego	11 04.7	63 58.8
Margarita, Pampatar	10 59.0	63 47.0
Margarita, Porlamar	10 56.5	63 49.0
Testigo Grande	11 22.0	63 06.0
Testigos, I. Noreste	11 25.0	63 02.0
Tortuga, Playa Caldera	10 57.0	65 13.8
Tortuga, Los Palanquinos	10 59.1	65 20.0
Tortuga, Cayo Herradura	10 59.1	65 23.4
Tortuga, Las Tortuguillas	10 57.7	65 24.8

readings.

One of the delightful things about this instrument is that enables you to know the strength and direction of the current as you sail. We find this particularly useful when beating into the prevailing current. It is often possible to tack to advantage in areas where there is no current, and even to some extent to keep out of the current. Conversely when the current is in your favor, you can use your GPS to stay with it to some extent.

We offer the following list of positions for planning purposes only. Check with the sketch charts to see where they were taken. We offer no guarantee of accuracy. We would be interested to hear how you found them so we can get a better idea of the accuracy of this method of navigation. If you send us information, please make sure your GPS is set to WGS-84 map datum.

PLACE	LAT (NORTH)	LONG (WEST)
Venezuela, west of I. de Píritu	**deg mins**	**deg mins**
Bahía de Buche	10 32.0	66 05.5
Bahía Puerto Cruz	10 32.8	67 20.6
Carenero	10 31.6	66 05.9
Chichiriviche	10 56.0	68 14.5
Ciénega de Ocumare	10 29.5	67 48.5
Ensa Cata	10 30.1	67 44.3
Puerto Frances	10 35.3	66 04.0
Islas de Píritu	10 09.7	64 58.6
Isla Larga	10 28.9	67 57.1
La Guaira	10 36.5	66 57.0
Marina de Caraballeda	10 37.4	66 50.9
Morrocoy Nat. Park, Boca Grande	10 50.7	68 13.0
Morrocoy Nat. Park, Boca Paiclas	10 48.5	68 16.0
Puerto Azul	10 37.3	66 44.9
Puerto Cabello	10 28.9	68 01.0
Puerto Calera	10 37.0	67 01.1

PLACE	LAT (NORTH)	LONG (WEST)
Venezuela, Mochima to Puerto la Cruz	**deg mins**	**deg mins**
Chimana Grande	10 17.0	64 39.0
Golfo de Santa Fe	10 18.0	64 27.0
Ensenada Tigrillo, north of Pta. Tigrillo	10 23.0	64 23.8
Ensenada Tigrillo, northwest of Punta Gorda	10 20.5	64 28.0
Islas Arapos, eastern end	10 15.5	64 28.0
Puerto La Cruz	10 13.7	64 38.3
Puerto La Cruz, off El Morro development	10 13.0	64 40.0
Puerto la Cruz, off El Morro Marina	10 12.0	64 42.4
Puerto Mochima	10 23.8	64 20.7

PLACE	LAT (NORTH)	LONG (WEST)
Venezuela, Golfo de Cariaco	**deg mins**	**deg mins**
Cangrejo	10 34.6	64 00.0
Carenero	10 26.5	62 02.4
Cumaná	10 27.8	64 11.9
Cumaná, Marina Cumanagoto	10 28.9	64 11.2
Cumaná, Navimca	10 29.8	64 08.5
Laguna Chica	10 34.0	64 04.6
Laguna Grande	10 34.5	64 03.0
La Marita/Sena Larga	10 34.5	63 57.3
Los Manantiales	10 34.3	63 56.5
Los Platitos	10 34.5	63 59.6
Marigüitar	10 27.3	63 54.8
Muelle de Cariaco	10 28.7	63 40.0
Pericantal	10 27.6	63 45.5
Puerto Real	10 33.8	64 07.6
Punta Cachamaure	10 26.7	63 49.2
Punta Cotua	10 28.1	63 42.7
Punta Gorda	10 27.9	63 44.7
Punta Tarabacoita anchorage	10 26.8	63 51.3
Sena Honda	10 27.0	63 58.4
Sena Larga	10 27.2	63 56.4
Sena Venado	10 34.5	63 58.6
Toldo	10 34.6	63 58.1
Venezuela Pen. de Araya/Paria	**deg mins**	**deg mins**
Cabo San Francisco	10 43.6	62 00.3
Carúpano	10 40.9	63 15.0
Ensenada Medina	10 43.0	63 01.4
Ensenada Mejillones	10 42.5	62 08.7
Isla Lobos	10 41.3	63 52.5
Isla Caribe	10 41.3	63 51.2
Isla Esmeralda	10 39.5	63 31.2
Isla Garrapatas	10 41.5	63 27.9
Venezuela Pen. de Araya/Paria	**deg mins**	**deg mins**
Peninsular de Araya, extremity of northwest shoal	10 40.0	64 19.5
Puerto Santos	10 43.7	63 10.2
Punta Pargo	10 43.0	62 03.4
Bonaire	**deg mins**	**deg mins**
Kralendijk	12 09.0	68 16.8
Southern tip	12 00.5	68 15.0

Space for your coordinates	deg mins	deg mins

Kavac, near Angel Falls

SIGHTSEEING IN VENEZUELA

While cruising Venezuela why not take a trip inland and see some of the interior? Venezuela is a large and magnificent country with every kind of landscape, from snow-covered mountains through dense rainforests to desert landscapes. Even the most impecunious can travel by hopping on a bus or por puesto and heading inland. But even more luxurious trips are excellent value.

Always carry your passport while traveling in Venezuela as there are occasional police checks.

Angel falls

The most popular trip is to fly to Canaima to see the Angel Falls, the highest in the world. The best view of the falls is from an airplane. A single day trip can include this and a canoe trip to a water fall where you can swim. You can also spend several days in the interior, traveling to the base of the falls in a canoe. Keep in mind it tends to be warm by day but cool by night so warm clothes are essential. You can also just spend one night there and see some of the interior as described in the following report from Jeff Fisher who made the trip from Margarita (It can even more easily done from Puerto La Cruz or Cumana):

We boarded a brand new single engine Cessna that had a capacity for 12 passengers, the plane was full.

We headed South, overflying isla Coche, then passing a thin strip of the Venezuelan mainland that encompasses the Golfo de Cariaco. We progressed into a mountainous area that is ideal for the cultivation of coffee and cocoa, this section was lush and green. After a few mountain ranges the ground became flat and dirt roads could be seen forming large squares, here is were they grow pine trees for paper and furniture. The Orinoco was next, a brown slow moving, wide river, on whose shore is Ciudad Bolivar where we set down to refuel. This first leg took about an hour.

We continued South and soon found ourselves looking down on some dark brown rock formations; iron-ore, jutting out from a flat arid looking land. This was interlaced with thin lines of bright green vegetation created by hundreds of small rivers and streams. These soon gave way to small lakes which became bigger and more numerous as we continued. Dried up trees could be seen jutting from all parts of

the lakes. These wetlands are a result of the recent completion of the second most powerful hydroelectric damn in the world which is built on the Caroni River. The dam took 20 years to build and has been in service for 10, it produces enough electricity not only for domestic use but to sell to both Colombia and Brazil.

After these flat wetlands we see denser vegetation and curling narrow rivers that have bright white sand beaches at the arc of every turn. Majestic flat topped mountains rise thousands of feet straight up. Our guide explained that these mountains, called Tepuis, had been raised from the surrounding land by geological forces a millennium ago. This effectively isolated each mountain top permanently, creating a unique environment on every one.

Angel Falls, the highest in the world cascades down the side of one of these Tepuis. It is called Auyantepui and has a surface area of 740 square kilometers and the waterfall is a result of this rain catchment area. The pilot maneuvered the plane between two adjacent Tepuis, close to the top so we could see the falls. Being the dry season, the fall was not as large as in the rainy season, but still incredibly spectacular. The river poured off the top, a massive waterfall at first, but as it went down, unhindered, it became like mist or fog, undefined. At the bottom of this long decent you could see the river continuing. Other tepuis could be seen spilling water off the top, in long misty threads. We circled around, descending to the other side of this plateau landing at Kavac which is at the bottom of the tepui and on the edge of a great savanna, a flat grassy area dotted with forests. Our overnight camp was a dozen thatch roofed, adobe huts.

We donned walking shoes, bathing suits, hats and cameras and set off following the Kavac river upstream. Moriche palms grow along the banks. Indians have traditionally used the leaves of these palms for thatching their huts. The rocks in the river are various shades of red and pink, a result of decaying vegetation and the presence of tanic acid from the iron ore upstream. We cool off in a series of pools and small cascades. Eventually we reach a place of many palms, and there comes a mixed sound of rustling palm leaves and rushing water.

We strip down to our bathing suits and give ours camera to the Indian guide who has come prepared with a couple of large plastic bags. We venture up an amazing passage through a gorge carved out by centuries of this running water. It is only about ten feet wide, but over a hundred feet straight up on each side,

The overhanging vegetation at the top obscures the sky. The water is deep and running, we swim and pull ourselves along a rope for about a hundred feet. We clamber over some rocks and rope our way through the water along the next stretch. Water drops like rain are continually falling off these sheer vertical walls and the sound of thundering water bounces off of them. A gap appears in front breaking the overhead vegetation. We see the sky and a giant fall which cascades a hundred feet into a deep swim hole. The Indian guide shows off his climbing and diving skills by scaling the rocks and diving in.

We made our way back to the camp along

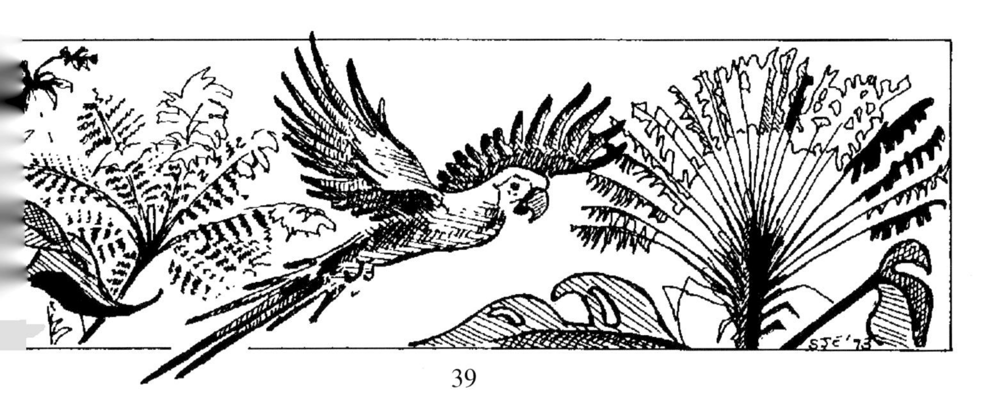

the same route, to a late lunch, after which those of us that were staying the night were showed to our huts. Mine had two parrots in it, one in the rafters and one chewing on my complimentary bar of soap.

After a brief rest we went off on another exploratory walk across the open llano to look at a small typical Indian village and their farm plot. These farm plots are carved out of a forest area and the trees burned, they are cultivated for only 5 years before becoming exhausted. They were growing yucca, a root used as their staple diet, wild pineapple, wheat, dates, cotton and corn. Evening found us walking back to the camp, I heard parrots squawking in the date palms and saw a falling star drop over a tepui.

The following day rose to a light rain which soon cleared. We set off on a steep climb that afforded spectacular views of the camp, the llanos behind and tepuis in the distance. Our first destination was to hike up and around to view the gorge waterfall from above. We continued upstream through another smaller swim-only gorge until we got there - a beautiful water fall straight down and uninterrupted, shafts of light found their way through the overgrowth to illuminate the falling water, the sound was deafening.

Guácharo Caves

While visiting Cumaná it is worth making time to visit the guácharo cave near Caripe. It is eight miles long, one of the world's largest and most magnificent caves. (Once you've done this one you'll never need to do another.) It is inhabited by some eighteen thousand guácharo birds, strange creatures that live in the dark and echo-locate like bats. They only come out at night to feed on fruits. They are sensitive to light, so no lights or cameras are allowed. You follow a guide who holds a dim oil lamp. The strident cry of what sounds like all eighteen thousand guácharo birds calling at once adds to the atmosphere. There are wonderful stalagmites and stalactites. The cave floor is muddy and it is best to bring boots. If you forget, you will discover, like many before you, why Caripe has so many shoe shops. The tour takes you a mile back inside the cave and lasts about two hours. There is a nominal entry fee.

Caripe is set amid beautiful mountain countryside and it is well worth staying there overnight. The bus takes four hours from Cumaná, and you should choose one that runs along the Golfo de Cariaco for the best scenery. Taxis can make it in two and half or three hours and are not overpriced. If you are cruising Golfo de Cariaco, then the trip to Caripe is much shorter from Muelle de Cariaco.

The Andes

For a real change in climate, visit the Andes. The central town here is Merida and you can get there by bus, plane or rent-a-car. If you fly, beware of afternoon departure and landing times as Merida is often fogged in. There is a mountain just outside Merida which is 15,634 feet high and snow-capped year round. A cable car takes you up some of the way. (The final stage to the snow has been broken for some years.) There is a fascinating side trip to an Indian village called Los Nevados which is a five hour walk or donkey ride along a precipitous path. In the picturesque village there are several houses that take guests overnight and feed them. It is like being in the family. There is also a road to Los Nevados, but few taxis are willing to go and the road trip is far more terrifying than the donkey ride. You need good sun protection for the long trip to Los Nevados. For those who want to do things the local way, this trip can be done by bus to Merida, early cable car to the top platform and then a talk with the waiting donkey drivers.

If you rent a car in Merida, stay at least one night in Los Frailes, a wonderful hotel built out of an old monastery dating from 1643. It is set amid bubbling streams and fields of yellow and blue flowers. (Book a room through any Avensa agent.) Take sedate horse ride in the magnificent countryside around the hotel and go in the morning as it often mists over in the afternoon. Drive to El Valle or La Azulita. Tr to avoid the busy holiday seasons (Christmas, Easter, and July to September). The days are often warm and the nights cool, so take some warm clothes and a raincoat. While in the Andes enjoy the wonderful trout (trucha), a local speciality.

If you are touring around and you come to a village where there is no obvious hotel, ask "Hay habitaciones?" and you will often find there is a little guest house (posada). If you are planning to get off the beaten track, best do it in the dry season as some roads wash out in the rains.

A little known fact about Merida is that it has a bull ring. Ask at the local tourism office.

Orinoco Delta

Deep in the Orinoco Delta amid thousands of miles of waterway live many indigenous people. Among these are a group called the Warao which means "people from the canoe". It is now possible to visit the Warao as a tour. You can ride down miles of waterway to see the flora and fauna of the region including monkeys, parrots and little crocodiles called Babas. You can visit a local village, built on stilts above the rivers highest flood levels. The adventurous can overnight in an Indian encampment. You can swim, fish and buy local handicrafts.

Tour Operators

Many people start their inland trip from Puerto La Cruz because of all the marina facilities. There are several people here who can be very helpful for inland tours.

Marisol Nuñez (T:081-69 334/21 625, VF:77) is a first rate travel and tour agent who can do wonders. Marisol has details on practically everything that is available and will be happy explain it to you in perfect English.

Steve Patterson (T/F:081-65 33 71) is an excellent ex-US airline pilot who has his own plane and can also rent larger planes should you need them. He does several trips, including a day trip to the Angel Falls. You will not find a better person to go with, or a more reasonably priced trip.

Chaser Tours (T:016-80 20 79, F:081-68 45 82/74 49 03, VHF: 77) is operated by Jim and Linda Chase who came here to retire and after traveling through Venezuela extensively for two years wanted to share and help others experience what they had. They have a couple of vans that can take groups as big as twenty or as small as four.

Leslie's Limo (VHF:77) is a 12-seater bus driven by Leslie who speaks good English and is used to working with yachting people. If it is close enough to travel to by bus, Leslie is your man. His rates are very reasonable and he often takes people to Caracas and Cumaná.

EATING OUT IN VENEZUELA

Restaurants in Venezuela are plentiful, good and inexpensive. You may like to know about some local specialties:

Arepas are corn meal griddle cakes, often sliced and filled with butter, cheese, meats and fish. In Venezuela, arepas are used as bread and filled arepas make a complete meal.

Pabellón criollo is a staple dish in Venezuela and consists of shredded meat, fried plantain, rice, black beans, white farmers cheese and arepas.

Ayacas are mainly served around Christmas and are made of corn meal, chicken, olives, spices and raisins which are wrapped together in a banana leaf and steamed.

Paella, the popular Spanish dish of rice with meat and seafood, is equally popular in Venezuela.

Bienmesabe is a coconut cream trifle whose name means "It tastes good to me."

Another popular Venezuelan dessert is flan, a custard with caramel topping.

Punta Elvira, golfo de Cariaco

ANCHORAGES IN VENEZUELA

Regulations

Before you go to Venezuela you must have valid up-to-date yacht documentation and current visas in your passports. You can get visas at any Venezuelan embassy. They now normally issue them for 12 months. Always get a multiple entry visa and allow a few days for the paperwork. Charges and procedures may vary from embassy to embassy. Expect to pay in the region of $38 US per person. You will need 2 passport photographs, ship's documents and passports. You have to make the visa payment to the embassy bank in town and bring them the receipt. After doing that, the visa takes 24 hours.

While the law has been changed so that people on yachts can enter on a tourist card without a visa, no mechanism has been put into place to make this work, so until you hear differently you still need a visa unless you fly in.

Yachts can stay up to 18 months, which is a reasonable time for leaving your yacht in dry storage.

When you enter Venezuela, immigration normally stamps you in for two or three months (this depends on the officer). After this you can leave the country and come back in again for another two or three months. The length of stay out of the country does not matter. You can also come in for two or three months and then apply for extensions of up to a month at a time. You have to clear in and out of major ports visited in Venezuela. (See also cruising information.) You are allowed to stay over in most offshore islands on your way in or out of Venezuela. Ports of Clearance include: Puerto Cabello, Carúpano, Cumaná, La Guaira, Pampatar/Porlamar and Puerto La Cruz.

The taking of conch is illegal throughout Venezuela at this time. It is only legal to buy or catch lobsters from 1st November to the 31st April.

In planning your cruise, keep in mind that you now need a permit to visit Los Roques. Any of the clearing agents can arrange this for you.

Holidays

Jan 1st - New Years Day
Carnival - Monday, Tuesday and Wednesday 40 days before Easter
Easter - Easter Thursday to Sunday
April 19th - Declaration of Independence
May 1st - Labor Day
June 24th - Battle of Carabobo
July 5th - Independence Day
July 24th - Birth of Simón Bolívar
October 12th - Columbus Day

Shopping hours

Most shops open 0800-1200 and 1500-1800, but there are many individual variations. Banks sometimes cannot change money until a new rate arrives and this can be anywhere from 0900-1100. Some shops are open Saturday mornings and big supermarkets often open at 0900 and stay open till 1900 or 2000, Monday to Saturday.

Telephones

The Venezuelan telephone system is run by CANTV. There are many card phones and the cards are available from CANTV outlets in the larger cities and some hotels and other shops. They are not always easy to find, so buy a good supply. Make sure you are getting them from an official card agency and that they are wrapped and sealed in the original packing. You may occasionally meet on old style card phone in which your cards will not work. These old style phones are no use for overseas calls and are being phased out.

You can directly access an ATT operator from some card phones without using a card by dialing: 800 111 20/1. Many CANTV offices in larger towns have USA direct phones. USA direct is written above the phone and you just walk in and pick up the receiver. This is good for reverse charge and ATT card calls. For Canada direct call 800 111 00

If you are using a card phone you usually dial 00 to get an overseas line and then the country code (1 for USA and most Caribbean islands, 44 for UK, etc.). However, read the directions.

A Venezuelan telephone number begins with an area code (e.g.093). You do not dial this if you are in the same code area. If you are dialing from overseas leave the first zero off the area code. This is followed by the Venezuelan numbers which is 5 to 7 digits.

The country code for dialing into Venezuela is 58. Thus if the Venezuelan number is 093-663 156, from the USA you would dial 011 58 93-663 156.

Currency

Currency in Venezuela is the Bolívar. In the last ten years the exchange rate has gone from 30 Bs to over 500 Bs to the dollar. It could vary greatly in the next few years, but whatever the rate, you can expect US dollars to have excellent buying power when converted to Bs.

Transport

Venezuela has several large airports with international links as well as local flights between cities. Inexpensive round trip tickets are often available between Valencia Airport (nearest seaport is Puerto Cabello) and Miami.

Renting a small plane is often the best way for a small group for sightseeing trips.

Regular taxis are not expensive. You can bargain for whole day trips. It is usually less expensive to hire a taxi for a day than to rent a car. The taxi will be older and have many more miles on it, but it comes with a driver who knows his way around.

Unless you know what the local taxi rates are, you should always ask "Cuanto Cuesta?" (how much?) before you get in the cab. Otherwise you risk being overcharged.

The mainstay of the local transport system is buses for long distance and "por puestos" for short and medium distances. Por puestos are taxis that ply particular routes and pick up passengers along the way. They will often drop you off at your destination even if you are a little off their route. Longer trips (to distant towns) are usually made by bus. In most towns you find the buses in a bus station. Both buses and por puestos are very inexpensive.

Venezuela had a thriving Indian community before Columbus arrived. The earliest European settlement was in Venezuela on the island of Cubagua where the attraction was the rich pearl beds. Indians were conquered and used as slaves, so the Spanish never needed to import African slaves. The Venezuelans broke free of the Spanish in 1811 after a long, hard revolutionary struggle. Simon Bolívar was a major leader in this fight for independence.

Today Venezuela is a thriving modern country with a Spanish tradition and language. It is a major oil producer and industrialized enough to be self-sufficient in most respects.

One difference between Venezuela and the Eastern Caribbean is that in Venezuela there is little awareness that yachts spent considerable sums. You are not regarded as a source of income and whatever relationships you form will be spontaneous rather than commercial. This is refreshing, but it also means that you will not be specially catered to, and while your dollars will buy you much, they don't mean much. Most Venezuelans are very warm, generous and hospitable, but a few of the richer Venezuelans are not particularly tolerant. They have welcomed cruising yachts before and found them wanting. Many private yacht clubs regard a cruising yacht much as the US coastguard views an old fishing vessel overloaded with Haitian refugees.

There are one or two private yacht clubs where foreign flag vessels are allowed and we have found the people in these very welcoming. However, there are some members who would prefer not to be bothered and they are looking for reasons to exclude foreign yachts. Try not to help their cause. Although you may pay fees in a yacht club, it is a private club and not a

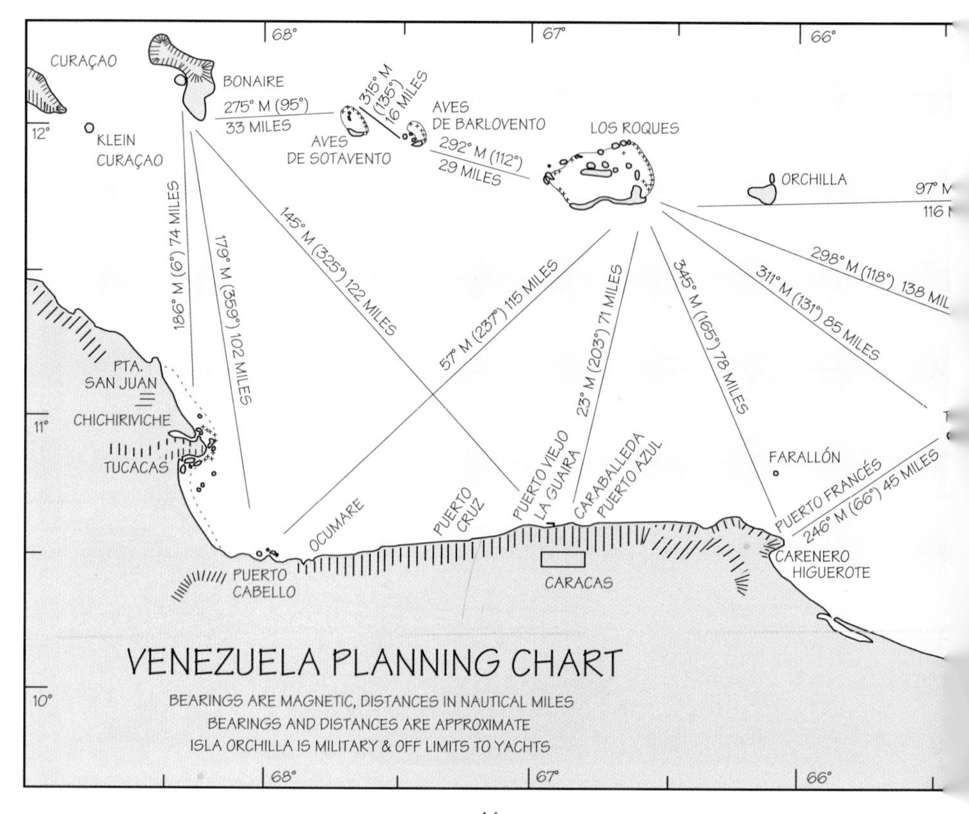

commercial marina. You cannot make demands and complaints will just make you unpopular.

While Venezuela has excellent medical services, many small fishing villages are so far away from large towns that the locals have a hard time getting to a doctor. So if you have medical skills and stock up on extra first aid gear, you probably can make a contribution in some outlying areas.

ORGANIZATION OF VENEZUELA IN THIS BOOK

Venezuela is a vast cruising area and it is doubtful that any two people will follow the same route. We have organized this book in a simple fashion. We describe the anchorages going westwards along the outer islands and returning eastwards along the mainland shore.

PASSAGE FROM GRENADA TO TESTIGOS

It is an easy sail to Los Testigos, with wind and current on your side. The distance from Prickly Bay to the nearest Testigos is 80 miles, but it is another five into the anchorage. The current often reduces the distance sailed by 15 or 20 miles. This was a bit too much for one singlehander who underestimated the current and was wrecked while still asleep.

The course is 245° true (258° mag). Most yachts sail overnight, leaving Grenada just after dark. For yachts that go 6-7 knots a magnetic course of 245-250° usually gets you in sight of the islands the next morning. If visibility is bad it is better to err to the south of Testigos. Here your echo sounder should pick up the 25-foot bank which extends some 15 miles south of the islands.

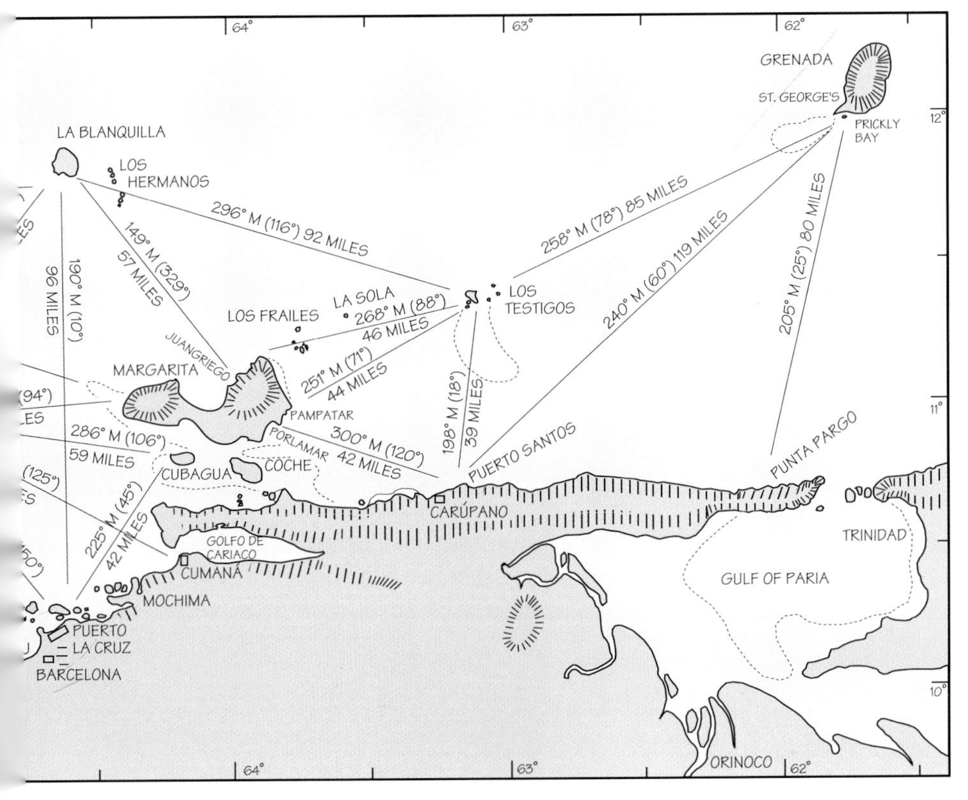

This will get you back on track.

Generally the winds will be in the easterly quadrant and they sometimes get lighter as you go south.

Testigos has a light some 807 feet high with a 10-mile range which flashed every six seconds last time we looked. It has been fairly reliable. However, time your arrival after daylight for this is no place to navigate in the dark.

Testigos, showing Isla Langoleta anchorage to Isla Iguana

LOS TESTIGOS

Los Testigos (The Witnesses) are a delightful group of islands with about 160 inhabitants who live by fishing. They live here year round and have a school and church, but for shopping or for an outing on a public holiday they zoom over to Carúpano in their pirogues.

Natives of Testigos can apply to build a house anywhere in the island group. Most choose to live on Isla Iguana or on Playa Tamarindo. However some have built elsewhere and a few houses are now dotted in other areas.

Since there is no ferry and no airport, yachtspeople are among the very few outsiders to visit. So far things have gone quite well between the locals and the yachting fraternity, and we should all do our best to make sure it stays that way. Under no circumstances should you take garbage ashore or get in the way of any fishing boats. Be sensitive if you are using a camera. Most of the people are friendly and more than reasonably patient with those like me who speak "poquito Español." Those who speak Spanish will obviously find it easier to communicate. One or two yachtspeople with medical skills have offered a helping hand and given yachting a good name.

You will find gorgeous beaches, huge sand dunes, lots of fish, interesting snorkeling, magnificent views and a vast colony of frigatebirds. Los Testigos make a convenient first landfall from Grenada and are a wonderful introduction to cruising in Venezuela. We have not heard of any security problems here.

Navigation

Currents set to the northwest and are strong usually one to two and half knots but up to four knots have been reported. Avoid getting set to the northwest because you will have to struggle to get back. Engineless yachts would do well to come in from the southeast with the current. If approaching from the north, pass to seaward of all the little islets around Testigo Pequeño, then power or tack close to shore

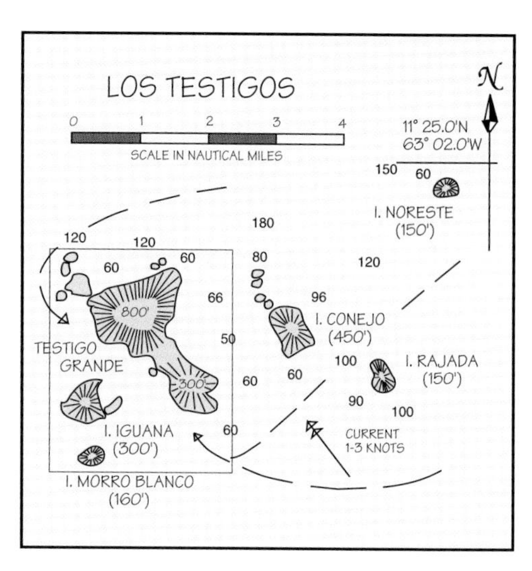

to stay out of the current. Narrow passages between islands are best avoided as the currents create overfalls.

Every few months the wind will switch to the southwest and blow quite hard for a few hours. Should this happen, head for the Isla Iguana anchorage (see below).

There are several anchorages, all of which roll from time to time. You can often improve the situation by using a stern anchor to keep you head to the swells.

Anchorage off Isla Iguana.

You can anchor off the village at Isla Iguana. This is fine for checking with the coastguard or for a brief visit to the village, but it does roll. It is much calmer if you tuck up close under the lee of Isla Cabra (Goat Island) though this is often full of the local fishing boats.

Isla Langoleta Anchorage.

This is a popular anchorage. You are within reach of the sand dunes, the walk up the mountain, Playa Tamarindo and the main village on Isla Iguana is within dinghy reach. A stern anchor can help cut the roll. For visiting the sand dunes you can take the dinghy pass inside Isla Langoleta through a cut in the reef quite close to shore.

Balandra Bay Anchorage (Sloop Bay). The best spot is right down in the southeast corner and it is calmest if you take a line ashore.

Playa Real (Royal Beach) Anchorage. A picture-perfect soft sand beach and inviting water colors make this anchorage the most beautiful in Testigos. Anchor close to the gap between Testigo Pequeño and Testigo Grande. Here waves crash on the windward shore just a few feet away. The holding is good, there is plenty of room, but it does roll a bit. The calmest anchorage is a quarter of a mile southwards, tucked into a small bay off Testigo Grande, with a line ashore. However, this can be out of the breeze. There is more room and it is still reasonably calm in the same area but anchored little farther out.

There is also room for one boat to anchor in the charming little bay between Isla Calentador and Testigo Pequeño. Note that although there is a deep water passage

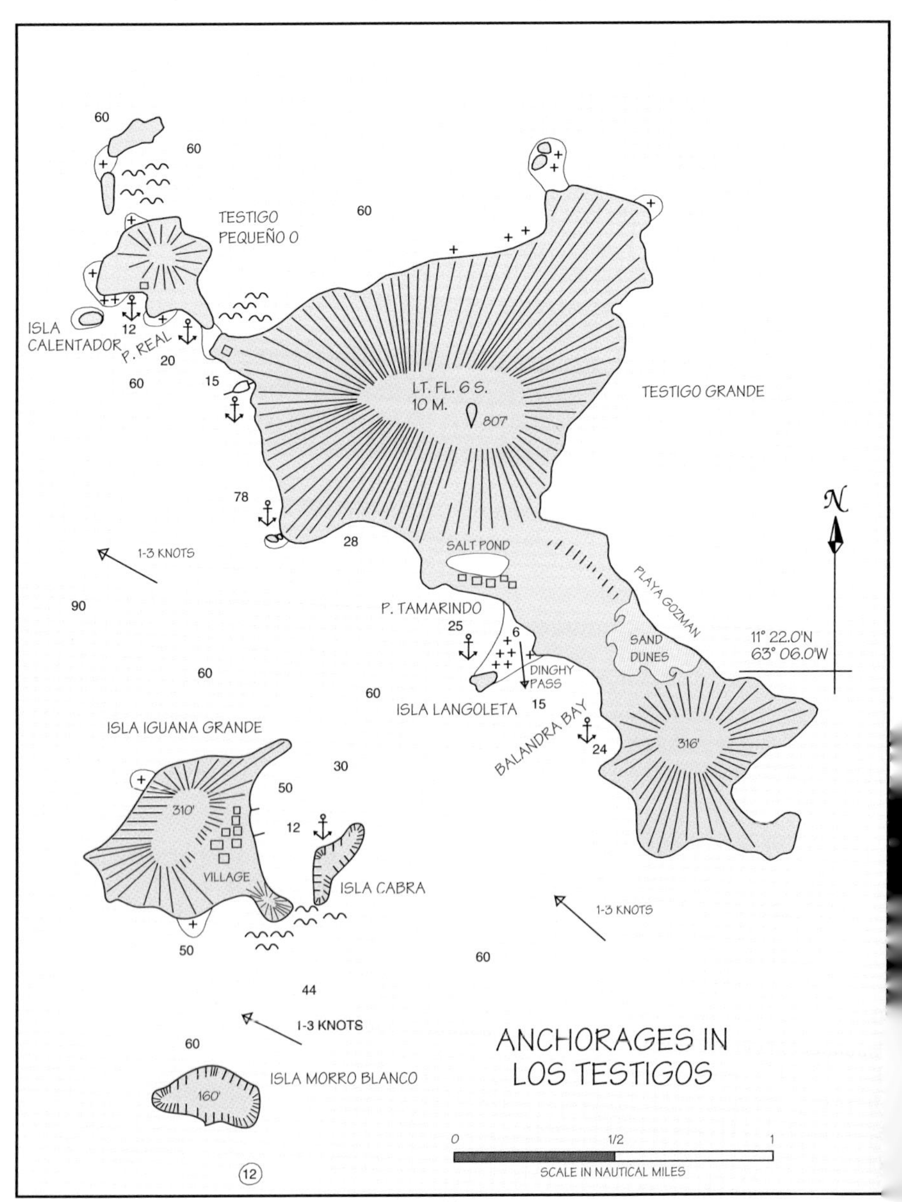

between Isla Testigo Pequeño and Isla Calentador, there are isolated rocks that stick well out from either shore. Explore by dinghy or snorkel before bringing the yacht through.

Regulations

There is a small coastguard outpost on Isla Iguana in a round building under the Venezuelan flag. They stand by on VHF:16 "Guardacosta." You can anchor where you like, but you should then visit the coastguard immediately. You can outboard over from most anchorages, but those who row should go in their yachts as the current in the channel is strong.

It is up to the coastguard officer to decide how long you can stay before carrying on to a proper port of entry. This can vary as the coastguard officers are rotated to different posts every few months. They will probably give you 48 hours. If you are enjoying it so much that you want an extra day, you can go back and ask. If you really want to stay longer than that, the best thing is to sail over to Carúpano and check in. It is a pleasant reach each way. You can then come back and stay up to your visa expiry date.

Los Testigos are a protected area. You are welcome to troll for fish, or hand-line off your yacht, but spearfishing is strictly forbidden. Scuba diving is also against the law as it is felt that some yachts were depleting the lobster population.

All garbage must be retained on board and taken to the next port when you go. Under no circumstances should it be dumped in the sea or left ashore.

Ashore

There is one small shop in the main village which is so basic that you may not find much more than a cold drink. You can buy fish from the fishermen year round and lobster in season (Nov 1st to April 31st). One or two locals prefer to swap the lobster for liquor, and they may approach you.

Those stout of heart and shoe should make the hike up to the lighthouse (allow two to three hours round trip). The path begins at the northwest end of Playa Tamarindo on the northwest shore of the salt pond. It is rough and involves scrambling in places. You may occasionally lose your way and have to backtrack to the last mark. The cliff-hanging view from the top is dramatic enough to make the climb worthwhile, especially if you remember to take your camera. The path is marked in three ways; blue painted rocks, notched trees and little heaps of stones. If you get lost go back to the last mark and keep looking until you find the next one. There are many cactuses, balsam plants and Spanish moss on the trail. You may see big iguanas.

There are wonderful sand dunes at Playa Gozman. They top the hill and you can see them from Balandra Bay. The swimming and body surfing looks exciting and there are acres of sand to play in. The sand gets the hottest hot so take shoes. There is a tiny beach for the dinghy in Balandra Bay and the trail is quite clear.

Snorkeling all around is pretty good. During the rainy season the water is sometimes greenish owing to effluent from the Orinoco, but the abundance of fish makes up for it.

MARGARITA

Margarita is the biggest and most important of Venezuela's offshore islands. It has a carefree holiday atmosphere and is the most popular holiday destination for Venezuelans. A major attraction is that it is duty free and watches, electronics and jewelry are cheaper here than on the mainland. Venezuelans are limited by how much they can take back each time they visit, but they are not limited on the number of visits they make. It also attracts many international visitors who are more interested in the warm dry climate, the lovely beaches and interesting mangrove channels.

Gambling has come to the island in a big way recently and casinos are everywhere.

Enjoy some of the island's attractions while you are here. One of these is the capital, La Asunción, which is back in the mountains. La Asunción was founded in 1565 and its pretty white washed buildings with red tiled roofs are a refreshing change from all the modern high rises in Porlamar.

Do not miss the Playa La Restinga and Laguna Grande. We put this under our Bahía Mangle anchorage, but you could also make the trip by taxi.

There is an informal marine net that operates on VHF:72 at 0800, with weather and an exchange of views, ideas and cultural events. This is run by yachtspeople and is dependent on how many are in the harbor, so there may not be a net when the yachts are scarce.

Regulations

At the time of going to press you could clear in and out in either Pampatar or Porlamar. There are agents in both places to help you and we strongly recommend you use them. However, if you want to do the clearance yourself, go to Pampatar since this is in fact the official port of Margarita and all relevant offices are there, and you may have to arrange for the doctor and customs officer to visit your yacht. The charges are variable. If you do it yourself you should ask for and keep a receipt for any money paid out.

Navigation

If you are approaching Pampatar or Porlamar from the east, Los Frailes show up clearly as do the mountains on the northern part of Margarita. As you get nearer, Pta. Ballena will appear as a distinct headland just to the south of the mountains. The land to the south is lower and one can see huge blocks of multistory buildings before the land itself. Isla Farallón makes another feature, it is a small, but distinctive white Island (Isla Blanca on some charts). From a distance Morro de Puerto Moreno looks like an

Pampatar

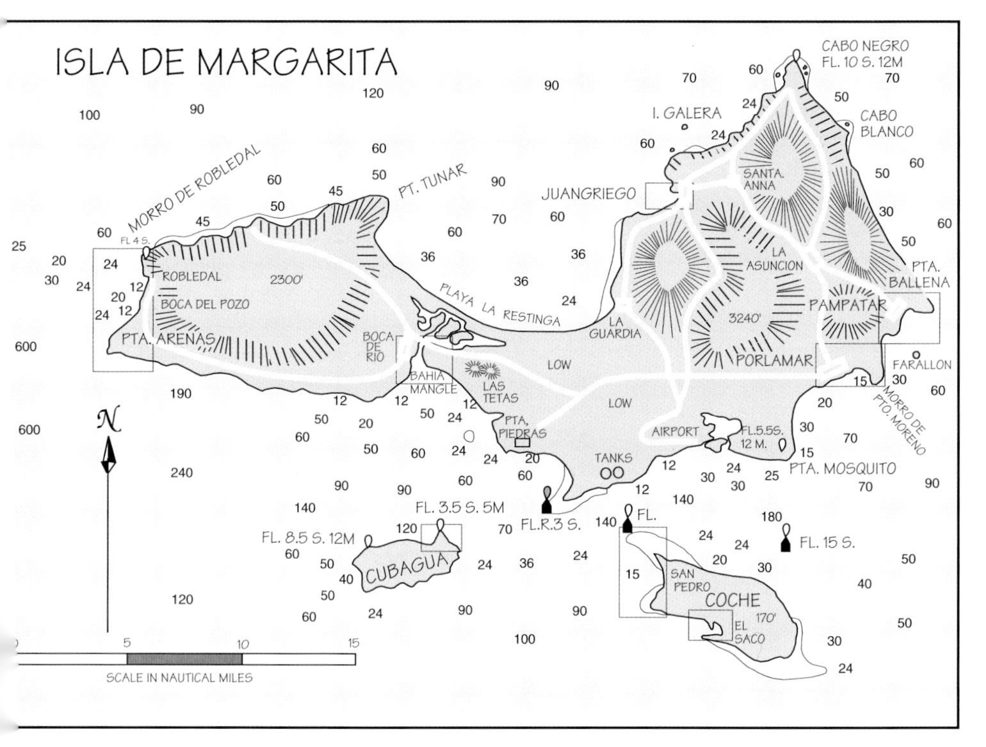

island.

It is about 44 miles from Testigos to Pampatar. The course is 239° true, 251° magnetic. Most people steer 240-245° to allow for the west northwest current. Porlamar is about four miles beyond Pampatar. You can change course and head for Morro de Puerto Moreno when you see it.

Do not approach Porlamar or Pampatar at night. Many fishing boats set nets in this area.

PAMPATAR

Pampatar is a quiet, picturesque fishing town with several beaches. Historically it was important because of its deep water harbor. At the head of the big new dock you will see Castillo San Carlos de Borromeo, a castle with ornate turrets. This was built in 1662 after the Dutch sacked the town and destroyed the original fort. The fort enabled the Spanish to fight off many hostile attacks, but they were driven out by Simon Bolívar in 1817 during the struggle for independence. The Spanish tried to blow up the fort with 1400 lbs. of gunpowder but the fuse didn't work. It has been renovated and is open to the public. From the top you get a commanding view of the bay.

Navigation

The harbor is wide open and easy to enter. Anchor where you find space. Pampatar is open to the southeast and can be rolly when the wind is from that quarter. With two anchors you can arrange your boat to face the swells. If a tropical storm threatens, head for the new marina next to the Hilton hotel, Coche, or Bahía Mangle.

Regulations

Customs and immigration are in Pampatar. There is an agent here who can help you (see services) and we recommend you use him, it will be much easier and quite possibly cheaper. If you clear customs yourself, start with customs (take three crew lists). They will give you an entry paper that you have to get stamped by immigration, the port captain and, finally, by the national guard over in Porlamar.

Unfortunately, clearing in is only good for Margarita. When you want to move on, you have to clear out. When you do this you can get a clearance to some distant port. This covers you for anything in between, except stays in other major towns like Puerto La Cruz, where they will insist you do it all again.

Services

Intmar Yacht Services (T\F 095-62 35 27, VHF:72, E-mail: hart@enlared.net) is just off the beach on the other side of the road, opposite the public phones. Intmar is a clearing agent and will handle in and out customs and immigration work for both international and national clearance. Owned by David Hart who speaks English and Spanish they will also help with water, ice, diesel and laundry, as well as fax and E-mail services. He has a small guest house with 4 rooms next to his office where he offers shower facilities. He is the agent for the Windward, a ferry that takes passengers and cargo from Margarita to the windward Islands.

Ashore

Take your dinghy in to the Trimar Restaurant and they will have someone look after it. In addition they offer water for the taking as well as showers, if you want ozone treated drinking water, they will give you that too as well as sell you ice. Pampatar has a pharmacy and several stores where you can stock up on Polar and other basics. For a complete provisioning take a bus or por puesto in the direction of Porlamar and get out at the big C&M sign on your right. Here you will find a complete shopping center and the huge C&M supermarket. You can usually find a taxi there for the return journey.

There are a few restaurants for a meal ashore. The Trimar (T:095-62 33 32, $D, cc:V) is a seafood restaurant that has stood

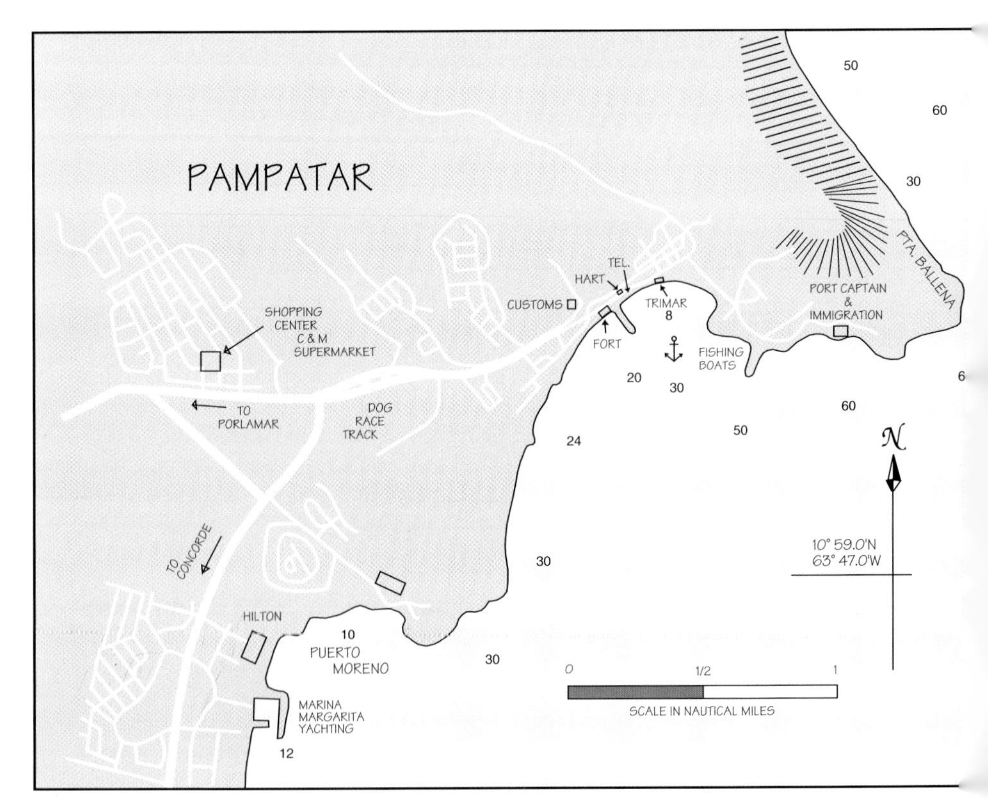

the test of time. They have a lovely location right on the beach and are open daily for lunch and dinner. To the left, on the beach is another restaurant called El Rincón de Antonio ($D), it has tables on the beach as well as inside seating.

PORLAMAR

Porlamar is the largest and busiest town in Margarita. It is very modern with smart shops and fashionable restaurants. The eastern part of town is full of impressive tall buildings that are either hotels or apartments.

Navigation

There are no problems entering. Anchor off the docks beside the Concorde Hotel. While Porlamar is a little better protected than Pampatar, you may need a second anchor to hold your bow into the swells when the wind comes south of east. The closer to the docks you can get, the less rolly it is. However, beware of the big shoal patch in the northeastern corner of the bay, and the other large shoal farther west off the main town.

This second shoal only really affects those who want to go into the town dock for fuel (see services). This is no problem as long as you approach in the right way. When you leave the anchorage stay well out in water that is at least 16 feet deep until you have gone right past the fuel dock. Then swing back in and approach directly in line with the dock, lining up the fuel hut with the lighthouse at 45° magnetic. This is the only sensible way to approach the town dock. It will keep you in a wide

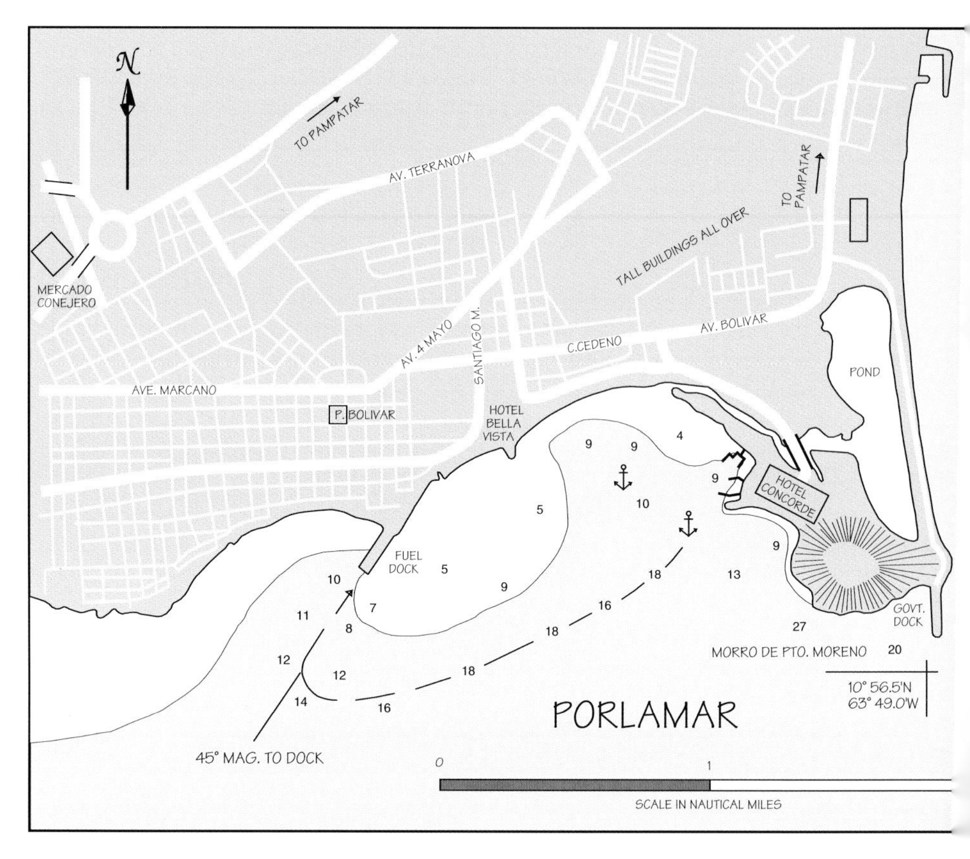

channel with depths of 12 feet most of the way in and 9-10 feet right up to the dock. On arrival drop anchor and go bow or stern to.

Every few months the wind will switch to the southwest for a few hours and make the anchorage unpleasant, though not usually untenable.

Regulations

You can bring your boat in here to clear in, but you should get VEMASCA to do it for you, they do it as a service at cost.

Services

Marina Deportes Nautico (Nautical Sports Marina, sometimes known as the Concorde Marina) stands by on VHF:16 and is run by Carmelo Acosta, they have about 30 to 40 slips with water, electricity (110volt, 60 cycles) and a guard. They have a maximum of eight feet at the end of the dock and they can do mechanical work.

Iodona Tours is a small store that has basic foodstuffs, ice and will fill your propane and arrange for gas. They are located next to Margarita Divers, in the long building that runs along the waterfront.

Water, diesel, gasoline and engine oil are available at the main town dock in Porlamar. It is easy to get there but you must go in the right way (see navigation).

There is a USA direct phone at the CANTV office near the Plaza Bolivar. You can get a USA direct line from a card phone by dialling 800 111 20 or 21. You can get cards for the card phones from the CANTV and other card agencies scattered about.

If you need to get anything sent from the USA quickly, there is a Federal Express office in town (T:095-63 35 78). A DHL and a UPS service as well as Domesa, local international courier service.

Marine Tech (T&F: 095-61 12 24) is modern high tech catamaran building company using computerized design systems and strip plank epoxy construction. Catatumbo, which at 71 feet is the larges

ɪerformance day charter sailing catama-ʼan in the world, was built by Marine Tech. ɬhey and Vemasca (T:095-63 10 72, ꜰ:095-63 20 80, VHF:72) are a hundred ʏards along the road into town from the marina. Vemasca is a wonderful modern chandlery and it is open everyday except sundays from 0830 onwards and they will do your in and out clearance at cost as well as provide office services. Among other lines they stock Ronstan, Profurl, Perkins engines (sales and installation only), Tasker spars, Norseman terminals, Trace invertors, water makers and electronics. Because they are a building company, resins, glass, kevlar and other building materials are on hand. Marine Tech has a complete machine shop and can do all kinds of welding and fabricating. Anything they cannot make or do not have in stock, they can order with guaranteed duty free delivery. Don Harris, a rigger works in conjunction with Vemasca and has metal working machines capable of taking care of your rigging problems. Many of the personnel speak English and you can also have your mail sent here: c/o Vemasca, Complejo Imica, Ave. Raúl Leoni, Near edif. Kokomar, Porlamar. Margarita, Venezuela.

In the same complex is Lilos Marine Services (T:016-95 10 55/ 64 55 65, VHF:72). Lilos is run by Jose Lopez, a well qualified engineer who will undertake a wide range of jobs including diesel and outboard mechanics, electrical, upholstery, glass and paint work. If something breaks take it to him first.

Marina Margarita Yachting (Tel:016-95 33 38, 016-95 33 36, T/F: 095-61 02 13) is in the final stages of construction next to the Hilton Hotel. This should come on line sometime in 1997. This is a large, very well protected man-made harbor with a capacity of 230 boats up to 180' and with a depth of 12 to 18 ft. They plan to have a complete line of services including port clearance, fuel, water, chandlery, several restaurants and more. It also serves as the base for the annual June yacht race event called SCOR that takes sailors to various points between Margarita and Puerto La Cruz.

Buses into town stop regularly in front of the Concorde hotel. Every day at about 0915 a bus operated by the Proveduria, a large supermarket and liquor store, takes passengers for free from outside the Concorde to their store and brings them back loaded with liquor and groceries right to the docks.

Changing money in a bank in Venezuela can be excruciatingly slow, and not all banks change money. You will probably get the best rate from Banco Union, but it may not be worth your time. For a slightly lower rate you can change money at a cambio fast and easily. Cambio Febres Parra in Hotel Bella Vista is convenient. They open Saturday mornings. In cambio you need your passport to change traveler checks, legally nationals cannot sell US$ so technically you need your I.D. to change cash but it seems not to be enforced.

If you need to get money from a credit card there is the big American Expres

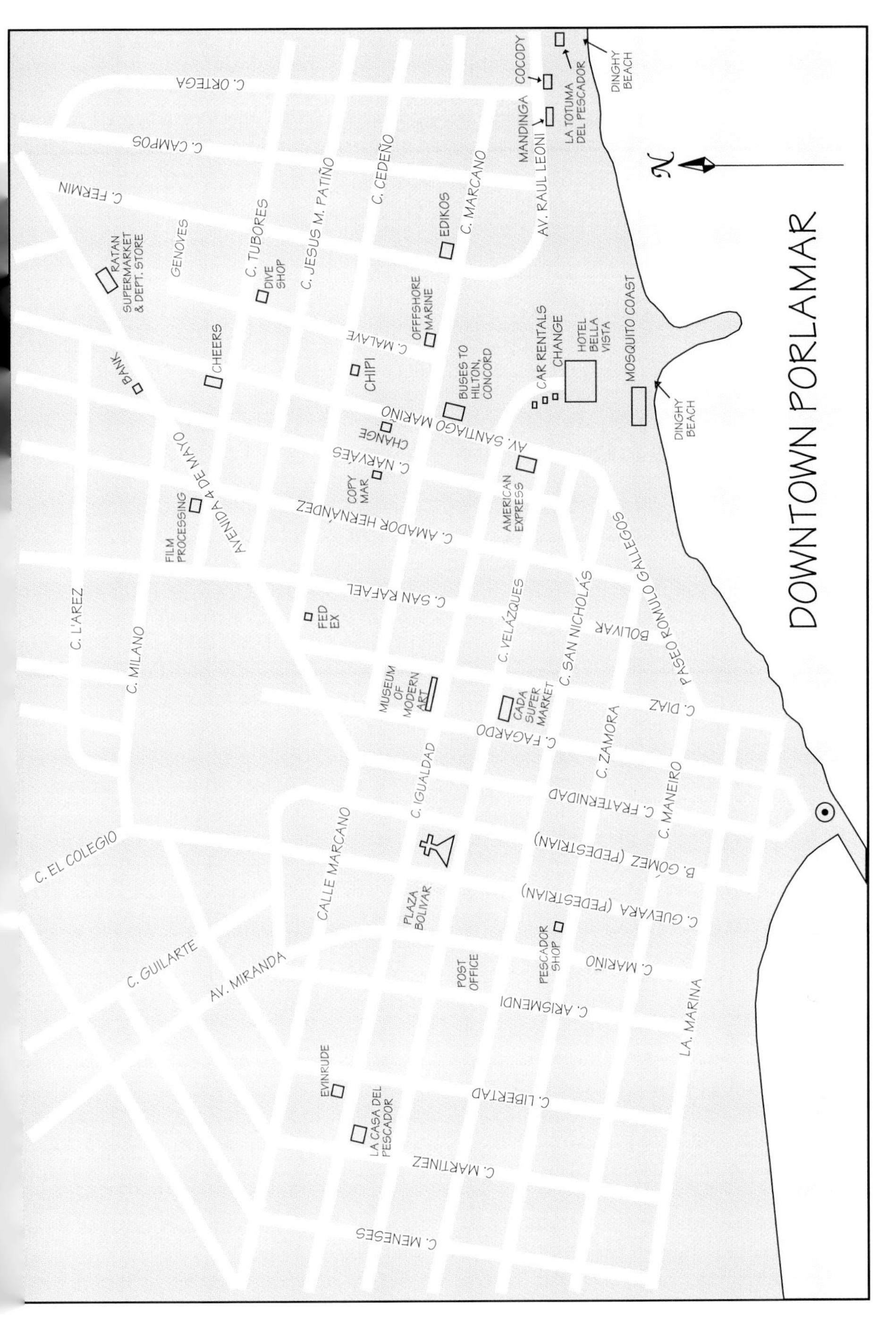

gency at Banco Consolidado (T:095-61 6 22/61 94 43).

There are three marine stores in town.)ffshore Marine (T:095-63 43 22/63 15 82 'HF:11, cc:V,M,A) on Calle Marcano is geared to yachts and has a wide range of general chandlery, including guides, water makers, electronics, fishing gear, coolers, ropes and are the agents for Mercury outboards. Margarita Island Imports ("todo para el pescador" or "everything for the fisherman") includes many essential items from anchors to paints. The other shop is two blocks past Plaza Bolivar on the corner of Igualdad and Martinez is called La Casa Del Pescador (095-63 93 05) they are the agents for OMC Johnson supplying parts as well as service. They have Caribe inflatables, some electronics and fishing gear.

Provisioning is a breeze at the two large supermarkets. The newest and fanciest is Ratan (T:095-61 79 11, cc:A,V,) on Ave 4 de Mayo, open Monday to Saturday from 0900 to 2100 and on Sundays from 0900 to 1300. This is both a large food shop and a complete department store with everything from household goods to bicycles. The goods are stacked so that unopened cases lie above items on display and there are discounts for buying by the case. You will be able to find someone who speaks English, and you can find a cab on the street outside. Cada (T:095-61 87 13) on Calle Velasquez is another big supermarket and they have a seafood counter which Ratan does not. They open daily 0800-1300 and 1430-2000 except Sunday when they open mornings only.

The most interesting places to shop for food, handicrafts and clothing is the Mercardo Conejero (Rabbit Market). It is best to go early in the morning when everything is in full swing. The market is a riot of color and movement as everyone wanders from stall to stall looking for bargains.

The boutique shopper will have a ball because Porlamar is one vast shopping mall. A good place to start looking for bargains is along Blvd. Guevara and Calle Gomez which are both pedestrian streets lined with shops. Santiago Mariño and Avenida 4 de Mayo have many fancy shops. Clothing and leather can be good buys. There are huge variations in both prices and quality.

Hotel Bella Vista (T:095-61 72 22, cc:A,V,D) is a useful landmark and meeting place as it is near the main shopping area. Many car rental agencies, are placed outside and a whole range of shops and services, including a travel agency, are inside. In the cool of their air-conditioning you can find comfortable arm chairs in which to sit. They have restaurants and an oyster bar out by the pool where dozens of succulent oysters can be had for just a few dollars. There is a variety of entertainment at night.

There are hundreds of restaurants in Margarita which open, close and change with astonishing rapidity. We mention a few that are currently good value. Most of these restaurants open daily at midday and stay open through the evening. El Chipi (T:095-63 61 01, $C-D, cc:V), on Calle Cedeño, has broken the rule about quick changes under the ownership of Luis Lopez for 28 years. Casual atmosphere and good seafood. If you are dying for Italian food, try Restaurant La Italiana (T:095-61 27 56, $C, cc:A,V,D) a smart and reasonably priced restaurant on Avenida 4 de Mayo. Just down the road Dagenaro Pizzeria (T:095-61 76 68, $D) cooks pizzas in two big wood-fired ovens. For that special night out, visit the Chalet (T:095-61 68 84, $B, cc:A,V, evening only). Expensive by local standards, it is reasonable by international standards and offers gourmet French style cuisine which is beautifully served. Cheers (T:095-61 09 57, $C, cc:A,V,D) is a pleasant place for lunch or dinner. Heavy duty air-conditioning and ice cold beer make a welcome break from the heat of the city. They serve good steaks and seafood, rice and pasta dishes, but save some room for something off the dessert trolley. Cocody (T:095-61 84 31, $D, cc:A,V open evenings only) is on the waterfront. You can even pull your dinghy up on the beach outside. They have an open air deck over the sand with an attractive white fence around it with access to the beach, which is nicely landscaped and well lit. They serve French, National and International food, and offer live music.

If you look from the anchorage toward the fishing fleet to the east of town, you will see a sandy path going up a hill. The Cinderella laundry is to be found up this hill, like most laundries in Venezuela you need only bring the dirty clothes, they supply the soap and will wash, dry and fold for you. A couple of blocks into town is a more modern laundromat called Ediko's that offers both do it yourself or drop off service and is air conditioned. On the beach is La Totuma del Pescador ($D) where you can land your dinghy and have a very good local seafood lunch and cold beer. A lot of yachtspeople come here where a cluster of palm trees close to the water provides natural shade and allows the breeze to keep things cool, traditional Venezuelan music completes the atmosphere. Here you can also top up your jerry cans with water.

For a more varied and formal meal, with authentic local entertainment and music, just down the beach is the Mandinga restaurant (T: 64 30 03, $C-D, cc:V)

For a switch of atmosphere try the Mosquito Coast restaurant (095-64 14 04/64 00 86, F: 095-63 48 18, VHF:72, $D, cc: A,V) for TexMex and Peruvian food with very attentive service. For the younger at heart there is a disco that gets going after dinner into the wee hours. They have a well lit little beach with a guard for your dinghy and a red flashing beacon on the roof to lead you in.

While wandering around town check out the Museum of Contemporary Art (closed Mondays) on Calle Igualdad. The downstairs contains the work of Francisco Narvaez who was born in Margarita and before his death became one of Venezuela's most sought after artists. His work often fetches higher prices than the most famous European artists. Upstairs the museum shows exhibitions of other modern artists.

Water Sports

Why not try diving in Venezuela? There are two dive sites within easy reach of Porlamar and others which are a longer boat ride away. The close ones include Farallón, a small island between Porlamar and Pampatar. You dive to about 40 feet. This is the site of a curious underwater religious statue put down by the first divers to dive here. (There is a similar one on the island.) In addition, you will see enormous brain corals, large sea fans and lots of reef fish including barracudas. In the same area there is an underwater patch of rock called Mucura. Here are huge boulders riddled with holes and home to many reef fish, including really large brightly colored parrotfish. It is somewhat farther away to go to Los Frailes. The current there is strong so it is for advanced divers only and is usually done as a drift dive. There are moray eels, really big barracudas and lots of oysters (See also Isla Cubagua).

Walter Vedovello's Margarita Divers (T&F:095-64 23 50, Cel. 016-95 33 41, cc:A,V) at Concorde Marina can take you on any of the above dives. They normally do two-tank dives. They will also fill your tanks and help however they can.

There is another dive shop down town in Porlamar called Venaquarium (T:095-63 93 96, 095- 63 11 60). They take groups to Frailes, Cubagua, Testigos and Blanquilla. They use helicopters as well as power boats and for longer stays they have a couple of sailboats. In addition, they have a well stocked shop for buying diving gear.

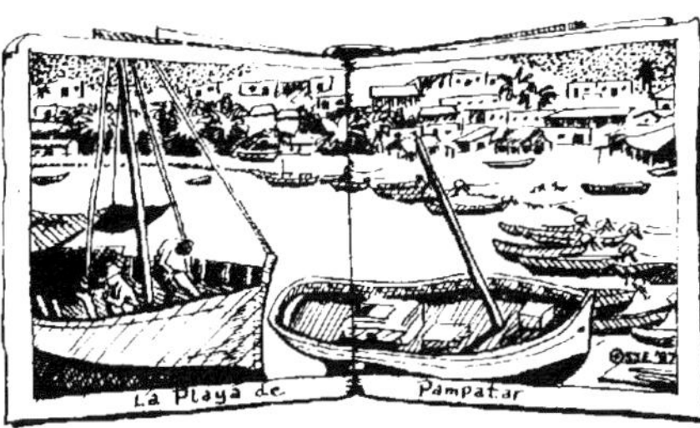

JUANGRIEGO

Juangriego (John the Greek) was named after a Greek pirate who was shipwrecked here. It is a delightful town with a touch of the Riviera. It is peaceful and pleasant, yet there are enough shops to satisfy most needs, a picturesque church, many brightly

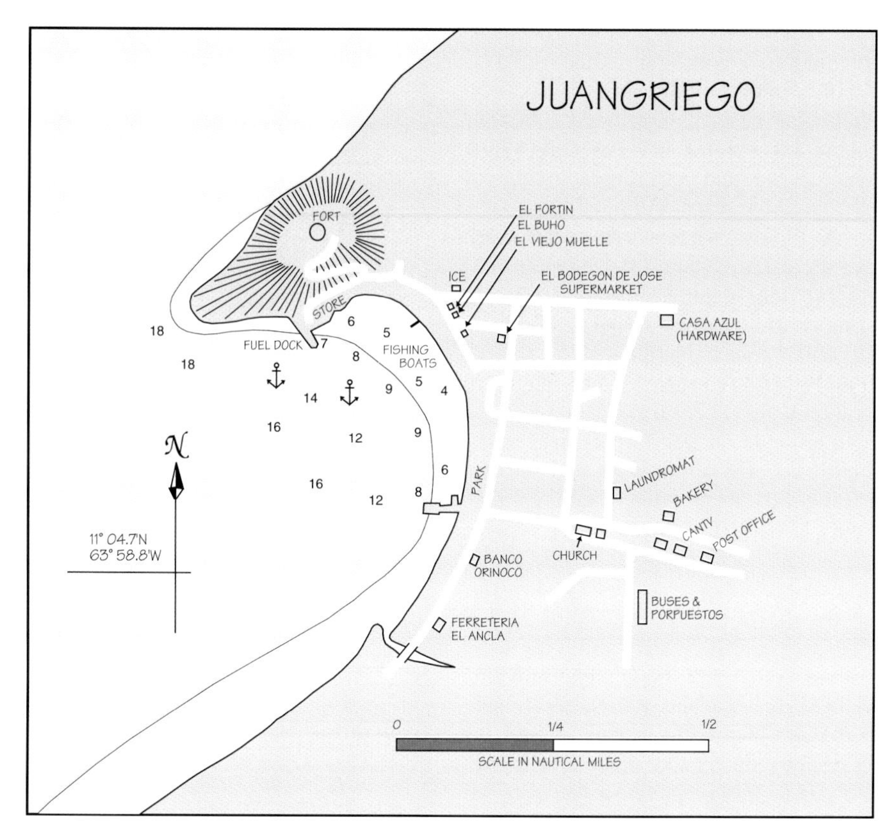

painted fishing boats and some cozy waterside restaurants. There are good shops for clothing, watches and souvenirs.

Navigation

Juangriego is open to the northwest. You would not want to be here during a northerly swell when bad seas can flood the town. In the spring and summer it is perfect, and far more comfortable than Porlamar and Pampatar when the winds switch south of east. Anchor anywhere in the bay clear of the fishing boats. Do not obstruct access to the fuel dock. You can pull your dinghy up the beach, or anchor it and take a line ashore like the local fishing boats. As you come in with the dinghy, watch out for long lines streaming from the fishing boats.

Services

You can get fuel on the fuel dock. There is seven to eight feet off the dock, but there may be scattered boulders on the bottom left over from building the wall, so approach slowly.

There is a small store at the head of th dock, they do yacht clearance and ca arrange for help if you have any maintenance problems

There is an ice factory close to the waterfront, or you can get it from the ice truc that supplies the fishing boats on the fue dock. Telephone calls can be made fro the CANTV office near the post office o from the card phones scattered around The laundromat shown on our sketch char is open 0900-1230 and 1430-1800.

Ashor

There are several small supermarket the closest is El Bogedón de Jose (T:095-5 386/55 714, cc:V) and they promise special discount if you mention this guid Although there are no chandleries, the are two good hardware stores in town.

Several agreeable little restaurants a clustered up in the northeast corner of th bay. El Viejo Muelle (T:095-55 073, $D), El Fortin (T:095-55 092, $D, cc:A,V,D) and El Buho (T:095-55 879, $D, cc:A,V,D) all serve good seafood and are beautifully positioned on the waterfront to sit and watch life go by.

El Fortin (Small Fort) de la Galera is a short walk up the hill which is rewarded by good views all around. This little fort played an important part in the Venezuelan struggle for independence. In 1815 while Bolívar was in exile in Haiti, his cohort, Juan Bautista Arismendi, mounted an attack on the Spanish garrison here and killed all the soldiers. This provided a stronghold for the return of Bolívar, who landed here in 1816 with 4000 rifles and a small force supplied by Haitian President Tion. He gathered up a small army and headed for Carúpano. The war of independence continued and in 1817 the Spanish general Pablo Morillo recaptured the fort and slaughtered hundreds of patriots. If you look down you can see a lagoon. It is said this ran red with blood after the slaughter and is called Laguna de Los Mártires (Lagoon of the Martyrs).

BOCA DEL RÍO, PLAYA LA RESTINGA & LAGUNA GRANDE

Your visit to Margarita will be more fun with a visit to the intricate mangrove channels in Laguna Grande and the beach at Playa La Restinga. This can be done by car, but you can also sail right up into Bahía Mangle and anchor in the mouth of the lagoon.

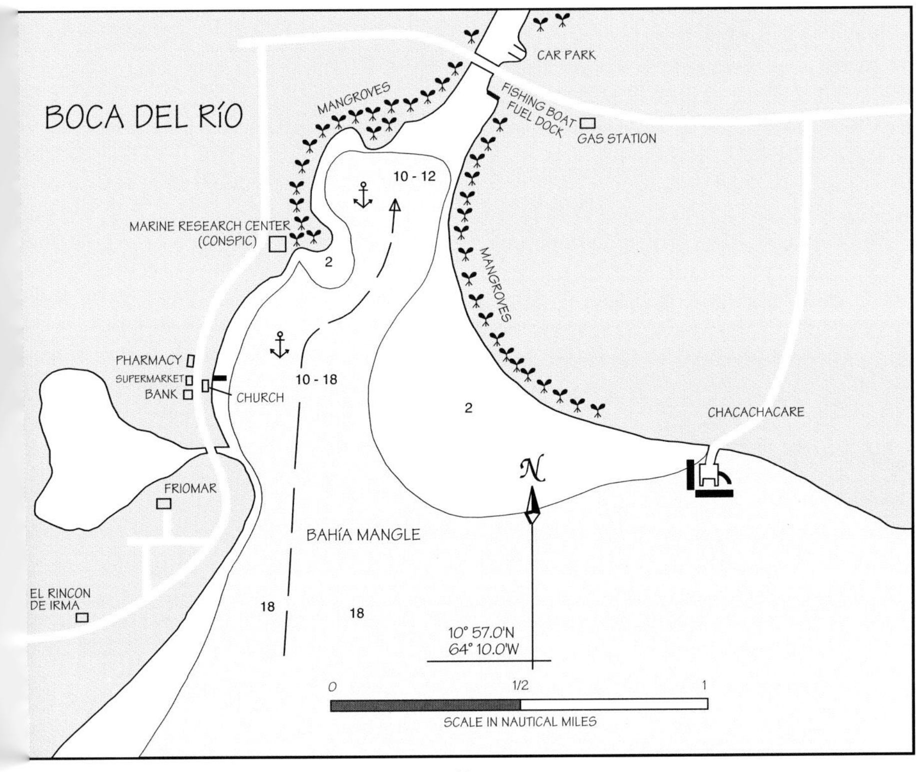

Navigation

The entrance to the Boca De Río (Mouth of the River) anchorage is not difficult, but unfortunately the water comes in patches of green and brown which bear no relation to the depth. As you come in Bahía Mangle favor the Boca del Río side of the bay, but do not hug the shore too closely. You can anchor right off the town. This is sometimes a lovely anchorage, especially in the winter when the winds are north of east. However, in the summer months this bay is subject to a nasty chop so it is better to continue up into the first mangrove bay which is completely sheltered. There is a shoal that extends about 120 yards to the south of the mangroves on the western shore. When you get about 200 yards from the entrance, swing out into the middle of the channel to avoid the shoal (see sketch chart). As the water is murky I would recommend a slow approach, taking soundings. Alternatively, if you anchor off the village, you will probably be approached by one of the men who do the river trip. They will guide you up into the bay in return for being chosen to take you to Playa La Restinga. If you are going up in the mangroves take mosquito coils for the night. Chacachacare, on the eastern side of Bahía Mangle is a busy fishing port. Yachts seem out of place here.

Services

You can jerry jug diesel, water and possibly arrange for ice at the small dock just before the bridge. Go to the dock and ask on the nearest fishing boat. There are two fishing hardware shops in Boca del Río.

Ashore

The trip through the mangrove lagoon to Playa La Restinga is not expensive and should be done with a local guide, on one of their boats, which might be described as "Lagoondolas." They are small open boats with a protective canopy and big outboard. The journey through the mangroves takes you along miles of twisted maze-like channels. There are placid lagoons, narrow tunnels formed by mangrove branches and pretty canals that have been called such names as "tunnel of kisses" and "canal of lovers." Huge pelicans perch in tiny branches, looking as out of place as a bank manager on a seesaw.

Your destination is Playa la Restinga. This is an almost deserted ten-mile long beach. The only buildings are right by the landing and consist of a bunch of rough and ready restaurants open to the sea breeze. Stay for lunch as the seafood is good and prices reasonable. Langostinas are the speciality.

Playa la Restinga is exposed to the wind and as far as the eye can see waves break in white lines along the shore. You can enjoy body surfing and playing in the waves. The beach has thousands of shells with a few unusual ones tucked among the clams. An hour or two is not too long to walk here and you should keep this in mind when arranging the return time with your boatman. When you go back it is by a short and quick route.

Laguna Grande is also known for its scarlet ibis. This bird is best seen at dusk and you would have to arrange a special trip.

If you bring a bag you can collect your supper from the sea. Thousands of guacucos (clam-like shellfish) get washed up along the shore. You can take the live ones as they get washed in or dig for them in the shallows. You need 20-30 per person. Rinse them countless times, or leave them in saltwater overnight to get rid of the sand. To make a delicious soup for 3-4 pour a one-pound can of tomatoes, the same can full of water and the clams in a pot. Add half a can of white wine. Add salt pepper and a little thyme and garlic. Bring to the boil and simmer for 20 minutes (reject any clams that stay closed). If the clams are still sandy, just forget them and enjoy the liquid part of the soup.

If the soup isn't as filling as you hoped you may wish to eat out. El Rincón de Irma ($D) is set in a pleasant garden and open every day. There is also Friomar.

WEST COAST OF MARGARITA

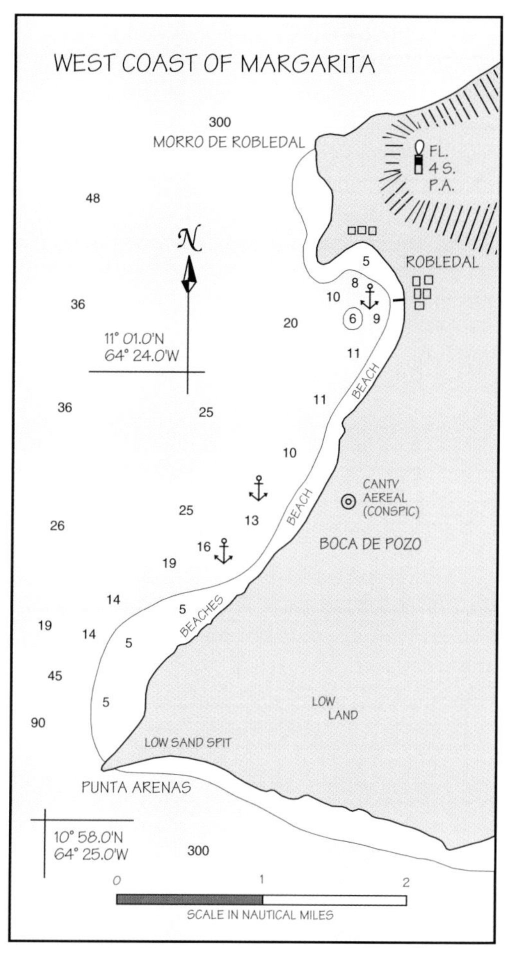

The west coast of Margarita has an attractive coastline backed by red mountains. You can find good anchorage here, though in the winter it should be treated with caution as it is susceptible to northerly swells. It is a convenient stopping place while circumnavigating Margarita and a stopping place en route to Isla Tortuga or Blanquilla. Punta Arenas (Sand Point) is very low with a lovely secluded beach. Along the west coast there are two fishing villages separated by another beach. The area is only occasionally visited by yachts. So far we have had no reports of security problems.

Give a good clearance to the southern part of the west coast as it is shoal. Keep in at least 14 feet of water. You can anchor anywhere else along the coast and the coast just south of Boca de Pozo (Pool Mouth) is especially attractive. If you want to visit the village of Boca de Pozo, anchor outside the fishing fleet in about 12 feet of water. You can carry on down to Robledal (Oak Tree) and anchor off the dock in nine feet of water. There is a six-foot shoal about quarter of a mile southeast of Robledal dock. It is soft mud. Your chart might show a light at Morro de Robledal. This has been replaced by one that flashes every four seconds and is situated on the hills above the point. The light is unreliable.

Ashore

You can find small shops and bins for your garbage in either village. Robledal is a little more picturesque with white washed houses set amid flowers. Here you will find a good general store, two bars, two pharmacies and a modern small hotel called L'Oasis (58 95 91-5339). It is owned by Dr. Santiago Lucques, a master mariner who is also a retired professor from Montreal and his wife Patricia, from Honduras, a professional hotelier. They run an excellent French restaurant, and are helpful with communications.

Boca de Pozo has a pharmacy, bread shop and a place to buy ice, all set round the square which is clearly marked by the huge aerial.

Isla Coche is an unusual island of dry hills in pastel hues of red, yellow and brown covered in dry scrub and cactus. It was originally inhabited by Indians and its name comes from their word for deer. It was colonized by Europeans in the 16th century when the pearls started giving out over in Cubagua and more were discovered in the waters surrounding Coche. It also proved a good source of salt, and they still produce salt here. It has a population of about 4500 and the capital, San Pedro, is a sprawling town of fisher folk which is reminiscent of Mexico in the 40's, an illusion that is aided by flocks of beady-eyed vultures that sit on roofs and stare. Hiking in the hills is really pretty, and the vultures take on a new look, soaring gracefully overhead. To the north of town, Punta Playa is a long and lovely sand spit. Coche is beginning to attract tourists both from the mainland and from Europe, though there is just one small hotel at the moment.

There are two main anchoring areas - the western end of the island and at El Saco on the south coast.

WESTERN COCHE PUNTA PLAYA TO PUNTA EL BOTÓN

Navigation

The high parts of Isla Coche can be seen from afar, but the low lying land, especially Punta Playa, can only be seen when you are quite close.

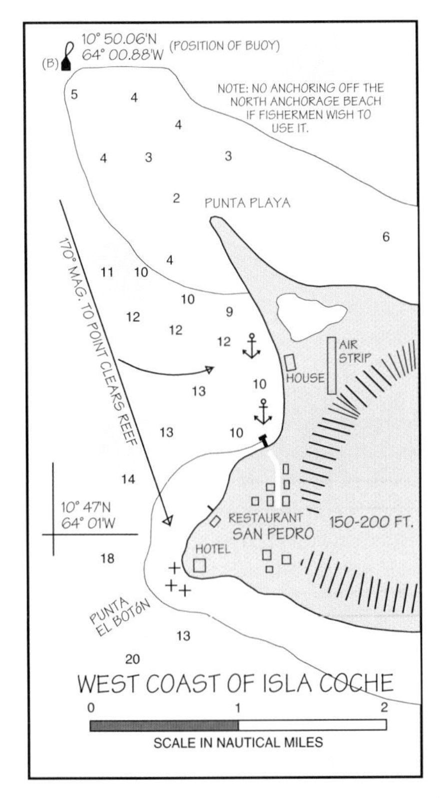

If you are coming from Porlamar, it is necessary to avoid the shoal that extends a mile and a half north of Punta Playa. If you round Punta Mosquito about a mile offshore and head due west, you should find it It is marked by a buoy at 10° 50.06' north and 64° 00.88' west. Once you have rounded the buoy with a reasonable margin, you can head toward Punta el Botón Should the buoy be missing or out of place then a course of 170° magnetic to Punta e Botón should keep you clear of the reef.

The strange castle-like building up in the hills is an abandoned government project intended as a holiday resort for unruly youths.

The Punta Playa anchorage is attractiv and in the early morning it is a pleasure t watch the pelicans and cormorants comin to work. It must be used with consideratio for the fishermen who fish all along th beach. Yachts anchored here are in thei way and they have even been known t move yachts quietly at night by pulling u their anchors and towing them. Day tim anchorage is no problem as the fishing nearly always done at night. If the wind howling out of the northeast (which it ofte does here), they will probably not be fis ing, and you can stay the night. If you s fishing boats with nets moored in this are move before dark. This is no problem as is less than a mile down the beach to the San Pedro ferry dock. There is a good anchorage north of the ferry dock in nine or ten feet of water and you will be out of their way. This is also a more convenient anchorage for visiting the town.

Ashore

If you run short on some essentials, there are several small basic stores in town. But why cook on board when there are two inexpensive restaurants ashore? El Bohio de Doña Carmen (T: 095-99 177, $D) is right on the waterfront and open to the breeze. You can tie your dinghy to the dock outside. They serve good fish and shrimp plates and are open every day from 0900-2100. Isla de Coche Hotel (095-99 118, $D, CC:A,V) is a new venture out on the point. They have mainly German clientele who come for the windsurfing. Meals are buffet style.

EL SACO

El Saco is a beautiful harbor on the south side of Isla Coche. It is open to the breezes but completely protected from the swells and large enough to house every cruising boat in Venezuela. It makes a great cruising rendezvous for a few days away from it all. The long thin land spit at the entrance often contains so many pelicans and cormorants that it looks brown.

Navigation

If you are sailing from San Pedro, keep about half a mile to a mile offshore to clear any shallow places along the coast. The white buildings of the disused sardine factory can often be seen when you round Punta El Botón.

While there is plenty of water in El Saco, you do have to cross a wide bar to get in. The depths on the bar vary from about seven to nine feet, with lots of bumps and dips. The deepest water seems to be on an approach of 50° magnetic toward the dock at El Bichar. There is a partially hidden red roofed church behind the dock which helps locate it. Binoculars also help. Approach the town dock until you are close, then head up into the lagoon. Once inside you have 10 to 18 feet of water in the first part of the lagoon. The prettiest anchorage is on the

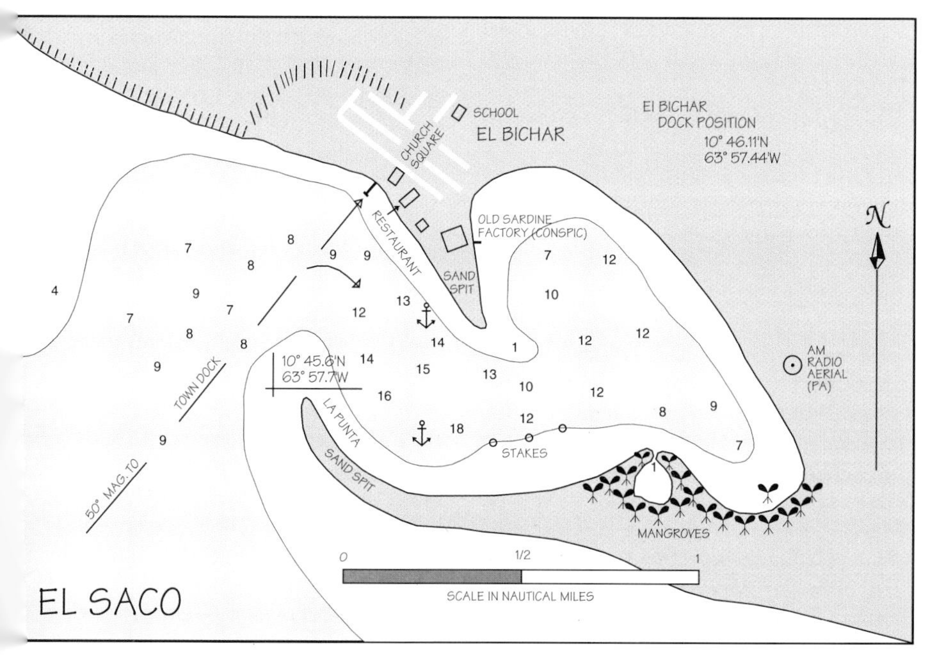

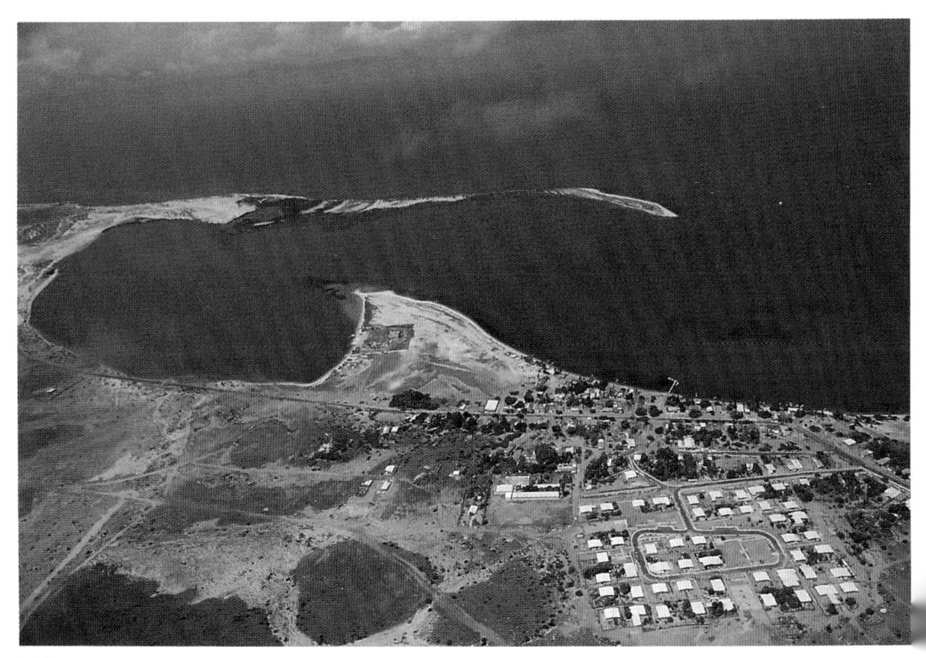

El Saco

south side of the harbor close to the southern sandspit which is so narrow that you can see the water on both sides. You can also anchor off the sand spit by the disused sardine factory, or anywhere in the bay.

If you are going into the second lagoon enter near the stakes as this has the deepest water. Inside our soundings showed most of the inner lagoon to be 10-12 feet deep. Proceed gently.

The inner part of this harbor is protected enough to ride out a tropical storm, but might be marginal for a bad hurricane as the low lying outer spit might be covered in a storm surge.

Ashor

The village of El Bichar sprawls up th hill. The waterfront, with a church an square and a street behind is the mos picturesque part. There are one or two smal stores, a couple of bars and a pleasant beac front restaurant called El Pescador de la Isl ($D). It is open daily from when the owner wake up to midnight. They keep plenty o cold Polar on ice and serve good inexpen sive fish and chicken plates.

The protected lagoon is ideal for dingh exploration and windsurfing. Ashore yo can hike into the dry hills.

ISLA CUBAGU

Isla Cubagua is a pretty island of sandy beaches and dry hills. The yellow-brown hills change color with the sun and on a clear day puffy white clouds perch on Margarita's mountains in a surreal way.

Isla Cubagua was the first European settlement in America. It happened because Christopher Columbus saw some natives with pearls along the Peninsula d Paria. Within a year, two adventurer Christobal De LaGuerra and Pedro Alfons Niño, discovered the source of the pearls be the pearl beds off Cubagua. In 1492 fif fortune hunters arrived and founded Nue Cádiz on the east side of the island. Th took Indians as slaves and forced them dive for pearls. They worked them so hard, whipping them when they would not dive, that hundreds of Indians died. At the height of the pearling industry Cubagua pearls provided Spain with a wealth almost equal to that of the gold transported from Inca lands. In one year alone Cubagua exported 820 pounds of pearls.

In 1520 a force of 300 well armed Indians attacked the town and forced the Spaniards to leave. But the Spanish came back in force and rebuilt the town stronger than before, fortifying their houses against attack. A fort was also built over on the mainland to secure a water supply.

After a few decades of heavy exploitation the supply of pearls decreased and new beds were sought in Coche and Cumaná. On Christmas Day in 1541 an earthquake and tidal wave destroyed Nueva Cádiz. Now Cubagua is uninhabited save for a small research station and a few fishing camps.

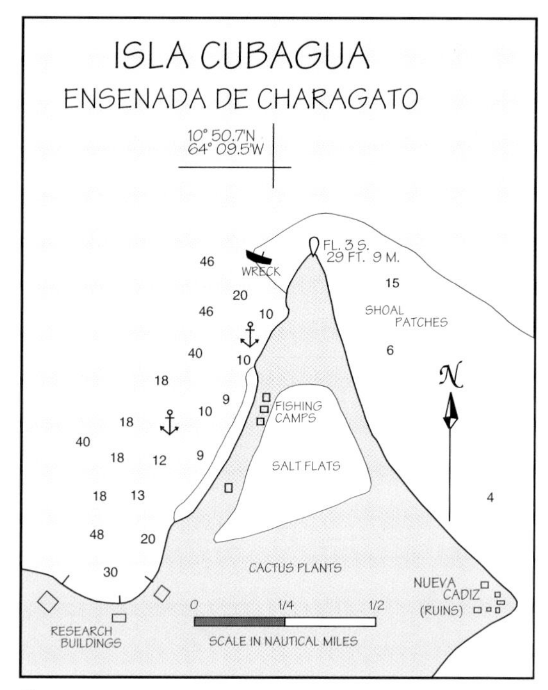

Navigation

The best anchorage in Cubagua is the Ensenada de Charagato at the north eastern tip. This is a large anchorage, well protected from the prevailing winds, and you can anchor anywhere along the shore.

As you approach you will see the con-

Isla Cubagua, Ensenada de Charagato

spicuous wreck of a car ferry. This caught fire in the late 70's. There were frequent explosions from the gas tanks of the cars on board, and it took a week to burn. Pass outside this wreck and sail up into the bay. The anchoring shelf is widest off the beach and holding is good in sand between the dense weed patches. Day charter boats use this anchorage, but there is plenty of room to anchor well away from them.

Regulations

Pearl fishing has been prohibited since 1962.

Ashore

The remains of Nuevo Cádiz are a 40-minute walk away. Skirt the salt pond and follow the shoreline south until you come to the ruins. Only the bottoms of the walls remain, but you get an idea of the size of the town and it continues down into the sea. The ground glints with reflections from thousands of oyster shell fragments.

Water Sports

The water is often refreshingly chilly here and the visibility is not always good, but snorkeling and diving on the big wreck are excellent, with lots of fish and reef creatures such as basket stars. You also see large star fish. Advanced divers can go inside the ferry hold and see the cars still sitting there. The wreck of a barge is close to the wrecked ferry.

PASSAGES BETWEEN MARGARITA, BLANQUILLA AND TORTUGA

The current in these passages is variable, and though it can be strong, it is sometimes half a knot or less. You occasionally get a reverse easterly setting current between Tortuga and Margarita. This reverse current is generally weak.

The shortest distance between Margarita and Blanquilla is from Robledal and it can be a pleasant reach in either direction. There is also no problem sailing from Juangriego or Pampatar, though you may want to do it overnight. From Robledal you can make either Blanquilla or Tortuga as a day sail, but be prepared to use your engine if the wind drops.

Blanquilla is low and cannot be seen until you are within a few miles, but it is easy to see Los Hermanos Rocks. They are about six miles east of Blanquilla and cover about six miles in a southerly direction. The largest one is 600 feet high and is easily seen from afar.

Tortuga is low lying and you cannot see it until you are within six or seven miles.

BLANQUILLA

Blanquilla is a delightful island, well off the beaten track, that lies about 50 miles north of Margarita. It is low lying, about 50 feet high. There are spectacular beaches, clear water and wonderful snorkeling. It would be easy to sit here a week or two, enjoying the water and watching the sunsets. The whole area is a national park, spearfishing is not allowed.

There is a small settlement around Playa Falucho with a few fishermen and a small garrison of National Guard. Wherever you anchor, expect the national guard to visit at some time to check your papers. If this is your first stop in Venezuela, you should check with them. In emergencies you could possibly find medical assistance and beg a little water. There is an airstrip by the village and a lighthouse that flashes every 5 seconds.

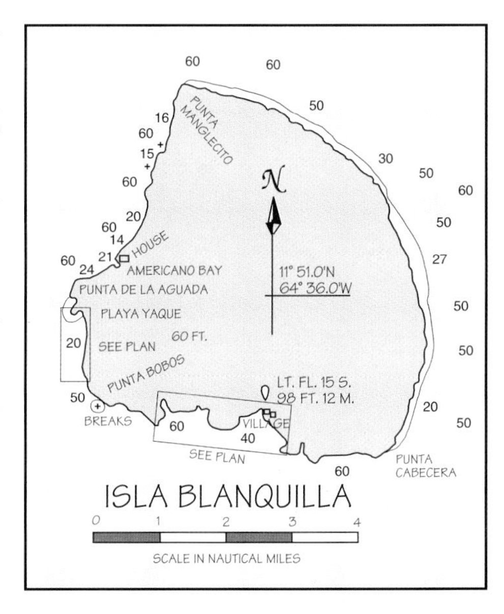

SOUTH COAST ANCHORAGES

Playa Falucho

The village anchorage is a sandy spot right at the head of Playa Falucho. The surrounding bay has a coral bottom 18 feet or more deep. The sandy patch is tiny and rather shallow. You can stop here for a short while, but if you stay long you will be in the way of the fishermen. A more secluded spot, still within reach of the village, is just inside the headland at the eastern end of the bay. Most of the bottom is coral but you can find a patch of sand just in front of the beach.

Snorkeling is good here and just around

the headland is an interesting fjord which can be explored by dinghy.

If you feel like walking, there is a road of sorts which goes over to Americano Bay.

Playa Caranton

There is a good little anchorage round the headland off Playa Caranton. It offers small fjords for dinghy exploration and good snorkeling.

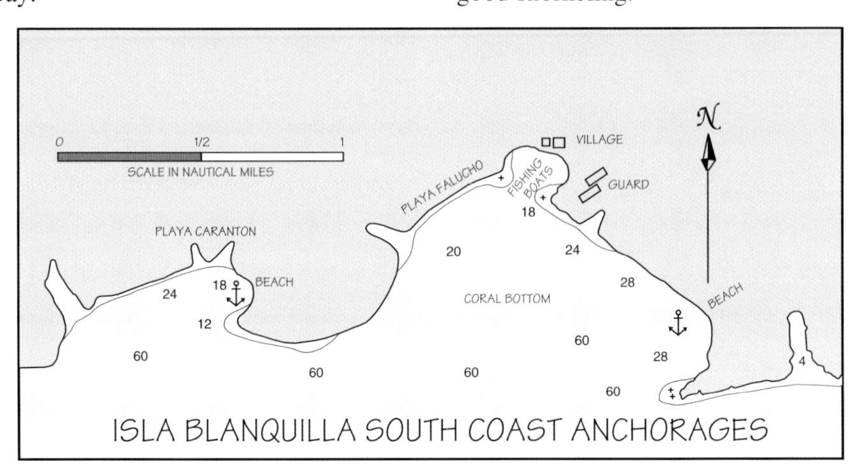

PLAYA YAQUE ANCHORAG

Playa Yaque is in the lee of the island. It is lovely, with gorgeous white beaches interspersed with rocks. There is plenty of coral and the snorkeling is excellent.

When approaching from the east beware of the little rock which breaks just belo the surface about a hundred yards offsho and a little to the east of Punta Bobos.

The seabed off the beaches is a mixture sand and coral. There are many cor eads that stick up within 4-6 feet of the urface, but these are mainly within a undred yards of the shore.

The north end of Playa Yaque terminates ı a strange point of sharp-pointed rocks. 'he most protected anchorage is inside ıis point, between it and the big flat rock vhich sticks out from the shore below the mall ruins. Enter in good light and stay ver the sand bottom. Unfortunately, more ıan two boats are a crowd.

Farther down, the prettiest anchorage is ff the best beach which is marked by a lump of palms in the middle. You have to ɔok carefully to make sure you are anhored on a patch of sand as much of the ottom is coral.

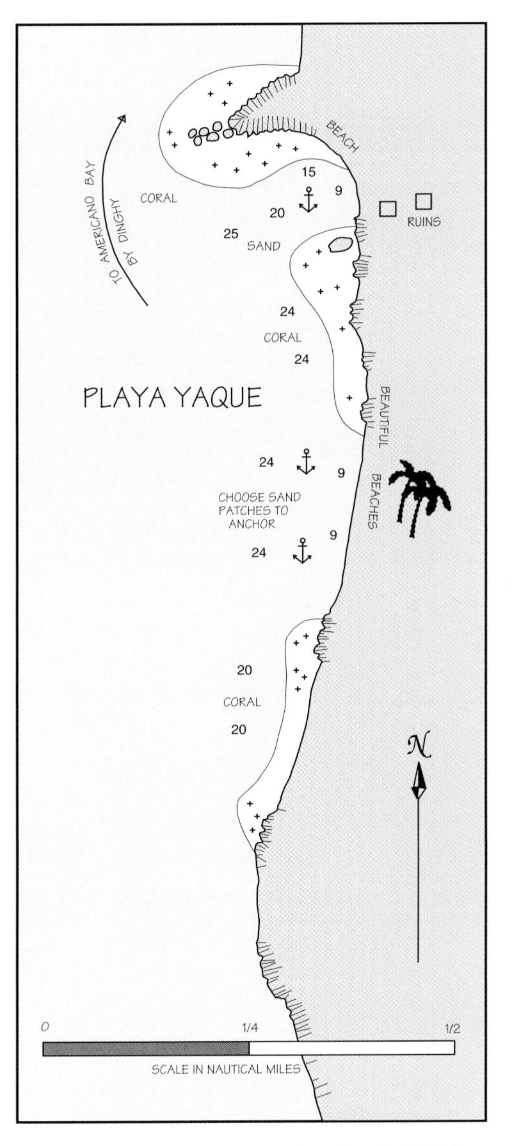

Ashore

You can enjoy walking over the flat dry ınd. The ground is covered with thouands of pretty flowering cactuses. These lants, which look so pretty in a pot, take n a different complexion when embedded ı your foot. Stout footwear is recomıended.

There is a great dinghy trip to Americano Bay. As you enter there are liffs on each side and a deserted beach at ıe head. On the south side is a deep cave ıat goes way under the rock. On the north s a spectacular natural rock arch.

The bay is named after the American, Mr. Blankenship, who built the little ouse here, long before anyone was using ıe island. He used to land his plane near ıe house. It is an ideal "away from it all" pot.

ISLA TORTUGA

Isla Tortuga is gorgeous. It is a low and ry island with sensational beaches, brilıant water colors, good snorkeling and nough anchorages to keep you happy for week or more.

Navigation

Tortuga and its associated islands are teep to within half a mile, so you can pproach from any direction. The only lace that may give trouble is Los alanquinos which are only a few feet high and difficult to see in some light conditions. If you are approaching from the north, you can gauge your position by taking bearings on Cayo Herradura. If you are approaching Punta Delgada from the north, you can usually distinguish it from the rest of the coast by dark green mangrove trees which stand out. It is sensible to approach Tortuga by day. If you must come in after dark, the best approach is around Cayo Herradura from the north because of the conspicuous lighthouse (as-

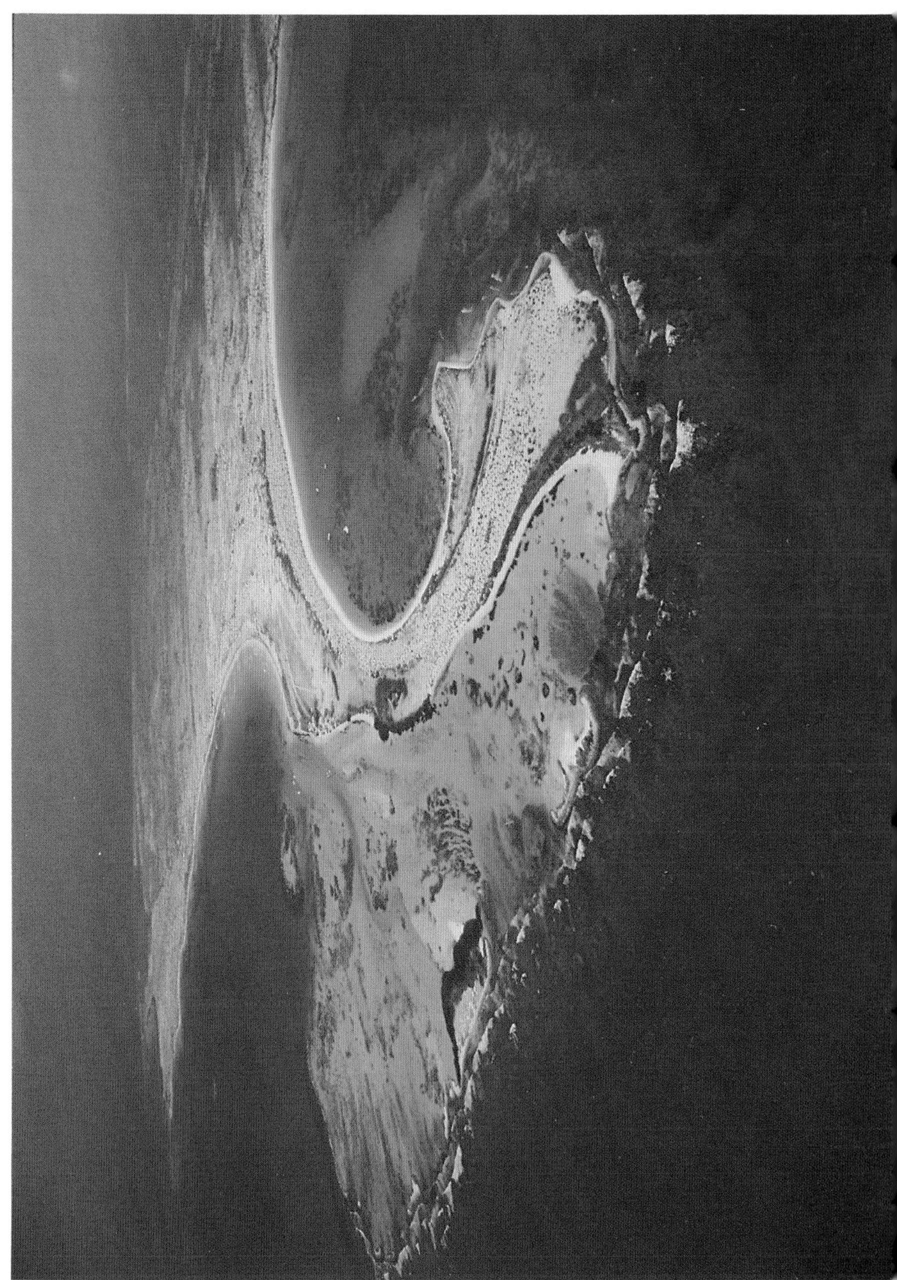

Playa Caldera

suming it is still working).

You can sail along either the north or the south side of Tortuga. The north side is best navigated when the light is not straight ahead so you can see your way past Los Palanquinos. You can stay fairly clos to shore, but there are a few reefs an shoals, especially east of Punta Rancho and along the shore off Los Palanquino and off Cayo Herradura.

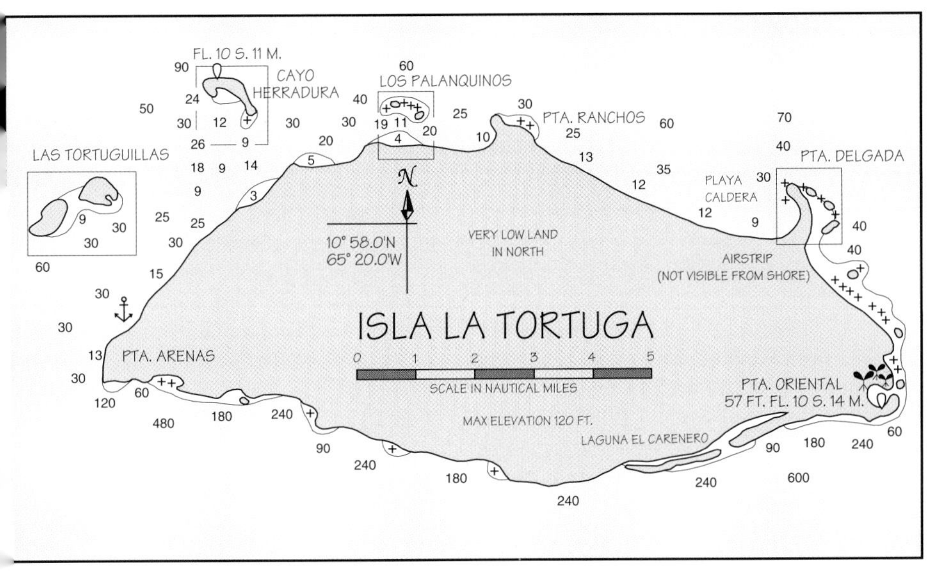

There are excellent anchorages in Tortuga for much of the time. However, northerly swells can make things pretty uncomfortable in most places and untenable in Playa Caldera. During the month of May there are often southerly winds for some hours. This can make Cayo Herradura and Las Tortuguillas uncomfortable, though not generally untenable.

PLAYA CALDERA

Playa Caldera (Cauldron Beach) is an outstanding half-moon beach of white sand over a mile long. Around noon the whole anchorage feels bleached and baked, heat shimmers and the houses look timeless and unreal. Distances become hard to judge.

The fishermen's shacks ashore are used

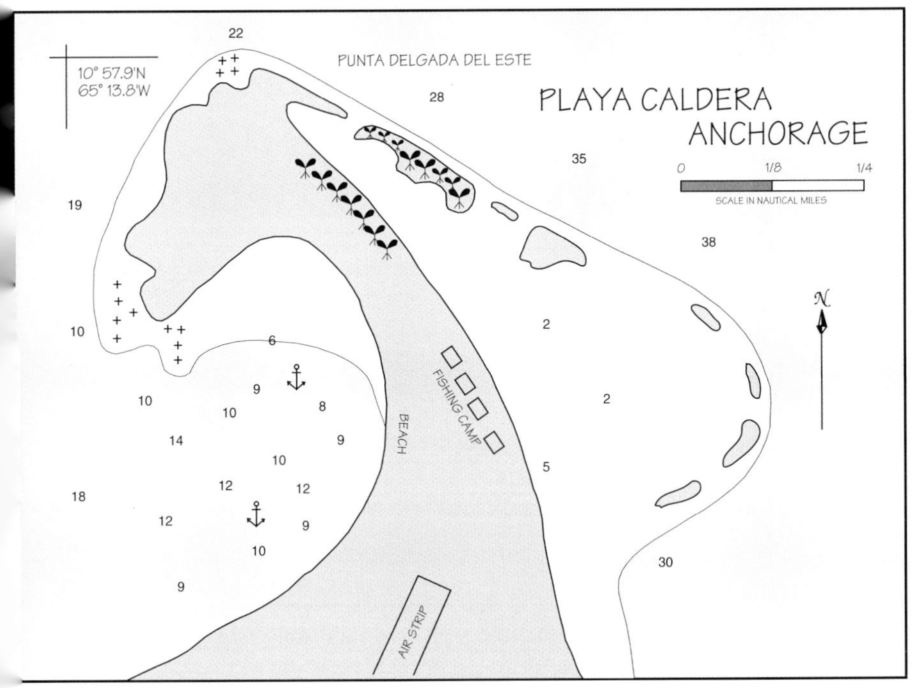

seasonally. A rough airstrip is used on weekends by people from Caracas who come in small planes to enjoy the beach. I am told that after a day's boozing and sunning, some pilots like to show off to their friends with low level aerobatics. I do not know whether this is true, but we did find the wreck of a plane on the other end of the island.

Navigation

If the light is good you can eyeball your way quite close to Punta Delgada. Stay a couple of hundred yards off if the light is poor. The reef does not extend far from the point, but the bottom is sand and weed, making it difficult to judge. Once you are right in the middle of the bay, find the best anchorage by feeling your way up into the northern corner and anchor in 8-9 feet.

Ashore

The beach here is stupendous, with dunes on the south side that are decorated by a variety of plants so tastefully arranged that a landscape gardener could learn a thing or two. On the windward beach you can walk for miles. A large lagoon to the east of Punta Delgada is formed by a group of small islands. It is very shallow and you can wade out along much of it. The fishermen bring boats in at the south end where the water is deeper.

LOS PALANQUINOS

Los Palanquinos is a mile beyond Punta Ranchos. It is an offshore reef with a few rocks sticking out. There is a generally well protected anchorage here with some good snorkeling and it is within easy reach of the shore for a walk.

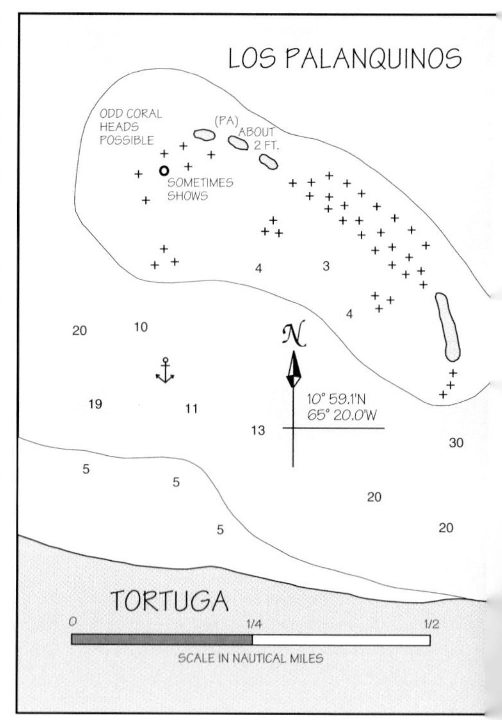

Navigation

This reef is hard to spot in some conditions, but easy enough to see when approaching along the coast in good light. If you are approaching from the north you can come around either side of the reef, but stay half a mile away from it. There is plenty of room to anchor between the reef and the shore, out of most of the northerly surge. The anchorage is weed and grass. Avoid the shoal area that extends from the Tortuga side.

The snorkeling here is well worth while. There are plenty of small barracudas out on the reef. Dinghy over to the Tortuga side for great walks, but if you plan to go far inland, take a compass and some liquid to drink.

CAYO HERRADURA

Cayo Herradura (Horseshoe Cay) is the most favored of the Tortuga anchorages. It is a mile long island made up for th most part of fine white sand. The island i quite popular on weekends with power boats from the mainland. At the north end there is a fishing camp, occupied for most of the year.

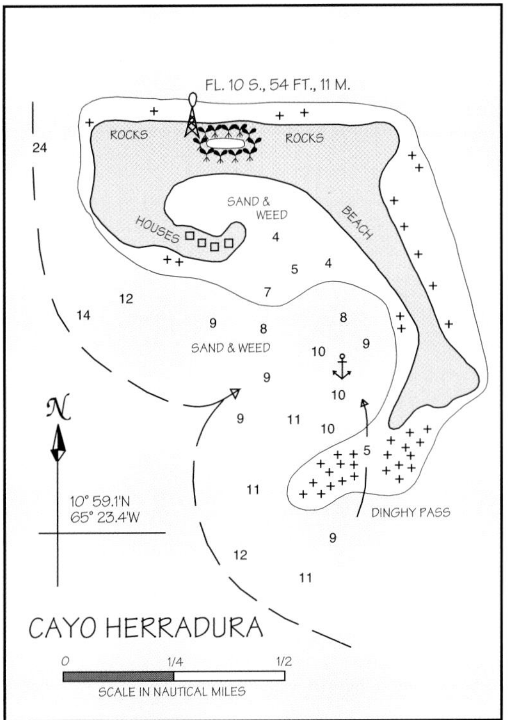

Navigation

There is a reef off the southern end of the island. This extends a quarter of a mile from the beach at most, not the three quarters of a mile marked on some charts. You can approach from the west or southwest but give this reef a fair clearance. It is usually quite visible, but sometimes hard to discern from the rest off the bottom which is sand and weed. Most of the bottom here is 10-12 feet deep with the odd patch about 8.5 feet deep. Boats drawing over eight feet might prefer to approach around the north of the island where they can stay in deeper water. You can approach the beach quite closely and anchor in nine or ten feet. The northern half of the bay is shoal and should be avoided.

There is an iron light tower on Herradura which flashes every ten seconds.

LAS TORTUGUILLAS

Las Tortuguillas (The Little Turtles) are two lovely deserted islands with phenomenal beaches and fair snorkeling reefs.

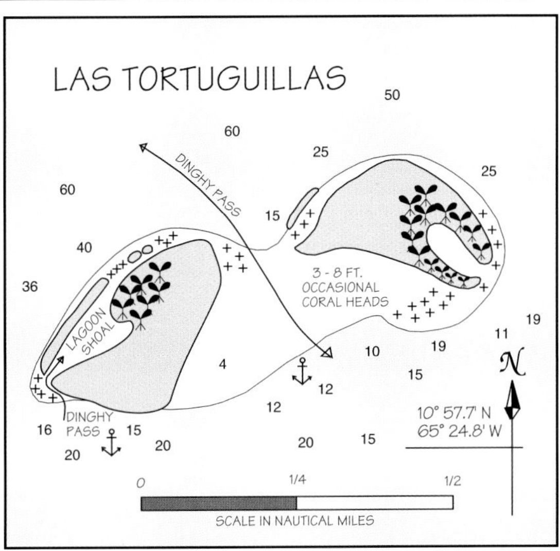

Navigation

Protection from the east comes from Tortuga and there is a two-mile fetch so you can get a chop in here. Some people anchor between the islands, edging in gently as far as possible. Remember that this is a lee shore. I have seen centerboard yachts tuck up behind the reef off the western island and still roll. A preferable anchorage, where the water is deeper, is off the southern side of the western island. If the conditions are not suitable for overnight anchorage, come and enjoy it by day.

Ashore

Take the dinghy into the lagoon behind the western island. The approach is right along the beach. The water inside is very shallow and warm. A great place to lie suspended with a face mask watching the little fishes below or to laze on the beach or examine the animal and plant communities ashore. There are hermit and soldier crabs and lots of birds. Red mangroves, saltwort, bay cedar, and joewood dominate the plant community.

ANCHORAGE NORTH OF PUNTA ARENAS

You can anchor anywhere along the west coast north from Punta Arenas. This is not a good anchorage in the winter when the wind comes from the northeast.

LAGUNA EL CARENERO

Laguna El Carenero

Some yachtspeople visit Laguna El Carenero (The Carenage Lagoon) on Tortuga's south coast. It is a good anchorage for power boats, multihulls and centerboarders. I don't consider this a good anchorage for other yachts because the entrance is tricky and the depths are marginal. There is a maximum of six feet at the entrance at low water. One boat has been wrecked here, and others have had close calls. The depths were too shallow to enable us to chart it, but for shallow draft yachts we include an aerial photo.

I can think of few places where I have had as much pleasure just sailing as among Los Roques. Stiff breezes, a flat sea and ever changing watercolors make it sheer bliss. Everything is so clear that you can often negotiate difficult reef passages under sail and tack between reefs right up to anchor.

Los Roques is an unbelievable cruising area made of about 14 by 25 miles of protected, reef-studded water, dotted with pretty little islands. The shallow reef areas reflect so much light that the clouds sometimes turn a green color and whole areas of reef seem to give off a greenish glow. Part of the attraction is that it is poorly enough charted that it is easy to find anchorages on your own and get the feeling that you are really out there on the edge exploring.

In many places the anchorages are from 40 to 50 feet deep. There is no problem anchoring in such areas - the holding is often excellent but you do need to come with enough anchor rode. Unless you have a reliable windlass, I would suggest anchoring with rope.

It is best to visit Los Roques in the spring and summer rather than in the winter. Summer winds are breezy and pleasant. Winter winds can sometimes turn the whole place into a kind of tropical roaring forties. While cruising is not a problem at this time of year, it is not as pleasurable. Northeasterly winds and northerly swells can eliminate many good snorkeling areas, make dinghy exploration difficult, and create rolly anchorages.

If you want to get the most out of Los Roques, I recommend temporarily rigging a few ratlines, just enough to get your feet about six feet above deck level. While this is not strictly necessary for navigation, it does make it a lot easier when exploring poorly charted areas and apart from that, you are going to love the way the view opens from just a few feet up.

For nature lovers there are some 80 species of birds that either live here or are migratory species passing through.

Los Roques is reputed to have the best bone fishing in the world, and aficionados stay in a special club on Gran Roque which caters to this sport.

Regulations

Los Roques is a national park and before you visit you have to get a permit from Inparques, The easiest way to do this is to arrange it though one of the clearing agents. You are limited to a two week stay. You will be charged a fee, these may well change but as we write it comes to about $1US per foot for the boat and $10 US per person. On arrival you have to proceed to El Gran Roque and check with Inparques, the Guardacosta and anyone else the Inparques direct you to. You will find them all strung out along the beach to the west of town. You can identify the coast guard by the big Venezuelan flag and the park authorities by the park flag.

Part of your fee goes to garbage collection and the garbage scow collects garbage about three times a week from yachts in all main anchorages. The exception to this is Gran Roque, where there are garbage bins ashore.

You cannot clear out of Venezuela from here, you have to go to the mainland to get clearance.

Spearfishing is not allowed (if you carry a speargun, the park authorities will probably hold it while you visit.) Collecting conch is forbidden. There must be no dumping of garbage or discharging oil. You can fish with a hand-line. Permits may be necessary for using a rod and reel - ask Inparques for details. You can anchor anywhere in the park except in the restricted areas where these activities are not allowed. Anchoring must always be on sand and never on coral.

Navigation

Unless you have a high powered speed boat, Los Roques is an overnight sail. When you are coming from the south or west, the light at Isla Orchilla is a great help. It is about 436 feet high, flashes every 13 seconds and has a 20-mile range.

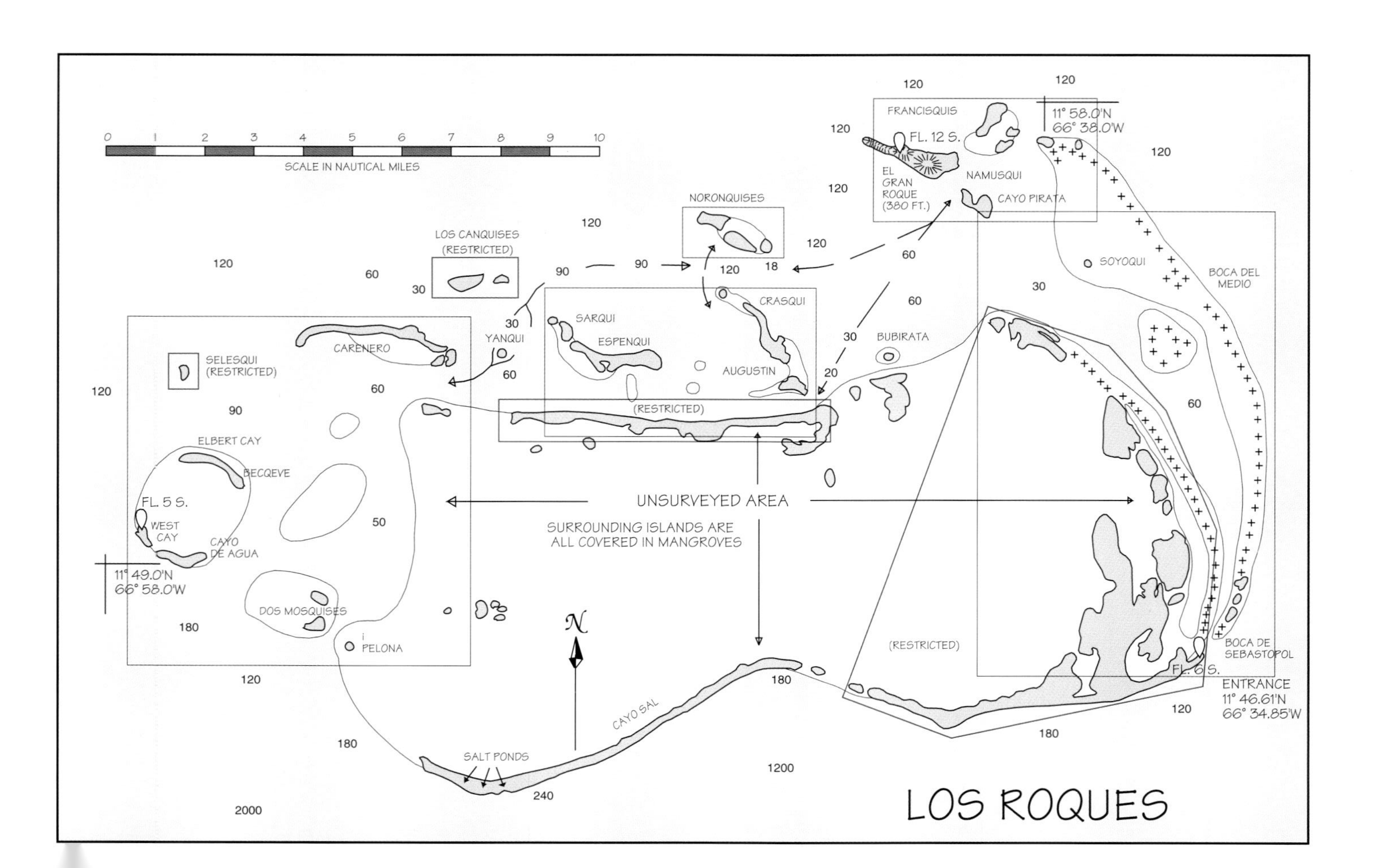
LOS ROQUES
SCALE IN NAUTICAL MILES
0 1 2 3 4 5 6 7 8 9 10
FRANCISQUIS
FL. 12 S.
EL GRAN ROQUE (380 FT.)
NAMUSQUI
CAYO PIRATA
11° 58.0'N
66° 38.0'W
SOYOQUI
BOCA DEL MEDIO
NORONQUISES
LOS CANQUISES (RESTRICTED)
YANQUI
SARQUI
ESPENQUI
CRASQUI
AUGUSTIN
BUBIRATA
(RESTRICTED)
CARENERO
SELESQUI (RESTRICTED)
ELBERT CAY
BECQEVE
FL. 5 S.
WEST CAY
CAYO DE AGUA
11° 49.0'N
66° 58.0'W
DOS MOSQUISES
PELONA
UNSURVEYED AREA
SURROUNDING ISLANDS ARE
ALL COVERED IN MANGROVES
CAYO SAL
SALT PONDS
(RESTRICTED)
BOCA DE SEBASTOPOL
FL. 6 S.
ENTRANCE
11° 46.61'N
66° 34.85'W

Lighthouses on Los Roques are unreliable. The one most likely to be working is the one at El Gran Roque because the officials notice when it goes out.

EASTERN LOS ROQUES

Eastern Los Roques is protected from the east by a long outer reef called Bajo de la Cabecera (Head Shaped Shoal). Once you are safely tucked behind the reef, this area is navigator-friendly in good light. The navigable water is deep and very blue and the shoal areas jump out as brown reefs or glow the color of the sand which covers them. This is the best area for exploring off the chart. You find some of the best anchorages yourself and the snorkeling is often excellent. Most charts have large areas marked as shallow, dotted with small reefs drawn all along the inside of Bajo de la Cabecera. The positions of the squiggly little reefs are generally pretty good, but the water marked as shallow on the chart is often 12 to 40 feet deep.

BOCO DE SEBASTOPOL (SOUTHEAST ENTRANCE)

Navigation

The Boca de Sebastopol entrance is convenient if you are approaching from the south. It is an all weather entrance, if somewhat hairy in big swells. You do need enough light to see the reefs and shallow patches, though these are clearly demarcated. From the southeast, the land is low lying and you will not see it until the last six miles. Once in view you probably can pick out the lighthouse against the trees behind. It looks very conventional with its red and white stripes, an illusion wrought of modern materials, in fact it is lightweight and made of fiberglass.

If you have been carried north and are approaching more from the east, another conspicuous feature is the wrecked trawler just north of Buchiyaco. Steer for the lighthouse until you get about a mile off and can

ooking south to Boca de Sebastopol. Both the Bajo de la Cabecera outer reef and the middle viding reef show up clearly.

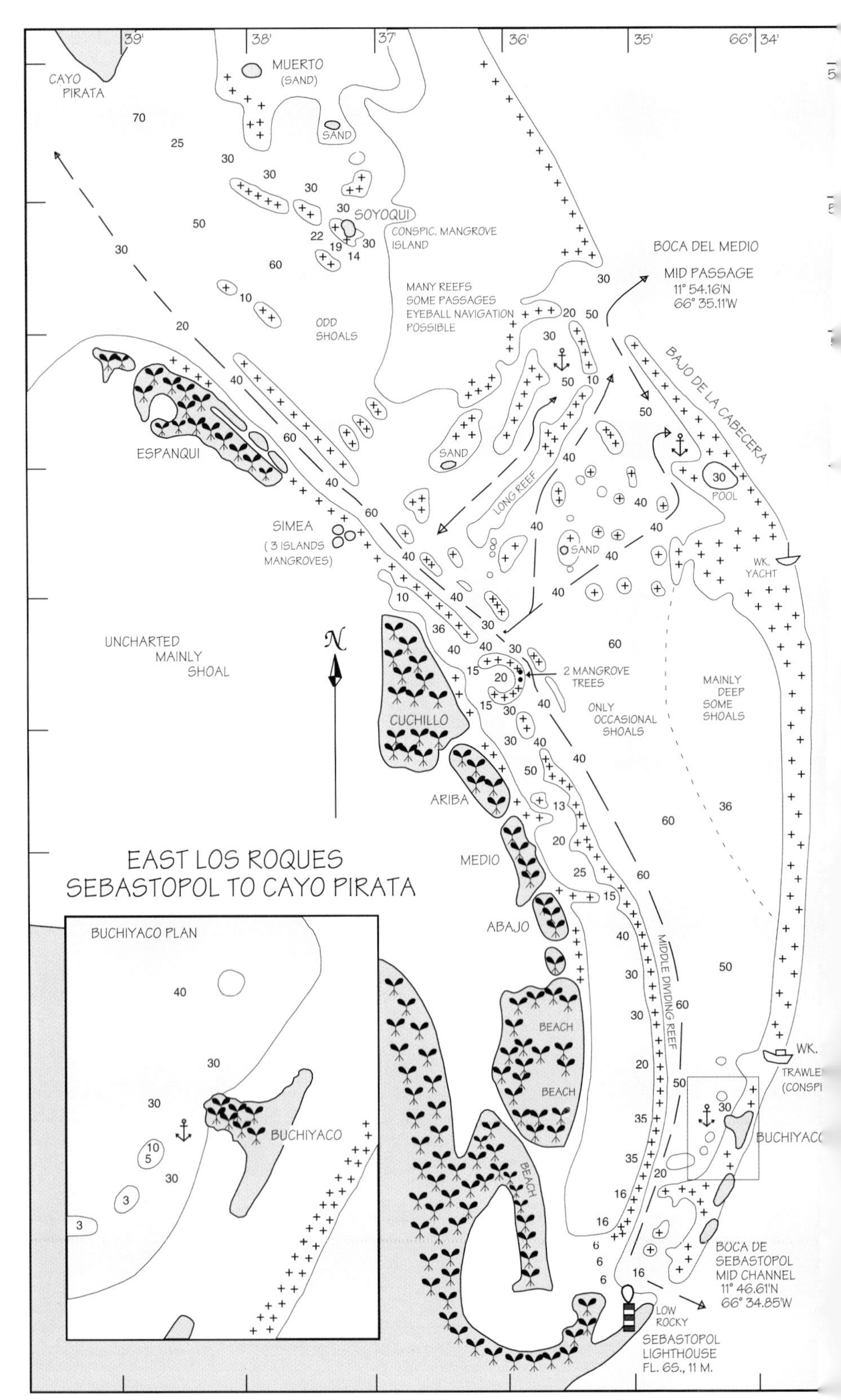

EAST LOS ROQUES
SEBASTOPOL TO CAYO PIRATA
CAYO PIRATA
MUERTO (SAND)
SAND
SOYOQUI
CONSPIC. MANGROVE ISLAND
BOCA DEL MEDIO
MID PASSAGE
11° 54.16'N
66° 35.11'W
MANY REEFS SOME PASSAGES EYEBALL NAVIGATION POSSIBLE
ODD SHOALS
BAJO DE LA CABECERA
ESPANQUI
LONG REEF
POOL
SIMEA
(3 ISLANDS MANGROVES)
WK. YACHT
UNCHARTED MAINLY SHOAL
2 MANGROVE TREES
ONLY OCCASIONAL SHOALS
MAINLY DEEP SOME SHOALS
CUCHILLO
ARIBA
MEDIO
ABAJO
MIDDLE DIVIDING REEF
BEACH
WK.
BUCHIYACO PLAN
BUCHIYACO
BOCA DE SEBASTOPOL MID CHANNEL
11° 46.61'N
66° 34.85'W
LOW ROCKY
SEBASTOPOL LIGHTHOUSE
FL. 6S., 11 M.

begin to see the entrance. The land that extends from the lighthouse to the entrance is very low and rocky, not easy to see until you are almost there. However, it is usually easier to see than the reef on the opposite side of the entrance. The entrance is about a quarter of a mile wide. When you can see both the end of the reef and the low rocky point off the lighthouse, enter midway between them. When you are past the entrance the sea begins to subside, but there will still be some left over swells. Look for the middle dividing reef that separates the two channels, and aim for the end of it. When you reach it, stay on the eastern side and follow it closely northwards. The depth at the entrance is 20 feet, and soon after you get in it shoals to about 16 feet. Then it gets deeper again and you find yourself in a wonderful area of very deep blue water, 30-60 feet deep and dotted with occasional shoals.

SEBASTOPOL NORTHWARDS

The clearest and easiest route is to sail northwards, keeping the middle dividing reef close on your port side all the way to Espanqui. From here you can head for Gran Roque. Up to Cuchillo you will see over the reef to the inside deep water passage. This passage stops at Cuchillo but the reef continues to Espenqui. This reef is very easy to see and is continuous except for a few cuts into the inner passage near Cuchillo and Ariba. Hug the reef, passing inside any off lying shoals along the way to Espanqui. This will give you the best and easiest passage in water mainly 40-60 feet deep. Unless the wind is against you, you can sail the whole way. You may notice this does not match most charts which show a detour outside a second set of reefs after Cuchillo. As far as we can see this is bad charting; use our sketch chart instead. You can also follow the route shown on other charts, but it is less clear and you have to dodge more reefs.

There is a good anchorage in the lee of Buchiyaco. There is a broad area of very shoal water extending from the reef. Behind that is a band of deep water then a few shoals with three to ten feet of water over them. Eyeball your way in, avoiding the shoal spots and anchor anywhere in the lee of the island. If it is blowing hard you can get a little lee from the mangroves. Holding is good in 30 feet of water.

You can also anchor anywhere along the reef, though if big waves are breaking over the top it could get uncomfortable. I would recommend looking for areas with depths of 30-40 feet to anchor in. The holding is often good in sand. Some people like to anchor "hanging off" the shallow areas - taking an anchor into the really shallow water. There are two potential problems with this. One is that the very shallow water is usually the top of a reef bank and consists of hard dead coral covered by a minimum of sand. The other is that often these shoal areas do have corals or sponges growing on them, and these are not always easy to see from a dinghy. So if you do anchor this way, use a mask and put the anchor down clear of any living creatures.

THE INSIDE PASSAGE WEST OF THE MIDDLE DIVIDING REEF

This long completely protected body of water is a great place just to explore under sail. This is all you can do because anchoring and fishing are forbidden here. Unless you are shoal draft I would not recommend approaching this area from the southern (Sebastopol) end. There is a bar at the entrance which is down wind in rough seas and only about seven feet deep at mid-tide which does not seem like an adequate safety margin for most keel boats. Even shoal boats would be better off trying this channel on their way out before attempting the downwind and down-sea entrance.

You can access the center channel through any of the three breaks opposite the islands of Ariba and Cuchillo. Enter one of these and eyeball your way down. You do have to steer round a few reefs (see our sketch chart) but this is easy in good light. There is an absolute minimum depth of 13 feet in the channel, but most of it is 20-40 feet deep. The passage goes right up to the north end of Cuchillo, but this is a cul-de-sac with little room to turn under sail.

BOCA DEL MEDIO AND NEARBY ANCHORAGES

Boca del Medio is an easy exit and not a bad entrance for more experienced reef navigators when conditions are reasonable and the light is right. Use your GPS to get you close to the entrance and eyeball your way in. Once inside, swing round the reef to the south until you are out of the seas. Getting back to the main channel is discussed below.

Navigating this area is strictly by eye and you should only do it when the light is acceptable. The positions of sand islands may be unreliable as these come and go. South of the reef we have called Long Reef on our chart, the reefs tend to be discreet so you do not have to worry about getting caught in a cul-de-sac. You can easily explore this area under sail with a good lookout.

You can choose your own passages between the reefs. The reef we have marked as Long Reef can be used as a highway - just follow it up or down. Another easy way through the reefs to or from the main channel begins just west of the reef with the two mangrove trees. From here a course of about 65° magnetic takes you pretty much out between shoals to the outer reef.

There is a delightful anchorage inside the outer reef just beside a deep pool surrounded by reef. The anchorage is 49 feet deep but the holding is good. You can swim or dinghy through to the pool. The water is clear and the snorkeling is excellent. Wherever there are patches of reef you find healthy corals, sponges, very tame parrotfish and doctorfishes, clams and pencil clams. This is also true on the reef outside the pool. More ambitious people might want to work their way down toward the entrance where the snorkeling is even better.

There is an area for excellent snorkeling right opposite Boca del Medio behind the next reefs. We show the two eastern entrances on our chart, but the southern one is only 10 feet deep and both are subject to rough seas as they are opposite Boca del Medio. It is safer to approach down the northern side of the long reef. Although the water is quite deep you need to send a snorkeller over before dropping your hook to make sure it is not in coral, as even the sand bottom here has some corals growing on it. There is lots of coral here, nearly all of it alive, and there are hundreds of colorful reef fish, including tame groupers.

We mention these two anchorages, bu one of the delights of this area is that it i not terribly well charted and there ar excellent anchoring and exploring possi bilities. You can find and choose your ow anchorage just about anywhere betwee the reefs, as long as it is outside the re stricted area.

The reef north of Boca del Medio als has many anchoring possibilities. A goo starting point is Soyoqui, a distinctiv small mangrove covered island that yo can see from afar. Soyoqui has many ar choring possibilities because there is channel all around and you can choos your spot to suit the conditions. It is easy t approach from Cayo Pirata or from th channel off Espanqui. From here you ca explore outwards and find your own spc

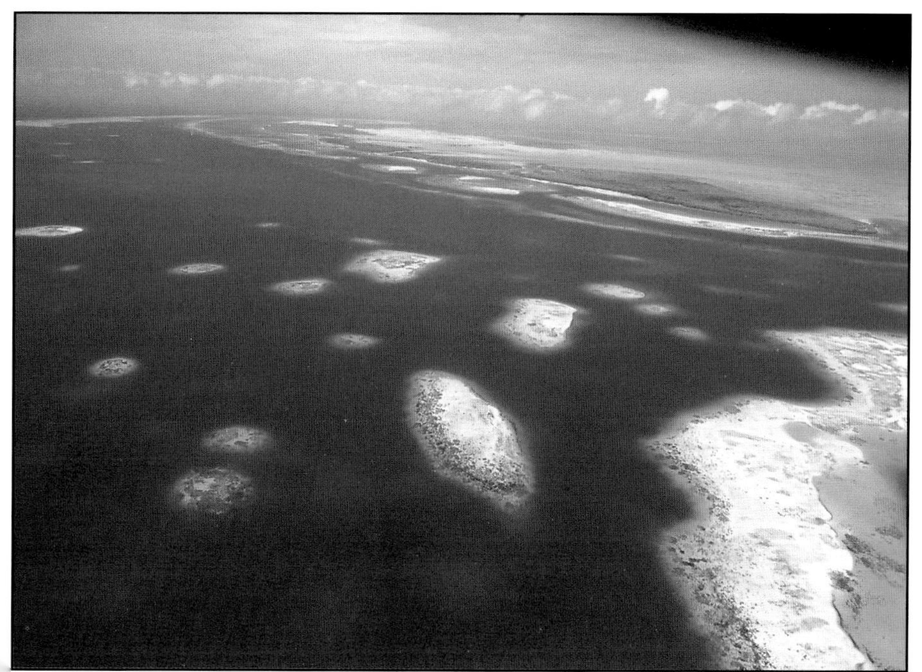

East Los Roques, looking south from Long Reef (bottom right).

NORTHEAST LOS ROQUES

There are several islands here and many good anchorages. Among them is the main island El Gran Roque. With hills about 380 feet, it is the only island in the group to attain any height.

EL GRAN ROQUE

With its 380-foot hills, El Gran Roque stands out like a beacon across the other flat islands. A very easy way to come in to Los Roques is to approach from the north. Just sail in round the west of El Gran Roque. It is impossible to mistake this island for any other in the group.

The other logical way to come in this area is by the northeast channel, between Fransiquies and Nordisqui. This is no problem provided you have correctly identified the islands.

Once you reach El Gran Roque, anchor off the town just south of the dock. There is a convenient anchoring shelf some 150 feet wide with depths of 10 to 13 feet. Outside this the depths plummet and inside they shoal rapidly.

Services

The local dive shop is helpful and sells desalinated fresh water. Take along your own jerry jugs or he will probably be able to lend you a 60 liter one.

Ashore

This is the only island with a village on it, and it also has the main airport. There are no cars and the streets are sand. Most of the houses were built as holiday homes for Venezuelans and they are simple but pleasant.

Salazar and Agusto are two supermarkets that get supplied from the mainland about once a week. Choice will be somewhat limited so it is probably best to arrive in Los Roques with most things you need. There are now two or three small restaurants in town. If things are busy, you may have to book a little in advance. Flights to Caracas can be arranged from one of the airline offices.

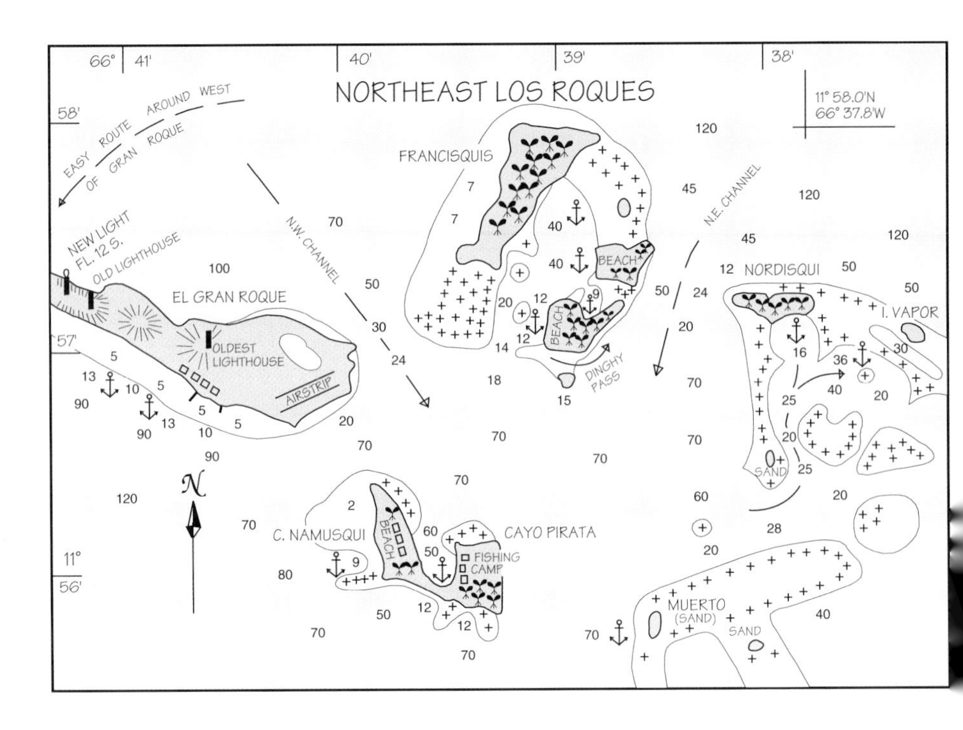

While you are here, follow the well marked trail up the hill to the oldest of the three lighthouses. Take your camera for a brightly colored all round view.

Water Sports

There is good diving and excellent diving in Los Roques. The good diving can be had by snorkeling anywhere that is deep

Looking east from the two eastern Fransiquis across the Northeast Channel to Nordisqui

enough and if it looks promising, go back for the tanks. One fine spot is off the northwestern point of El Gran Roque. The excellent diving is all along the south side of Los Roques, where there is a dramatic drop off. The best way to get there is to dive with the local dive shop, Sest Continte Dive Resort (T:014-24 18 53 or 02 731 1507, VHF:16). As it is a fair distance, they usually run a two-tank dive with a break for lunch. The manager is helpful and speaks English. He also rents and fills tanks.

FRANCISQUIS

These islands and their fringe reefs form a completely protected anchoring lagoon with lots of space. Powdery beaches, good snorkeling, and proximity to El Gran Roque, make this a favorite. There are one or two habitations, but not enough to spoil it.

Navigation

Enter from the south, eyeballing your way between the shoals. There is about 14 feet of water over the entrance channel. Once inside, there are a couple more reefs to dodge, and after that most of the lagoon is 40 feet deep with several good anchorages. For breeze and an open aspect the best is off the reef at the northern end of the lagoon. For beaches you can choose between the two eastern islands. The southern one is longer, prettier and has easy anchoring in 12 feet of water. This is probably why it is used by many day charter boats and why many cruising people go to the northern one. You can also carry about eight feet through the narrow cut into the mangrove lined lagoon between the two eastern islands. Once inside, the water is 10 to 12 feet deep. Some Venezuelans keep their boats here.

Water Sports

There is splendid snorkeling on the eastern side of the two eastern islands. While ashore look for a bird that looks like a great blue heron, except it is white. It is a variant of the great blue and this is one of the places you see it.

CAYO PIRATA AND CAYO NAMUSQUI

These islands are joined by a sand bar at their southern ends. You can anchor between them on the northern side. The water is 60 or 70 feet deep but you can edge gently into the shore until the depth gets to be 25 feet before dropping your hook. If you are staying long, a line ashore and an anchor in the deep water would be the best way to secure your boat. Ashore there is a fishing camp where you can buy lobster during the season.

Cayo Namusqui has a pristine beach, though there are a few houses here. The water off the northern end of this beach is very shoal, but you can eyeball your way in to the southern end between the shallow water and a reef. Anchor where the water is about nine feet deep.

MUERTO

Muerto is a sand bar and pleasant place to lie out and play in the shallow water. The water tends to be too deep or too shallow. Place one anchor in the shallow water and another in deep to keep you from swinging aground.

ISLA VAPOR AND NORDISQUI

There are quite delightful anchorages tucked up in the reefs by these islands. Start at Muerto, follow the reef it lies on eastwards. You have to dodge one side or the other of one little reef that might get in your way if you are under sail. When you get to the long reef that extends south of Nordisqui, follow it up on the eastern side, sailing between it and the next reef. If you want to be close to the shore, anchor off Nordisqui. If you like being in the open, anchor off Isla Vapor. Isla Vapor is a small island covered in seaside purslane, which is almost as good as grass to lie on. The island is inhabited by hundreds of terns. They will resent your presence if you go to the eastern side of the island, but if you stay near the beach they will leave you alone.

Between Isla Vapor and the anchorage is a pool of deep blue water some 30 feet deep surrounded by reef. The water colors are incredible here as they change from pale green to dark blue. The water in the shallows is warm enough to lie in all day. There is good snorkeling on the reef patches both inside the pool and out between the reefs.

ANCHORAGES IN NORTHWESTERN LOS ROQUES

This whole area is dotted with little islands, most of which have delightful anchorages. Usually the next island is no more than a couple of miles away. Since sailing is such fun in Los Roques, I recommend darting from one area to another rather than exploring systematically.

NORONSQUIS

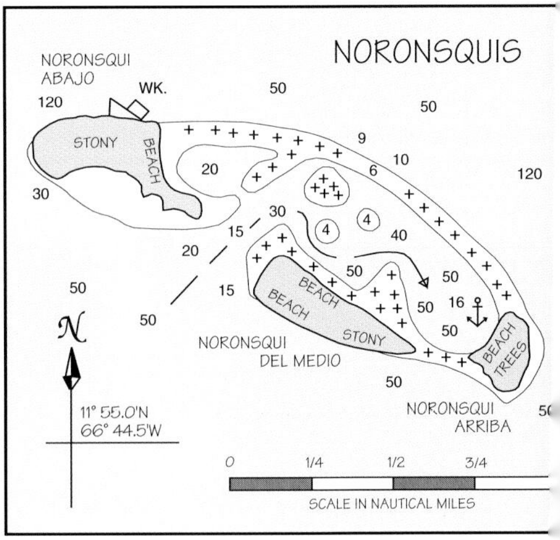

Three little islands and a barrier reef create a lustrous blue lagoon of deep water surrounded by several unblemished little beaches. On the north shore of the western most island is the conspicuous wreck of a Venezuelan navy vessel that was being used to ferry supplies. It was anchored in Gran Roque when its mooring line parted. It somehow caught fire after grounding which added to its problems and it is still sitting on the shore.

Navigation

Sail to the south side of the island group and enter midway between Noronsqui Abajo and Noronsqui dcl Medio. Depth over the bar is about 15 feet. Inside, the lagoon is mostly about 50 feet deep. Stay in deep water, closely following the reef along the north shore of Noronsqui del Medio to avoid the two 4-foot reefs in the middle. The calmest anchorage is off the tiny beach on the west side of Noronsqui Arriba. The water is deep and you can take a line ashore or into the shallows.

There are great beaches to explore an the snorkeling is good, though much of th coral inside is bleached. When snorkellin look out for the huge midnight and rain bow parrotfish along the north shore c Noronsqui del Medio. Weather permi ting, you can dinghy out through the (break in the reef for advanced snorkelin on the outside.

Looking southeast at Noronsquis. The wreck shows up clearly in the foreground

CRASQUI

Crasqui has a picture perfect beach which seems to go on forever. While there is no snorkeling on the lee side of the island, aficionados can dinghy to the windward side where the snorkeling is good. This is a very popular anchorage with Venezuelans and will be crowded on weekends, though there is plenty of space. A hotel and restaurant opened here for a while, but it has been closed by Inparques in an effort to preserve the natural state of the island.

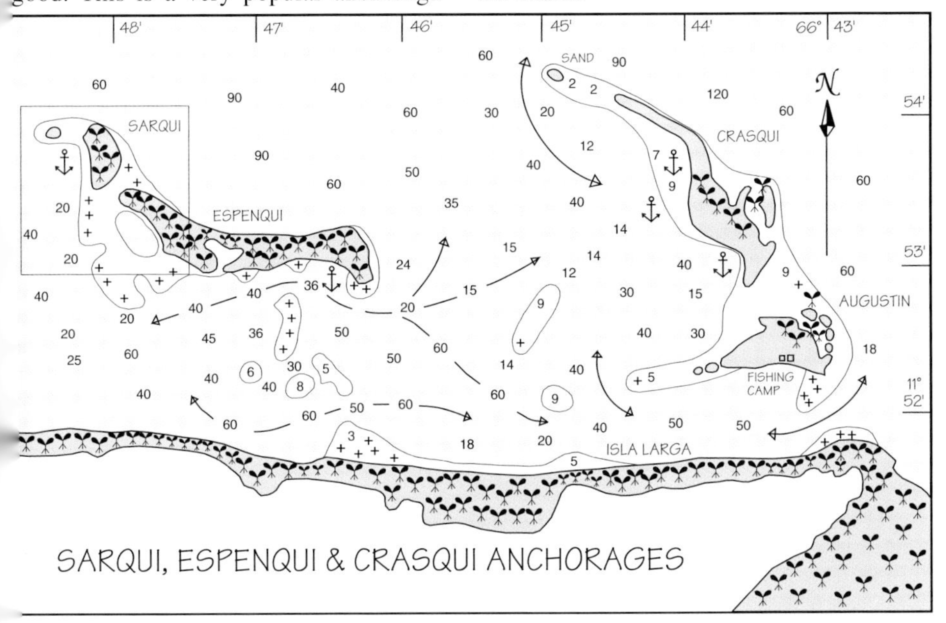

Navigation

If you are approaching from the north, pass to the west of the sand cay to the northwest of Crasqui. Anchor anywhere along the beach. If you are approaching the beach at the north end you have to ease your way in gently as it gets shallow a fair way out. There is deeper water down at the south end.

If you are leaving to sail south and east round the south end of Augustin, note that there is a long shoal that ends in a reef extending to the west of Augustin. You may find eight feet of water cutting inside the shoal, but it is hard to read the depths and not worth it. When you pass between Augustin and Isla Larga you have to sail closer to Isla Larga to avoid the reef off Augustin. It is best to do this in good light. There is plenty of room for most modern yachts to tack through under sail. Give the eastern side of Augustin good clearance.

If approaching southwest round the south side of Espenqui, avoid the reef half way between Augustin and Espensqui.

ESPENQUI

Most charts do not give details on this area, but you should find our sketch chart adequate. There are several shoals between Espenqui and Isla Larga. The easiest route is to follow the southern coast of Espenqui. However, the shoals are easy to avoid in good light and you can pick your own route between them. The minimum depth in any passage between two shoals is 15 feet.

There is a good little getaway anchorage in Espenqui tucked up into the eastern end of the south coast. Lots of birds live here and snorkeling is worthwhile around the eastern end of the island.

SARQUI

Sarqui has a superb, if somewhat small, anchorage. If you are approaching from the south, give a good clearance to all the reefs that extend south of Sarqui and west of Espenqui. The anchorage is right at the northern end of the island, protected by the reef that extends eastwards from Sarqui to a small island. You can anchor here in sand in 10-16 feet of water. Do not anchor south of the sandy area as you will be on coral which is not allowed.

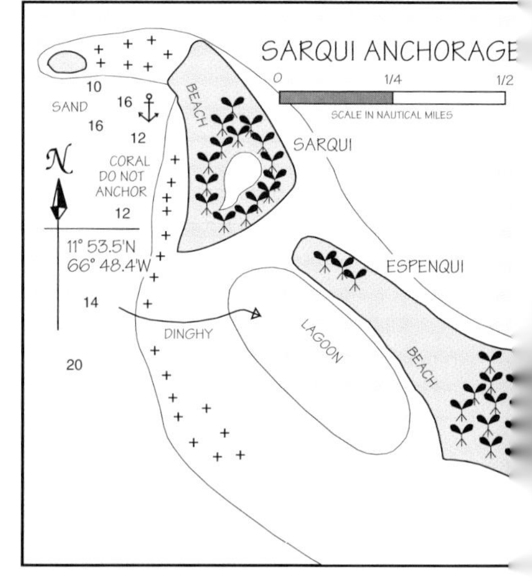

This is a great place to sit and watch all the birds in action and to go for a snorkel. Snorkeling is good both over the coral in the bay and out around the north and east side of Sarqui. There is also good dinghy exploration into the lagoon at the north end of Espenqui, where there is a delightful beach and bathing pool.

LOS CANQUISES AND SELENSQUI

These islands are restricted areas and anchoring is not allowed. Los Canquises is full of birds and during the winter from January to March flamingos are seen here. Dinghy exploration is allowed, but the passage across can be rough. If you do visit, do not disturb the birds.

ANCHORAGES IN WESTERN LOS ROQUES

There are delightful anchorages in western Los Roques. This is far from El Gran Roque, so there are often only a few boats around.

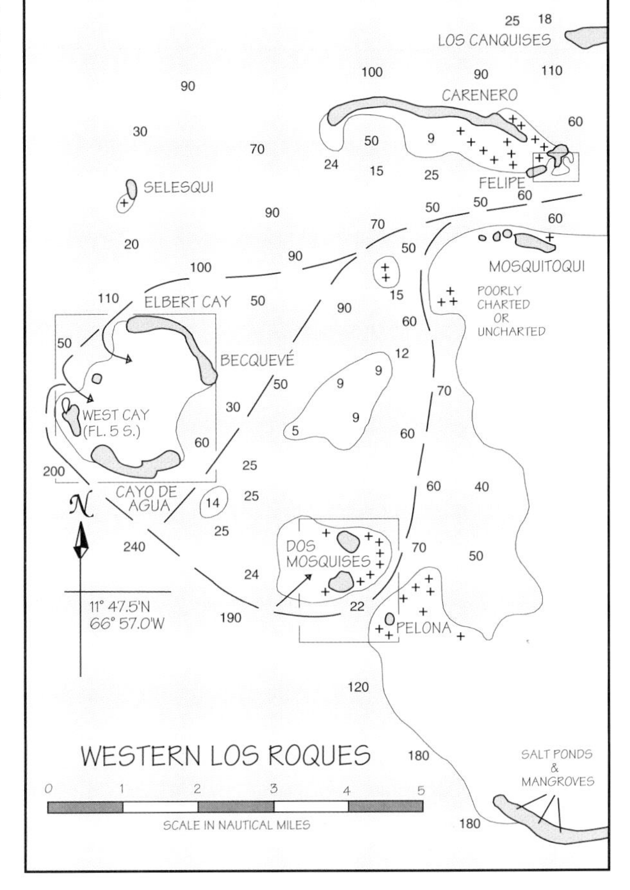

ISLA CARENERO

Cayo Remanso and Felipe are two small mangrove islands at the eastern end of Carenero. Between them is a perfect lagoon anchorage. Approach from the south and eyeball your way in. There is a four-foot shoal in the middle of the entrance. The deepest and clearest route is to the east of the shoal.

Once inside you will have a beach backed by mangroves on the eastern side and a lovely open vista across miles of blue and turquoise water to the west. The seabed in the lagoon is sand and you can easily see the 20 feet to the bottom.

The snorkeling is excellent as you follow the reef out of the bay to the northeast.

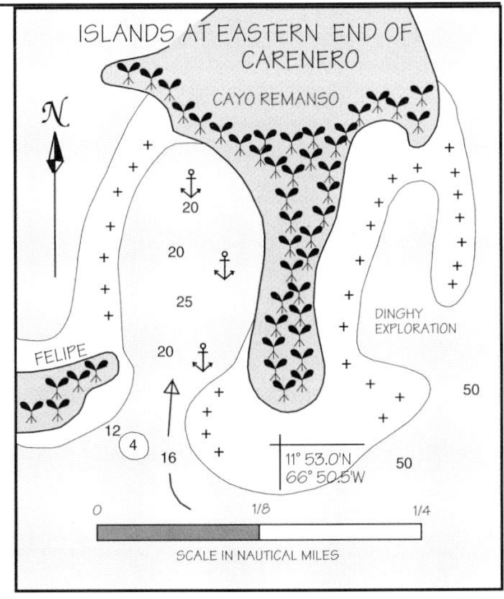

There are more than enough fish to make up for the fact that much of the coral is bleached or you can take the dinghy over to Carenero for a long walk.

You may not have this anchorage to yourself. It is not only very popular with yachts, but fishing boats often come in here for repairs.

DOS MOSQUISES

Dos Mosquises are two pretty islands sheltered by a protective barrier reef. This was where the Amerindians chose to live when they inhabited this area. They arrived in huge dugout canoes that carried fifty people and stayed for the fish, conch, lobster and turtles. Dos Mosquises was a good choice, conveniently close to Cayo de Agua for water, and the nearest island to the mainland. They were close to the natural salt ponds which enabled them to salt their fish, and there are plenty of mangrove trees close by, which could be used for making fires and building.

Nowadays Mosquise Sur houses a small research and fisheries station. On the fisheries side they take turtle eggs, hatch the turtles and keep them until they are one year old and then let them go. Many people come here to do research on all aspects of the area. It is a good place to come for natural history information, but what you find will depend on who is there at the time.

Navigation

Enter Dos Mosquises from the south (if coming from the north you can pass between Isla Pelona and Dos Mosquises to get to the south side). The entrance is a little worrisome as you have to cross an area of reef. While this is about nine feet deep at low water, it is impossible to tell if one coral head is sticking up more than the others and coral does grow. Therefore if you have 6-7 foot draft, I would suggest crossing the bar at high water which will

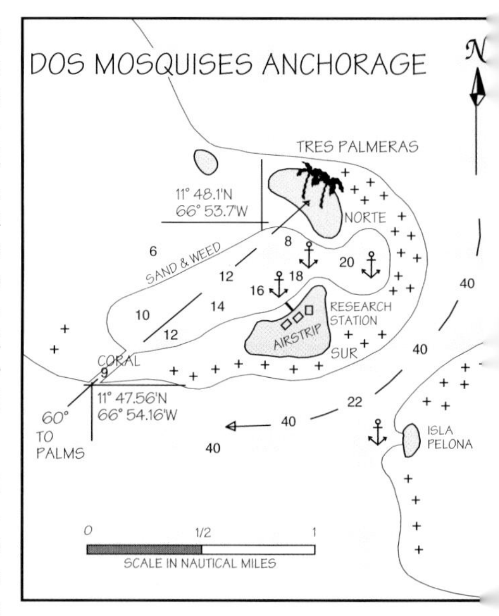

give a safety margin. The best angle o approach is with the palms on Tre Palmeras bearing about 60° magnetic Once over the reef there is plenty of wate inside and you will find depths from 12 t 25 feet. You can go past the islands an anchor in the lagoon. It gets much shal lower towards Tres Palmeras (Mosquise Norte), though you can edge in towards th beach at the eastern end.

Ashor

The research station welcomes visitor Tres Palmeras is deserted with a fabulou beach. There is good snorkeling on th reefs all around, particularly excelle along the outer part of the reef south of th south island.

ELBERT CAY TO CAYO DE AGUA

This little archipelago consists of four islands, Elbert Cay, Bequevé, West Cay and Cayo de Agua, along with many reefs. It is a delightful area with good island exploring, fine snorkeling, and excellent fishing.

Navigation

While the outer edges of the archipelago are deep, the water between the islands is rather shallow with lots of coral. To make things worse, it is littered with grass beds which makes it harder to read. Nonetheless, if you follow the main routes into the anchorages as shown on our chart you should not have a problem

Bequevé

Bequevé and Albert Cay are currently joined by a sand dune and will probably stay that way. The only anchorage is close to where the two islands join. It is a good anchorage and well protected from trade winds. You do need to arrive in good light. Enter between Elbert Cay and the little coral island. Head southeasterly until you are on a line between the coral island and the southern tip of Bequevé and then keep on this line. You should be able to make out the shoal we have marked "easily seen" on our sketch chart. Eyeball your way up into the anchorage. The entrance is quite narrow, with a reef to the south and shallow grass and sand to the north. At this point it is only about 8-9 feet deep. Once inside, the water gets a little deeper and there is plenty of room to anchor.

Ashore there are miles of fabulous sandy island to explore with beach front that will please the fussiest beach lover. When that tires there is snorkeling on all the reefs around.

Cayo de Agua

Cayo de Agua has two anchorages, one on the north side and the other on the west. The northern anchorage is much larger and better protected except in howling

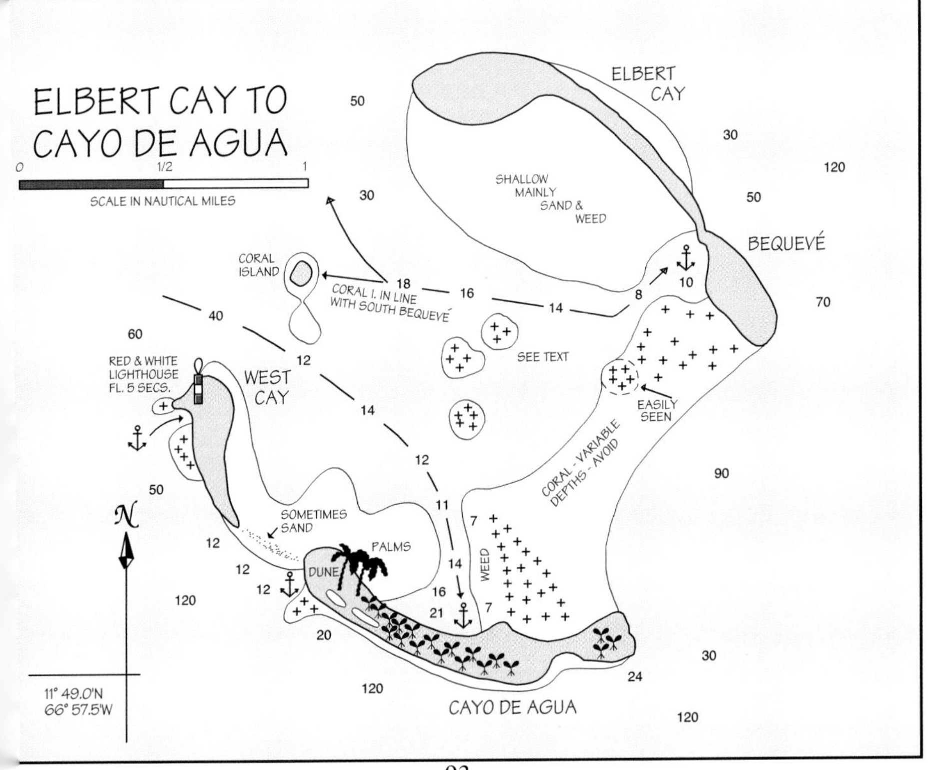

Crasqui anchorage

northeasters. Enter between the coral island and West Cay and head for the northeastern point of Cayo de Agua. After that just eyeball your way between the reefs. The eastern reef is flanked by a long shallow weed bank to its west. Treat this as part of the reef. The entrance is narrow, but once inside the water gets deeper and a large anchoring area opens up. The calmest water is close to the beach and the reef at the eastern corner.

While it is possible to eyeball your way between this anchorage and Bequevé, I would not recommend it as you have to pass over many banks of coral 8-12 foot deep and one never knows where the extra tall coral head is.

The anchorage on the western side of Cayo de Agua is good but only has room for two boats. It is right at the western end of Cayo de Agua, where it is closest to West Cay. Sometimes it is joined with a sand spit, and at other times there is a shallow sand bar.

The water is clear and the approach is easy. Just avoid any small coral heads and the reef to the south which provides the protection. To get out of the swell edge as closely as possible in to the beach. The water shelves gradually from about 12 feet so this is no problem.

There is also a very small anchorage under the lighthouse at West Cay. This is a one boat anchorage where you have to use one anchor in the shallows (or on the beach) and another to hold your stern as there is no swinging room.

Ashore

Cayo de Agua is a delightful island of tall sand dunes, a palm grove, mangrove trees, lagoons and water holes. The bird watching is tremendous with all manner of terns, pelicans, herons, oyster catchers and many wading birds in the lagoon behind and along the shores. Terns nest here so be careful not to disturb them.

You will notice lots of holes dug in the ground in the area of the palms. These were dug for water and one or two may have water in them. Cayo de Agua got its name because there is lots of fresh water a few feet down and it has proved an invaluable supply to the Amerindians, fishermen and the occasional desperate yachtsman. I was amazed to come here at the end of a very dry season and still find water that was only a tiny bit brackish in the holes.

Water Sports

The snorkeling and diving along the south coast of Cayo de Agua is excellent with a sand bottom and lots of thick coral patches. It falls off downhill steeply, but without a dramatic wall. It is a pretty area of coral gardens where the coral is alive and well and fish are bright and tame.

Trolling or hand lining from the dinghy in the same area will usually be rewarded with a fish big enough for dinner.

If you are anchored on the northern side, the snorkeling is good in places on the reefs all around. Hand line fishing is also very good in the region of the coral island.

These are two separate little island archipelagos, separated by about 10 miles of deep water. They got their name from the large number of birds that make them their home. They are conveniently placed en route to Bonaire and should not be missed.

AVES DE BARLOVENTO

A horseshoe reef gives protection to two islands and a few smaller cays. The birdlife on the southern island has to be seen to be believed. From afar you can see birds by the hundreds perched in the trees. The majority are various species of booby, but there are also other seabirds and herons. Close to they set up a wonderful chorus as they argue over branch rights and feed their young.

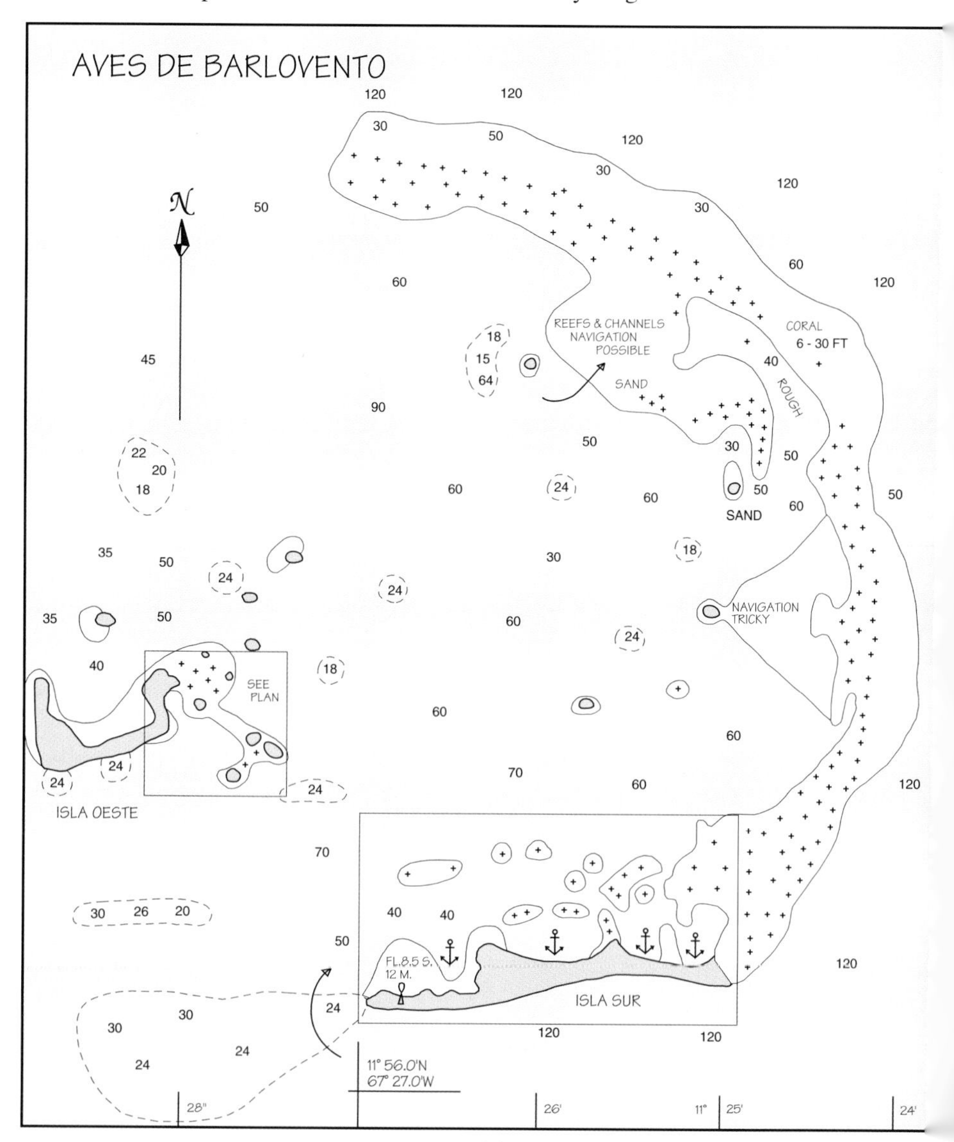

Navigation

Aves de Barlovento is relatively easy to navigate. For the most part the water is either very deep or shallow. The charting is not all that accurate and there are some shoals that are not marked. If you always keep a good lookout, sail when the light is reasonable and avoid anything that looks shallow, you should be all right.

ISLA SUR

Navigation

It is easiest to approach from the southern side as Isla Sur, the barrier island in the south, has 40-foot tall mangrove trees which makes it clearly visible.

The places we have marked shoaling on our sketch charts are living coral and considerably shallower than the charts show. It is best to avoid them, either by eyeballing your way round or making a sweep out toward the little island of sand and seaside plants.

Fishing boats often anchor in the first bay just east of the lighthouse. This anchorage is exposed and can be rolly. Much better to carry on to the east where there are three different bays behind the reefs which are reasonably well protected from all directions. It is easy to find your way through in reasonable light conditions, and you can enter the first one even in poor light, provided you can make out the very shallow reefs. While you can pick your own route through the reefs, I suggest you use those shown on our sketch chart for the first time.

The first protected bay is half a mile long, though it does have a five foot shoal in the middle which is a little hard to see. It is quite an experience to be anchored here with noise and sight of hundreds, maybe thousands, of boobies in the trees ashore. The water is deep almost all the way to the mangrove trees. However, I would not anchor too close in as you will probably get splattered by defecating birds and bitten by bugs. You should be fine on the north side of the anchorage and still close enough to see and hear the boobies.

If you leave this bay and follow the reef round you come to the middle bay. The entrance is narrow but there is 14 feet of water over it. Depths in the bay are 20 to 30 feet and you can anchor anywhere off the reefs. This bay also has mangrove trees and birds, but the action is not quite as

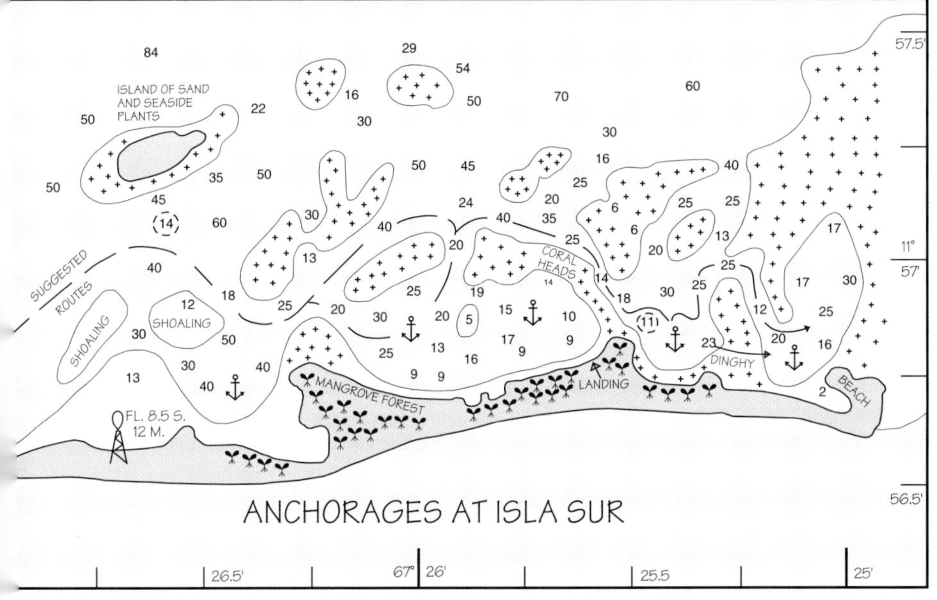

ANCHORAGES AT ISLA SUR

Baby booby,
Aves de Barlovento

intense as in the first bay.

The easternmost bay is probably the prettiest of the three. You have to wind your way down a narrow reef channel out toward the eastern end of the island. This end of the island is low, with only one or two small mangroves by the water's edge. You don't see so many birds, but you still get a few wading visitors along the shore. Access to the island here for a walk is easy via the beach. There is a dinghy pass through into the middle bay along the shore.

Close to Isla Sur, temporary anchorage is also available off the little island of sand and seaside plants. I would anchor on the south side in about 45 feet of water. Good snorkeling and interesting exploration.

Ashore

You can get ashore onto Isla Sur at the place marked on our chart from the first bay and from the beach in the eastern bay. The island is very colorful, with big patches of southern glasswort, seaside purslane and saltwort all in different shades of green. According to our Venezuelan book on Los Roques, saltwort is known as fisherman's tobacco, as it can be dried and smoked. Heaven knows what it does to your lungs.

This is an extraordinary place to watch birds. Many species use this island but boobies predominate and with a pair of binoculars you can watch the fluffy white chicks. (You can also walk up to them, but this is not recommended as in the long term it could affect where they nest). It is a great place to look at the red-footed booby as their feet are quite visible in the branches.

There are small pools with crabs and you will also see many hermit crabs in the grasses and bushes.

Water sports

The snorkeling is good on the reefs. Some spots are excellent, others drab. You have plenty to choose from.

Sometime toward dusk get out the hand line or troll round the bay. The fishing is excellent and the odds are you can leave that can of corned beef in the locker.

ISLA OESTE ANCHORAGE

There is a good anchorage at the eastern end of the Isla Oeste. If you are approaching from Isla Sur, pass south and west of all the little islands just off Isla Oeste. The anchorage is off the beach right up at the eastern end of the island. The water is very deep and the best way to anchor is bow or stern to the shore. There is only room for about two boats in comfort. You are protected from all directions except the south. If you wish to head out eastwards, note that the 60-foot channel shown on some charts between Isla Oeste and its offshore islands does not exist. Either the parrotfish have been very busy or the cartographer had a bad morning back in 1870 or whenever it was surveyed. A bank of sand and coral goes all the way across. You can get about 18 feet of water through here, if you avoid the coral heads.

The bay on the northern shore looks inviting, but it is full of coral and not a good place to anchor.

Ashore

This is a delightful spot with a pleasant each, plenty of islands for dinghy exploation and lots of snorkeling. Start with eef right off the south end of the beach. The fishing is superb so you shouldn't go ungry.

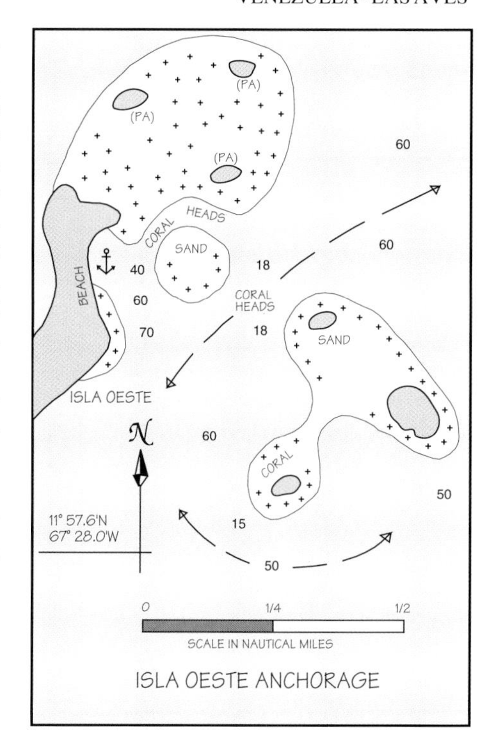

OUT ON THE REEF

Being anchored out on the reef is wonerful in fine weather with reasonable reezes. If the wind is howling from the ortheast, it is possible but uncomfortable. ou will find most anchoring spots in 20-0 or more feet of water and these will have e best holding.

You have to eyeball your way out and hoose your spot. Note that there is a break n the reef about a third of the way down. his is not deep enough to pass through, but it does let waves in which is worth keeping in mind when choosing your spot. The two little islands just close to this break are fun to explore with good snorkeling but the water is about 60 feet deep. There is a whole area to the northwest of this where you can get right among the reefs. Follow up inside the reefs to the northernmost little island. Eyeball your way in from here. There are deep passages between the reefs.

AVES DE SOTAVENTO

Aves de Sotavento lies about ten miles est and a little north of Aves de arlovento. It has some delightful islands d reefs, but navigation and anchoring e a little problematic because there are uch larger areas of shallow water and the ost protected harbor has a shoal approach which could be difficult if large vells are running. Most yachts anchor in the lee of the three pretty little islands. This is perfect in good conditions but uncomfortable in a northerly swell. The alternative is to go to the windward side of the small islands and anchor somewhere out on the barrier reef. This is fine if the wind is not blowing too hard, but in a howling trade wind you are going to get some chop and roll. In short, it is best to visit Aves de Sotavento in the spring or summer when there are no northerly swells and the winds are not too strong.

Navigation

You can approach around the northern or southern end. The northern end is easier because you stay in very deep water to the first anchorages. The Saki Saki light was flashing about every eight seconds, which is almost the same as Barlovento. I would suggest staying well away from this area at night.

Regulations

There is a coast guard station on Isla Larga. Call them on the radio when you arrive (VHF:16) and they will come and check you in. They also check you in for Barlovento, so if you are coming from this direction call in and see them.

Commercial fishing and the taking of any turtles or conch are forbidden.

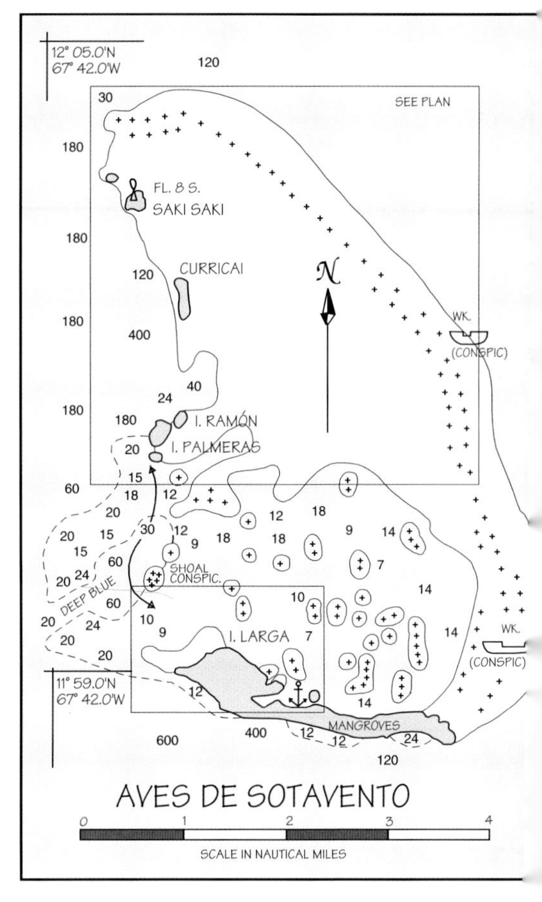

NORTHERN ANCHORAGES

Most people stay on the west side of the reefs and anchor in the lee of the little islands.

Saki Saki and Curricai

These two islands are photogenic with powdery beaches, lovely water colors and good snorkeling. The approach from the west is in deep water and presents no problems. However, both share the same problem for anchoring. The shelves on which one can anchor are mainly coral with patches of sand. This presents a headache for those anchoring on rope, as it will quickly get twisted around coral heads and chafe. Those with chain will have no problem, but the coral will. A sweeping chain can cut in seconds through structures that have taken centuries to build. If you anchor on chain, snorkel on your anchor and minimize damage in any way you can. A second anchor helps as it stops the boat swinging from side to side. If you are anchoring on rope, think about putting a buoy about 20 feet from the anchor to keep the rode lifted above the coral. Again two anchors will help.

Isla Palmeras

Isla Palmeras has two little sister islands, Isla Ramón to the east and another to the south. There are several good anchorages, depending on the conditions. There is a good little anchorage between Isla Palmeras and Isla Ramón. Approach from the Isla Palmeras side and ease gently, as the water keeps getting shallower. You can find good anchorage in 10-12 feet of water, with only a couple of coral heads to avoid.

You can anchor in the lee of Isla Palmeras. This presents the same coral and sand problem as in Saki Saki and Curricai, though here the patches of sand tend to be greater and the patches of coral smaller.

There is also an anchorage on the south side of the little island to the south of Isla Palmeras. This is generally sand or sand and weed with only a few coral heads, which can be avoided. It gives good shelter from the northeast, but if the wind blows hard from the east or southeast there will be a chop. If you do anchor here, snorkel on the little reef right off the small southern island. It looks like very little from the boat, but seems to house an astonishingly large number of colorful fish. From your yacht you will probably see a lovely looking deep lagoon just to the east of Isla

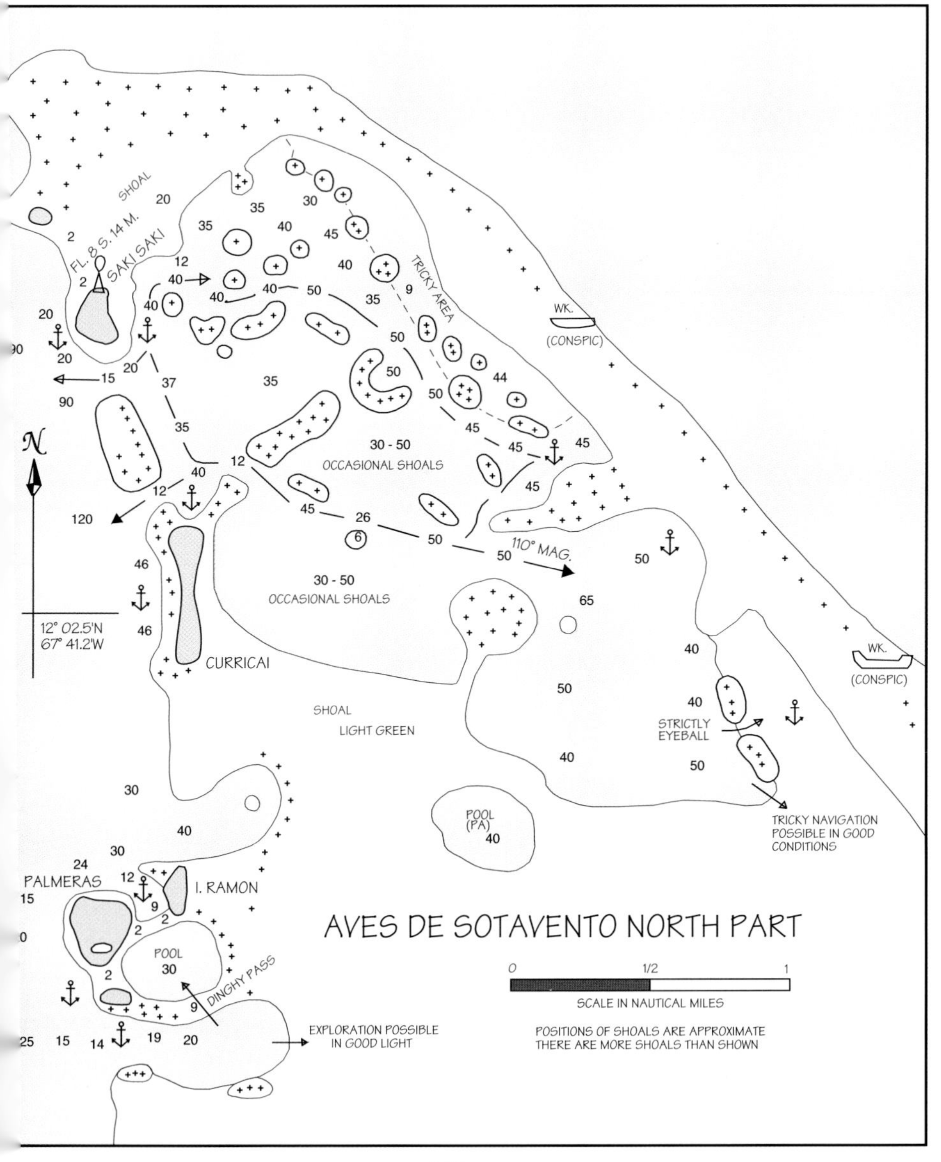

Palmeras. We sounded nine feet of water through the most obvious looking cut toward high water. But it is narrow, and the lagoon would not be all that well protected in a strong wind.

EAST OF THE ISLANDS

The northern part of Aves de Sotavento is much deeper than the southern part. Once you pass into the reef system there is a huge area between the islands and the barrier reef. It is easily accessible though two cuts. One is just south of Saki Saki with about 15 feet in the channel and the other is just north of Curricai with about 12 feet in the channel. Once inside you often have 40-50 feet of water which is deep blue and easy to tell from the many reefs. You have to be prepared to anchor in these depths as shallower water that is not part of a reef can be hard to find. We have shown most main reefs and passages on our sketch chart, but it should be emphasized that this area is strictly a matter of eyeball navigation in good light. You can anchor anywhere inside that seems reasonable for the conditions. You get the most protection at the outer reef, but it is still not that calm in windy conditions. This is a good place to be if big northerly swells start rolling in.

The easiest access to the outer reef is from Curricai. Enter through the pass, then the passage to get you just east of Curricai. From here if you head about 110° magnetic you have an almost straight shot out to the reef with just minor adjustments to avoid shoals along the route.

Nearly all the reefs provide excellent snorkeling .

ISLA LARGA

The Dutch once settled Isla Larga and mined guano. The ruins of three old forts are all that remain of their reign. Isla Larga, like Isla Agua in Los Roques, has water just beneath the sand. There are plenty of birds here, but not in the same extraordinary numbers that are found in Aves de Barlovento. The coast guard station is at the western end of the island.

Mangrove Bay

Mangrove Bay is the most protected anchorage in Aves de Sotavento, though the access is a little shallow. If you are coming from Isla Palmeras get into the dark blue water and follow it south until you see the

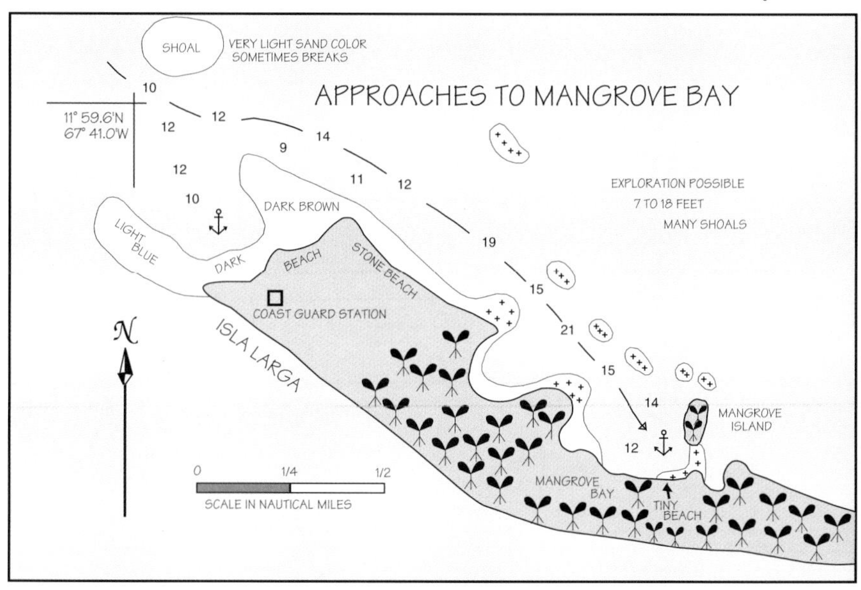

shoal about half a mile north of the customs station. It shows up clearly as very light colored water. Enter south of this shoal and head for the eastern most point of Isla Larga. Depths will be mainly 10-12 feet. When you get near the island follow it round into the anchorage. Shortly before the anchorage, pass close to the two obvious reefs extending from the two points of land. This avoids other, harder to see reefs farther out. You get good protection in the southern corner of the bay, but enough breeze to keep bugs away. This is a comfortable place to hang out and you can explore the island by dinghy. There are lots of reefs around for snorkeling.

Chichiriviche is about as far west as most people cruise in Venezuela. Farther west are the oil fields of Maracaibo, which is no place for a yacht. Those heading west usually follow the island chain out to Aruba before heading on toward Cartagena.

Chichiriviche and the Morrocoy National Park offer excellent cruising with small islands of beaches and palms, huge mangrove areas and the Golfo de Cuare.

Some people sailing from Bonaire to the Eastern Caribbean bypass this area because they can lay Puerto Cabello, which is farther east, on one tack. If you have extra time, a visit to Chichiriviche and the Morrocoy National Park is a good way to use it. Getting back to Puerto Cabello is not hard and you can most often make it in one fast, easy tack.

Navigation

From Bonaire or Las Aves, it is usually an easy reach to Chichiriviche. However, for those who are dogged by ill winds, a southerly is possible.

The whole offshore area is of mixed depths, mainly from 30 to 60 feet. Sometimes this area is calm, but a combination of uncomfortable swells and honking trades will produce conditions to delight the windsurfer and convert the pocket cruiser into a semi-submersible. If possible, avoid areas in the open ocean with charted depths of 24 feet or less as we noted considerable shoaling on some of them.

The easiest approach to Chichiriviche is from the east, entering the ship channel which is clearly marked by red and green buoys. If coming from the north, give the northern and western side of Cayo Borracho a wide clearance. The reef system going north from Cayo Borracho is the best part of a mile long.

From the north you can also enter inside the islands in good light. Pass fairly close to the western side of Cayo Sal (Salt Cay), then hug the western side of Cayo Los Muertos (Dead Men's Cay), before joining the ship channel.

You can anchor anywhere off town, but in a brisk easterly wind a surge does enter. One of the calmest anchorages for easy access to the town is off Cayo Los Muertos.

Lanceros run tourists all around the area in fast pirogues. They are usually happy to act as a water taxi and can be helpful for getting to town from Cayo Sal. They also make trips into Golfo de Cuare, should you not wish to take your yacht in.

In bad weather, you could not ask for a safer anchorage than the old sand dock on Golfo de Cuare.

All along the Venezuelan coast winds swing in every direction. This should be kept in mind when you anchor. Those using Danforth anchors which can trip should always set two anchors.

Regulations

Chichiriviche comes under the jurisdiction of Puerto Cabello which is a port of entry. There is no customs or immigration in Chichiriviche. The port captain (VHF:16) does not want to be bothered by yachts, but if you arrive from abroad he may give you permission to spend a day or two on your way to Puerto Cabello at his discretion. The port captain's office is in the blue and white building on the road immediately facing the dock. If you are leaving Venezuela from Chichiriviche get your clearance at Puerto Cabello before you come here. No need to check here.

Ashore

Chichiriviche has a large cement factory which brings in ships from all over the region. It is a fishing port with an active fishing fleet of open boats. Nowadays it is becoming a tourist destination because it is only 90 miles from Caracas and is the gateway to several pretty islands and the Morrocoy National Park.

You can beach your dinghy anywhere, tie it to the unfinished main dock, or the other small docks. Do not dinghy close to shore on the south side of the main dock as a reef comes a fair way out. The main dock is built for lanceros and fishing boats and it is in shoal water.

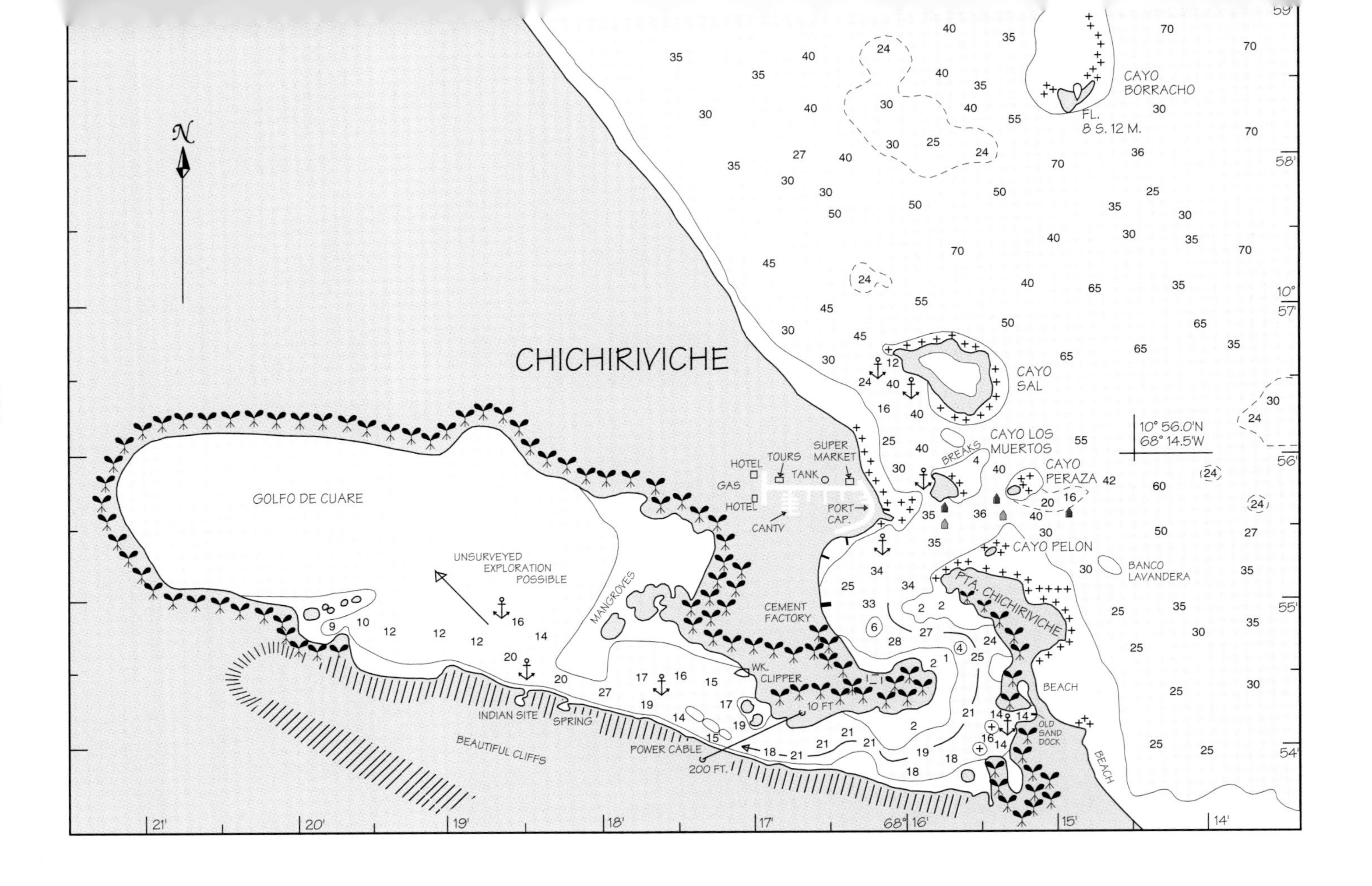
CAYO BORRACHO
FL. 8 S. 12 M.
CAYO SAL
CAYO LOS MUERTOS
CAYO PERAZA
CAYO PELON
BREAKS
BANCO LAVANDERA
PTA. CHICHIRIVICHE
BEACH
OLD SAND DOCK
10° 56.0'N
68° 14.5'W
CHICHIRIVICHE
HOTEL
TOURS
SUPER MARKET
TANK
GAS
HOTEL
PORT CAP.
CANTV
CEMENT FACTORY
WK. CLIPPER
10 FT.
200 FT.
POWER CABLE
MANGROVES
UNSURVEYED EXPLORATION POSSIBLE
INDIAN SITE
SPRING
BEAUTIFUL CLIFFS
GOLFO DE CUARE

Most things are strung along the dusty Avenida Zamora, the main road leading out of town which is a little north of the main dock (see our sketch chart). Near the beginning of the road is a supermarket and a liquor store that has cube ice if the supermarket does not. Opposite is a bakery. If you want block ice you can get it at the ice factory (marked ice on our chart). On the street leading to the ice factory is a shop selling bread and fresh meat.

CANTV has a bank of phones. The pharmacy and bakery sell phone cards, if CANTV does not. You can also try Varadero Tours (042 86 754/83 47 45) who may be willing to help you with an international call. They are also willing to change money. These are the people to go to if you need a taxi. They will call one from another town as there are no taxis here yet. Geramias Alveres in the office speaks English. Varadero Tours is open 0800-noon and 1500-1700. They arrange tours and rent diving and windsurfing equipment. If you are desperate for fuel, try the gas station at the end of the road near the big hotels.

There are several restaurants, some of which only open on weekends and holidays. Casa Vera Cruz ($D) is simple, inexpensive and on the waterfront with a dinghy dock next door. They have live entertainment on the weekends. Take bug spray in the evenings. Restaurant Txalupa ($C-D) serves good seafood and is open for lunch and dinner daily except Wednesday. There are many other small restaurants around town. There are also the big hotels (Hotel Garza and Hotel Mario), though these are a fair walk out of town and only make phone calls and offer general help to hotel guests.

CAYO SAL AND CAYO LOS MUERTOS

Cayo Sal and Cayo Los Muertos are both delightful islands with sandy beaches and coconut palms. They are popular on weekends and holidays, and Cayo Sal has a restaurant that opens when things get busy.

When passing between Chichiriviche and Cayo Los Muertos stay close to the island to avoid the shoals that extend out from the Chichiriviche side. Anchor toward the northern end of the west side in the calmest spot.

In Cayo Sal there is a good anchorage off the southwest coast in 35 feet of water or you can anchor right at the western end where the water is 12 feet deep.

GOLFO DE CUARE

Golfo de Cuare is a wildlife refuge and a marvelous place to spend a day or two exploring, bird watching and fishing. There are spectacular cliffs sculpted into caves, caverns, walls and steep valleys along much of the southern shore. Once the whole area was under water and the cliffs are limestone from old coral formations. About seven million years ago tectonic activity uplifted them to their present position. Acids, born by rain, have dissolved parts of the limestone, causing whole areas to fall away until they reached their present shapes. Much of the cliff bottom has been eaten away by sea action so there are low overhangs at sea level. These make a cheerful chuckling noise in small waves. The cliffs are covered in part by trees, vines and shrubs, mainly of the dry forest type. The whole area is decorated by white frangipani flowers. Among the trees are many birds, much more easily heard than seen. Hawks glide overhead, swallows flit out over the gulf and you may catch glimpses of woodpeckers and other brightly colored birds flying close to shore.

Navigation

Despite the large shoals, access to the gulf is easy and you can see all the shoal

in good light. If you make a mistake, most of the bottom is mud. The entrance channel is much wider than it looks on our small scale sketch chart. Pass close by the long shoal stretching southwest from Punta Chichiriviche, then head slightly east of center channel to avoid the 4-foot patch. It is a little harder to see than the other shoals. Stay in the middle of the channel, avoiding the shoals marked on our sketch chart. Electric cables run across the entrance of the gulf where we show them. They start very low on the northern shore and top the cliff on the southern shore. If you stay as close as you can to the southern shore we judged that you would have about 120 feet of clearance. This was done by comparing the height of the wires to our 52 feet mast as we went under from a distance.

The easiest and most interesting way up the gulf is to follow the southern shore. Stay about 100 yards off, just outside the shallows. You will pass a series of reefs to starboard, but the passage is amply wide. Farther up you pass another shoal to starboard which comes all the way over from the northern shore.

On your way back, remember the power cables! Stay to the cliff side of the bay as you go under them.

Ashore

You can anchor anywhere in the gulf but the most interesting anchorage is off the Indian site. Here the cliffs are at their most dramatic. Ashore there is a small jetty (hard to see) and a notice outlining the history. The cave was used as a burial ground by the Caquetios who lived here about 3400BC. There are quite a few rock carvings and if you walk back behind the jetty, you find yourself in a crater with sheer cliff sides some 200 feet high. Take bug spray. Look on the mangrove trees at the entrance for mangrove crabs and exotic spiders.

There is another wonderful grotto just a short distance east of the Indian site that you can dinghy right into, with shallow water suitable for lying in. This, too, has religious significance, judging by all the little statues and candles placed on the rocks. There is a little fresh water spring which comes out of the rocks behind a mangrove tree.

On the northern shore of the gulf, just northwest of two little islands is a large wreck with a clipper bow, apparently once a square-rigged ship.

There is another excellent anchorage off the old sand dock. This was used for shipping out sand mined from the beach, an activity which is now banned. From here it is just a few steps to the windward beach where you can walk for miles. There is also excellent dinghy exploration in several little mangrove lagoons. In the deep ones go slowly without creating a wash because sometimes there are people up to their necks in water, picking oysters off the mangroves.

Anchorage off Indian site, Golfo de Cuare

MORROCOY NATIONAL PARK

The Morrocoy National Park has some wonderfully calm yet breezy anchorages. The whole park covers about 25 square miles and consists mainly of mangrove islands with channels between them. Some outer islands and Cayo Sombrero have lovely beaches. Fishing is excellent and dinghy exploration never ending, with thousands of narrow twisty channels opening out into hidden lagoons. Some areas are roped off to protect the birds. You have a good chance of spotting a turtle. Before this area was made into a park there were some 1700 holiday homes, mostly on stilts. These were all pulled down to make this a park.

This whole area is very popular with Venezuelans and many Caracas residents keep small power boats here for weekend camping. It is a very cheerful place to be on the weekends, the beaches are decorated with sunshades and tents, and lots of small boats and a few yachts are anchored. Everyone seems happy.

It is an area that Inparques feels has come under too much human pressure and so they have put charges on yachts. At the time of going to press, local yachts were paying about $50 US for ten days and foreign flagged yachts were paying $140 US for ten days. By local standards this is high, but it is a beautiful area and if you like what it has to offer it is probably money well spent. For the moment, Inparques officials have been collecting from the yachts in the anchorage. Some people just staying there a night or two have not been charged. If you want an update on the situation call Inparques (Spanish only) at:042 83 00 69

Bird life is varied with pelicans, herons, egrets, cormorants, stilts, hawks and some scarlet ibis which fly by looking like little Father Christmases. The birds like the shallowest water so the place to see them is way back in the mangroves and the best time is early morning or late afternoon when they travel to and from their roosting grounds. Ensenada El Placer is a good place for viewing.

Lanceros take tourists out to the outer islands is small open boats. They can be useful as water taxis or for visiting Tucacas for shopping.

Navigation

If heading south from Chichiriviche, stay offshore enough to clear Banco Lavandera. As you approach Cayo Sombrero look for the small sand Cayo Nuevo (New Cay). Stick to the Cayo Nuevo side of the channel to keep in the deep water. Once past the shoal area, eyeball your way up to the beach on Cayo Sombrero. Along part of the beach the water is about 60 feet deep almost to the sand. This is the place to anchor. Though we have had reports that the holding is difficult here. Beware of the tempting little bay farther southeast. It is used by many power boats, but there are reefs off it. In calm weather Cayo Sombrero is a delightful anchorage. In a strong easterly wind some waves find their way along the shore. In these conditions you can get a much more sheltered anchorage behind Cayo Pescadores (Fishermen's Cay). The only trouble is the depth. The channel is some 50-60 feet deep all the way through. The shoals on both sides are so wide that taking a line ashore is difficult, so it is best to take enough line to anchor in the deep area.

The rest of Morrocoy National Park is a maze in endless shades of green. Clues to this puzzle are in the form of three main channels now marked with small beacons whose arrows point into the channel; false clues are given by older buoys which have been left to drift around. The buoyage system is simple and if you use our plan which shows where the buoys are supposed to be and use your eyes to gauge the depth, you can navigate through it without too much problem.

If you are coming from the north the logical entrance is Boca Grande. It is down wind and sea but the water is very deep and you soon get out of the swells. From the south the logical entrance is Boca Paiclas which is also very deep. If you stick to the

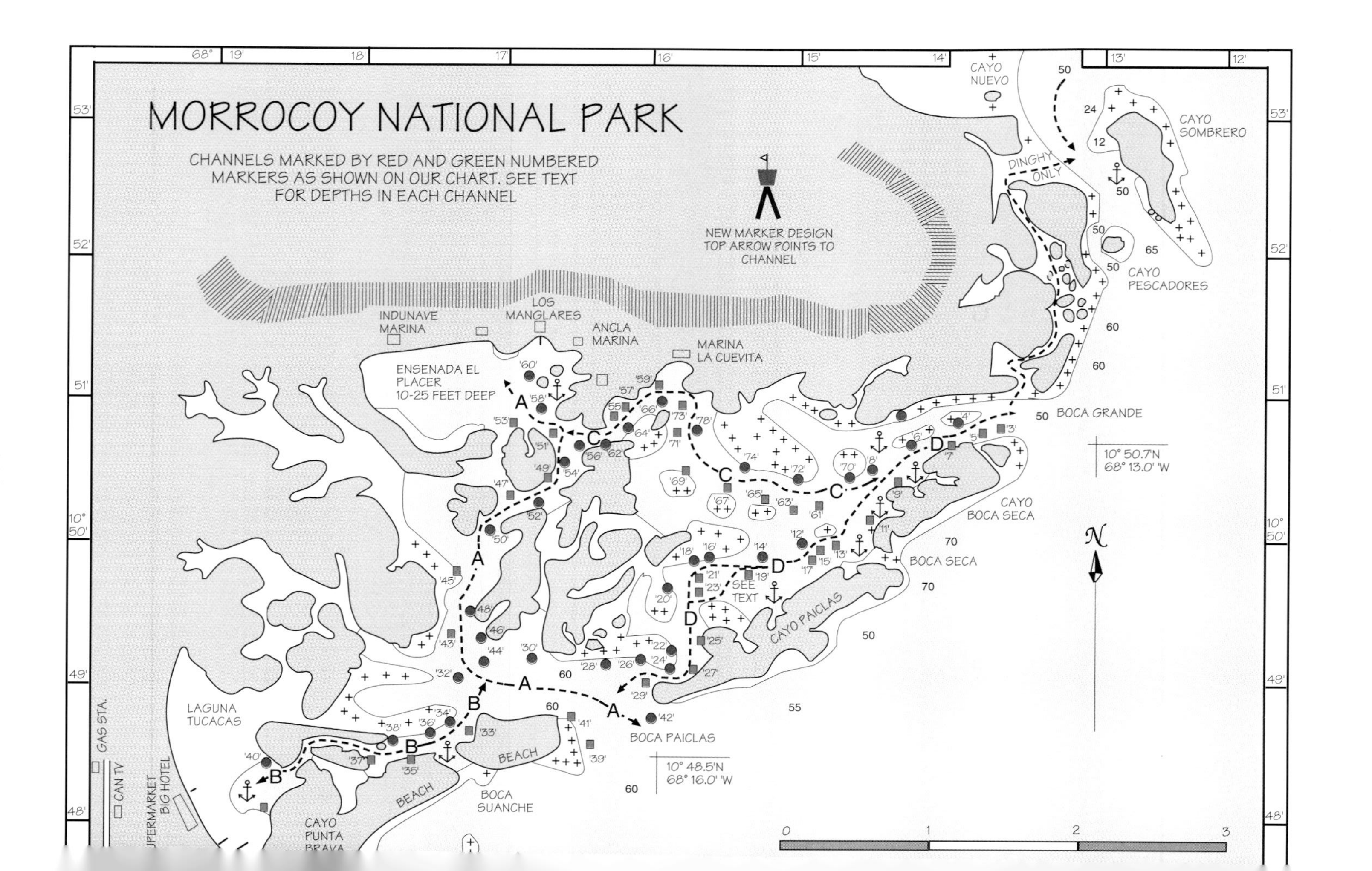
MORROCOY NATIONAL PARK
CHANNELS MARKED BY RED AND GREEN NUMBERED MARKERS AS SHOWN ON OUR CHART. SEE TEXT FOR DEPTHS IN EACH CHANNEL
NEW MARKER DESIGN TOP ARROW POINTS TO CHANNEL
CAYO NUEVO
CAYO SOMBRERO
CAYO PESCADORES
DINGHY ONLY
BOCA GRANDE
CAYO BOCA SECA
BOCA SECA
CAYO PAICLAS
BOCA PAICLAS
BOCA SUANCHE
BEACH
BEACH
LAGUNA TUCACAS
INDUNAVE MARINA
LOS MANGLARES
ANCLA MARINA
MARINA LA CUEVITA
ENSENADA EL PLACER 10-25 FEET DEEP
SEE TEXT
BIG HOTEL
CAN TV
GAS STA.
10° 50.7'N 68° 13.0' W
10° 48.5'N 68° 16.0' W
68° 19' 18' 17' 16' 15' 14' 13' 12'
53' 52' 51' 10° 50' 49' 48'
0 1 2 3
50 24 12 50 50 65 50 60 60 50 70 70 50 55 60 60 60
'3' '4' '5' '6' '7' '8' '9' '11' '12' '13' '14' '15' '16' '17' '18' '19' '20' '21' '22' '23' '24' '25' '26' '27' '28' '29' '30' '32' '33' '34' '35' '36' '37' '38' '39' '40' '41' '42' '43' '44' '45' '46' '47' '48' '49' '50' '51' '52' '53' '54' '55' '56' '57' '58' '59' '60' '61' '62' '63' '64' '65' '66' '67' '69' '70' '71' '72' '73' '74' '78'

eastern side you will quickly be in calm water.

It is best to navigate using the main channels. For gunkholing and anchoring look for a deep area outside the channels and eyeball your way in. In many places you have depths of 40-60 feet, making eyeball navigation easy. You can anchor anywhere you like out of the main channels, though for some of the best spots you should be prepared to anchor in 50 feet of water. To avoid confusion on our small scale chart, we have numbered the buoys and left out depths. We have also given a letter to each of the four channels. Channel A is the main channel from Boca Paiclas to Ensenada El Placer (Pleasure Lagoon). This has 60 feet at the entrance and 50 feet to Buoy #52 from where it shoals slowly to about 35 feet at the entrance to the lagoon. The lagoon has depths from 10-25 feet.

There is an excellent anchorage to the southeast of the two mangrove islands just as you enter Ensenada El Placer. This is a good bird viewing spot and sometimes scarlet ibis roost on the mangrove islands, so do not anchor too close.

Channel B runs from the main channel to Laguna Tucacas. Up to Boca Suanche there is about 30 feet of water. There are several good anchoring spots around Boca Suanche. Do not pass too close to Buoy #36 as it is shoal, though a little farther south there is over 30 feet of water. The shallowest part comes between Buoys #36 and #35. A boat drawing 6.5 feet can bounce gently over this on a low tide and is fine on a high tide.

Thereafter depths are 8-13 feet and remain this deep all the way. The twisty narrow mangrove channel just before Laguna Tucacas is a pleasure to traverse under a minimum of sail with the wind behind. It is best during the weekdays when there are not too many high speed power boats with which to share it.

There is a good anchoring area in Laguna Tucacas about half way between town and the channel entrance. If you go any closer to town it is shallow.

Channel C runs from Ensenada El Placer and joins the main channel off Cayo Boca Seca. This is an easy channel to follow. The depths jump around a lot, but we found nothing less than 15 feet.

Channel D runs from Boca Grande through to Boca Paiclas. There is between 30 and 60 feet deep near Boca Grande with many excellent anchorages behind the barrier islands. Pass very close to Buoy #13 as the channel is only 100 feet wide and 13 feet deep. The shallowest part comes between Buoys #21 and #23. There is only about 6.5 feet of water here at low tide. We found considerably deeper water (about nine feet at low water) fairly close to the north of Buoy #19, rejoining the channel just south of Buoy #23 (see the sketch chart). Eyeball your way through the deepest looking water. Once past Buoy #23 the channel deepens to 50 feet or more.

One of the nicest anchorages is close by Boca Seca (Dry Channel). The reef protects you from the sea and you get the full breeze.

Services

There is a fuel dock with 10 feet alongside called Los Manglares (VHF:77) in Ensenada El Placer. It opens weekdays from 0800-1300 and 1400-1700, weekends from 0800-1700. Owner Alfredo Ceasares sells gasoline and water (diesel is planned), engine oil, ice and has a marine store and restaurant ($C) which are open weekends only. Alfredo speaks good English, gives information, takes garbage and offers a telephone and fax service.

There are several other small marinas in the area, including Ancla Marina (VHF:74) where you can get fresh water and Indunave (VHF:16).

No restaurants or stores in the park are supposed to sell booze. However, neither Chichiriviche nor Tucacas are in the park, and there is no law against drinking.

Marina La Cuevita (VHF:72) is one of the larger marinas. They do not sell fuel, but they have a pleasant seafood restaurant ($D) and a small shop which stocks large quantities of ice and bug repellent. These are open all day from Friday to Sunday. The restaurant looks out over the water, is active on the weekends, and is a great place to visit for lunch. You can even buy a beer here.

Showers and bathrooms are open to the public all week long. There is dockage with up to 16 feet of water alongside. Boat storage and mechanics can be arranged.

If you run short of something, you may want to try Tucacas. There is no diesel on the waterfront and there are no taxis, but, if you ask the fishermen, someone may have a truck they are willing to use to run you a mile to the gas station where you can buy diesel. Before the gas station is a CANTV where you can make overseas calls. Tucacas has several supermarkets and liquor stores, many of which will deliver to the dinghy dock. A large local market close to the docks opens on Tuesday mornings. There are about a dozen restaurants.

PASSAGE FROM MORROCOY TO PUERTO CABELLO

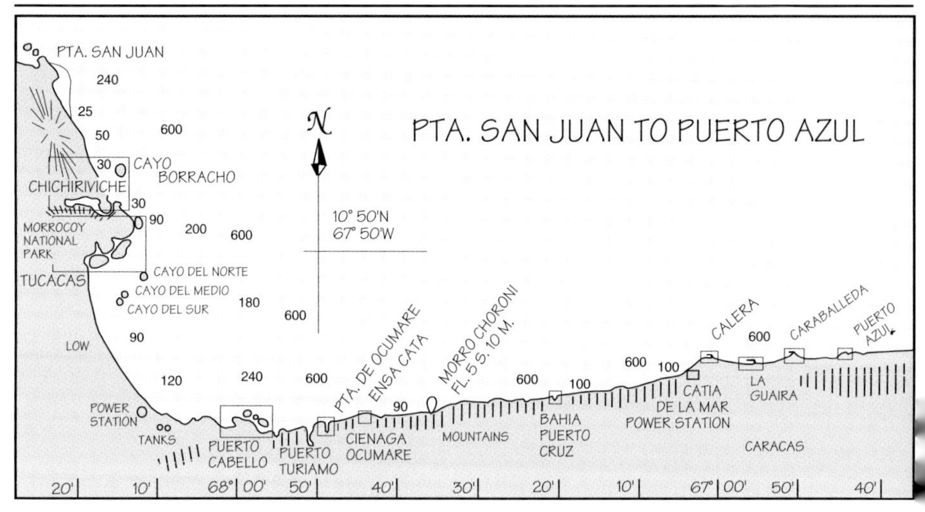

It is about 25 miles from Morrocoy National park to Puerto Cabello. You can often make it in one tack, and if you are lucky it will be a close reach. On the way there are three small islands; Cayo del Norte, Cayo del Medio and Cayo del Sur. None of them is large enough to have an acceptable anchorage, though local scuba boats visit for diving.

PUERTO CABELLO

Puerto Cabello is a pleasant town with some charming walkways. The area around Paseo El Malecón is especially attractive with well restored old buildings. The main drag in town for shops and restaurants is Avenida Bolívar. Puerto Cabello is a major port and the largest natural harbor in Venezuela. It is said that the name Cabello (One Hair) was given because it was so well protected and secure you would only have to secure your ship with a single hair to make it safe. Unfortunately this huge natural harbor has been taken over by the Venezuelan navy, so yachts are not allowed to anchor inside. Puerto Cabello is a major commercial port and a good place to provision and get things fixed.

Navigation

There is a breaking shoal just north of Isla Goaigoaza which is buoyed . The big semicircular buildings you see to the west of Puerto Cabello are part of a soap factory You must always go into the clearing dock for entry and dealing with the port captain After that you can anchor off or go into the marina.

Regulations

Puerto Cabello is a port of entry. The Por

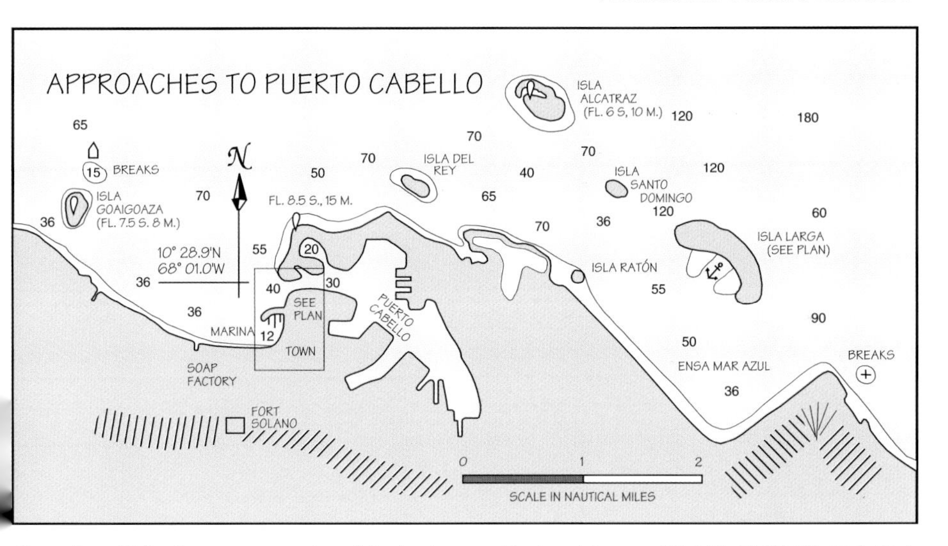

Captain will insist you come into his dock for clearance. If you want someone to do the paper work for you contact Carlos Alvarez (T:042 61 08 68, Cel:014 43 25 45). Marianella is now only there once a month but in case this changes her number is T:042 64 60 97. She is also happy to do it when she is there.

Services

Marina Puerto Cabello (T:042-61 72 77, VHF:71) is the best place to be while you visit Puerto Cabello. They do not have much spare room, but usually manage to fit everyone in. This is a private yacht club and some members have mixed feelings about visiting yachts, so please keep in mind that it is not a commercial establishment where you can demand services. Water and electricity (110/220 volt 60 cycles) are available on the dock. They have showers, ice, security, diesel and gasoline, and a helpful staff. The manager is Pedro Sanchez and he is assisted by Niuka Barrera. At the moment no one speaks English.

If you cannot get into the marina you could anchor between the marina and the beach, though anchoring yachts have reported late night thefts by people swimming out. You could anchor much farther out, outside the protection of the marina, but you would roll. If there is no room in the marina, I would consider anchoring off the marina for the day and going to Isla Larga for the night.

Carlos Alvarez (T:042 61 08 68, Cel:014 43 25 45, VHF:71 speaks English, and does all the paper work for yachts. Carlos is good at sourcing anything you may need at a reasonable price and is happy to take you on tours in the surrounding countryside.

Marianela (T/F:042 64 60 97) speaks perfect English and good French. Unfortunately she will hardly be around any more as she has accepted a job in the south and will only return once a month. She was very good at helping yachts in all ways including arranging medical treatment and finding whatever they needed. If you particularly want to be in contact with her, we suggest you do so long before you get to Puerto Cabello.

The navy yard is often willing to haul yachts. They will let you work on them yourself, or you can use their very professional team to get a first class job at a reasonable rate. Long term out-of-the-water storage can be arranged. They have two hauling methods. Yachts up to 60 tons are lifted by crane, 60- to 300-ton yachts are pulled up on a large railway. All kinds of painting and repairs can be arranged. However, because this is a navy yard, you are expected to be properly dressed at all times. Shorts and shirt are fine, but no bathing costumes, or sleeveless t-shirts. Since it is a long way to town, people on the hard are usually given permission to use the navy supermarket. Contact them direct

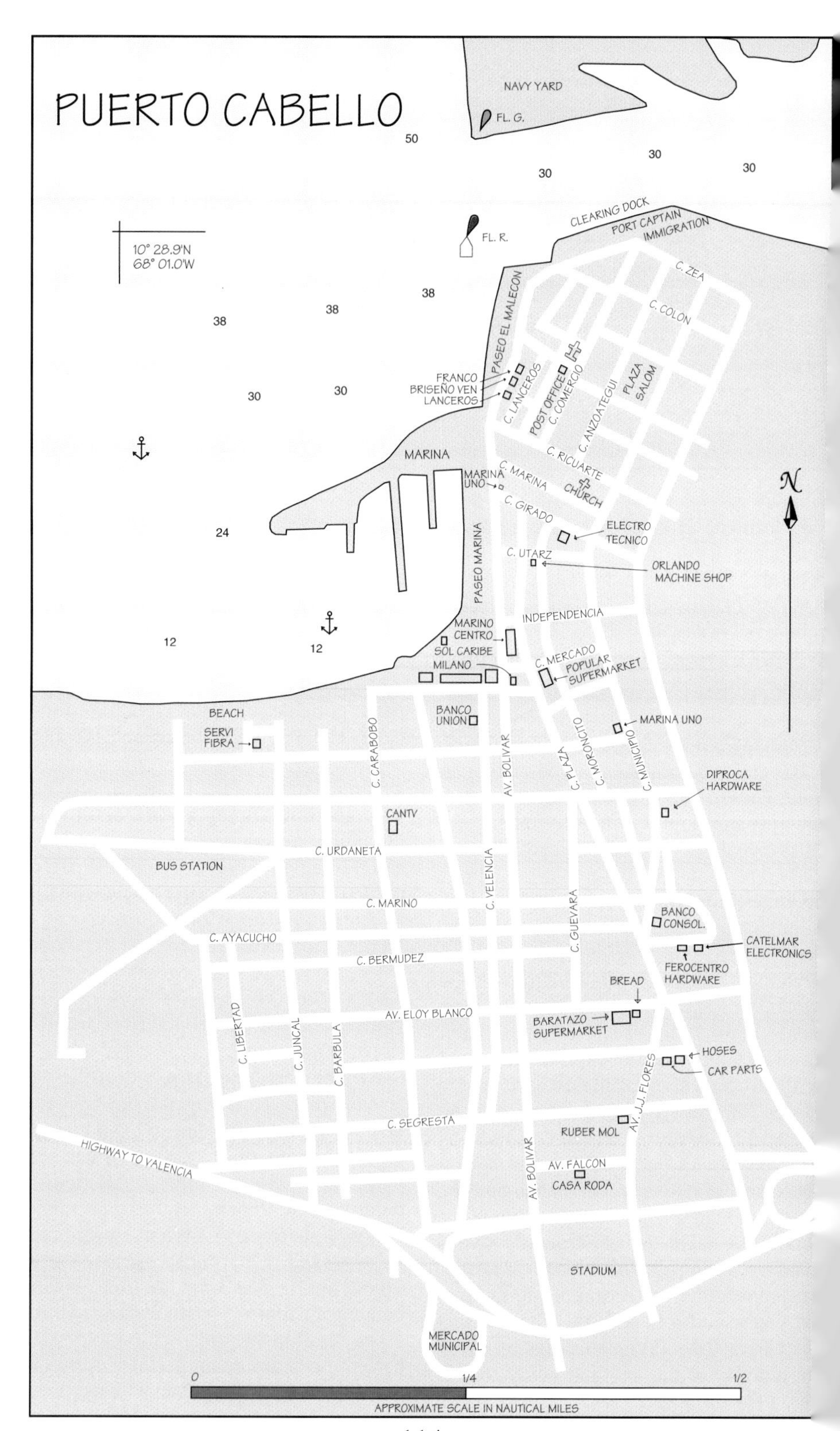
PUERTO CABELLO
NAVY YARD
FL. G.
50
30
30
30
CLEARING DOCK
PORT CAPTAIN
IMMIGRATION
FL. R.
10° 28.9'N
68° 01.0'W
38
38
38
30
30
24
12
12
C. ZEA
C. COLON
PASEO EL MALECON
FRANCO
BRISEÑO VEN
LANCEROS
C. LANCEROS
POST OFFICE
C. COMERCIO
C. ANZOATEGUI
PLAZA SALOM
MARINA
C. RICUARTE
C. MARINA
MARINA UNO
CHURCH
C. GIRADO
ELECTRO TECNICO
C. UTARZ
ORLANDO MACHINE SHOP
PASEO MARINA
INDEPENDENCIA
MARINO CENTRO
SOL CARIBE
MILANO
C. MERCADO
POPULAR SUPERMARKET
BEACH
BANCO UNION
SERVI FIBRA
MARINA UNO
C. CARABOBO
AV. BOLIVAR
C. PLAZA
C. MORONCITO
C. MUNICIPIO
DIPROCA HARDWARE
CANTV
C. URDANETA
BUS STATION
C. VELENCIA
C. MARINO
C. GUEVARA
BANCO CONSOL.
C. AYACUCHO
C. BERMUDEZ
CATELMAR ELECTRONICS
FEROCENTRO HARDWARE
BREAD
AV. ELOY BLANCO
BARATAZO SUPERMARKET
C. LIBERTAD
C. JUNCAL
C. BARBULA
HOSES
CAR PARTS
AV. J.J. FLORES
C. SEGRESTA
RUBER MOL
HIGHWAY TO VALENCIA
AV. BOLIVAR
AV. FALCON
CASA RODA
STADIUM
MERCADO MUNICIPAL
0
1/4
1/2
APPROXIMATE SCALE IN NAUTICAL MILES

Puerto Cabello

in Spanish only at T:042-61 01 11, F:042-61 58 86, VHF:07.

There is a USA direct phone at CANTV which is open every day from 0730-2300. There are also lots of card phones around.

You can get buses around town and to Caracas (mornings only) from outside the marina. For other buses go to the bus station. Taxis are available opposite the marina and at Marino Centro.

There are lots of places to buy gear or get things fixed. Try Carlos as your first bet. A reader particularly recommended a chandlery called Venecia Ship Suppliers and Duty Free (T:042 61 69 22/61 69 51). A representative came to the boat, the captain gave him three hard-to-find items they had been unable to get elsewhere, and he came up trumps for all.

Servi Fibra (T:042-61 71 23) has a small marine chandlery. They fix any type of outboard and do fiberglass repairs in their shop or on your boat. Navalmar, another marine store also fixes outboards, speak to Mr Benito.

Electrotecnico (T:042-63 861/779) is a big electric shop that can fix any kind of electric motor or generator, including starters, alternators, windlasses and electric pumps.

Orlando's Machine Shop (T:042-61 36 51) is a complete machine shop that can handle all kinds of welding and machining and the staff will even come to your boat to fix things if necessary.

Catelmar Representaciones (T:042-61 08 30, F:042-61 31 74) is one place for new electronics or any type of electronic repair. Another is Electronics Radio Marine (042-61-57-96), Mr Rasheed, the owner, speaks English.

There are excellent hardware stores all over town, including Ferreteria Errocentro (T:042-61 00 10), with fastenings, tools and an excellent stock of electrical fittings.

Diproca (T:042-61 22 22/23) not only sells hardware but keeps a good stock of oil and fuel filters, pumps etc.

Mangueras Oporto (042-61 51 20) is one of several stores specializing in hoses of many types, including all hydraulic hoses and their fittings. Rubber Mol is another. Casa Roda (T:042-61 48 45) specializes in all kinds of belts, hoses and seals.

Donato D'Andrea (T:042 64 01 98/64 02 29) is the man to check for computer gear and accessories or for sending e-mail or cybersurfing.

Ashore

Shopping is easily done at Popular

Puerto Cabello

(weekdays 0800-1230 and 1430-1930, Saturday open 0700-2000, Sunday open 0800-1200). Popular is big, close and well stocked. You can arrange a taxi to get your shopping back. Baratazo is another supermarket. There are bread shops all over town, including one opposite Marino Centro. Calle Mercado has lots of stalls selling fresh fruits and vegetables. For large orders of beers and soft drinks, talk to any liquor store near Marino Centro. Most will deliver to the dock.

There are several good restaurants right near the marina. Lanceros (T:042-63 634, $D) is a good steak and seafood restaurant with Spanish style cuisine. It is pleasant, local and inexpensive. About four doors down from Lanceros in a yellow building with no sign outside, Biseño Ven (T:042-63 569/707, $D) is an excellent Venezuelan restaurant specializing in local food. Lunch (100-1430) is the big meal and they have a wide choice. In the evening (1700-2130) they serve only arepas (the very best) with various fillings. France is Italian, inexpensive and good and Sol Caribe is also well worth checking out.

Marina Uno is almost a fast food place, but the food is good as well as inexpensive.

There are several interesting side trips while you are in Puerto Cabello. Take a taxi, arrange transport with Carlos or put on your hiking shoes and walk up to Fort Solano, about a mile south of town. Built by the Spanish in 1740 and still in use as a signal station today, this fort offers excellent views over Puerto Cabello.

The adventurous can try the three and a half hour train trip to Barquisimeto. This is a very local railway, the only one in Venezuela and not a luxury trip. Barquisimeto has good handicrafts shops and an ice skating rink. The train ride is an inexpensive way to see some countryside. The trains run about four times a day and the station is west of the bus station.

There are good hikes up a river with little waterfalls and pools where you can hear bellbirds and monkeys in the countryside around Puerto Cabello. There are also hikes on old Spanish roads. Very inexpensive round-trip tickets to Miami are available from Valencia. Contact Carlos for details on any of the above.

Valencia is only about 20 miles away from Puerto Cabello. It is a major shopping and industrial city.

ISLA LARGA

Isla Larga is one Puerto Cabello's alluring offshore islands and the only one open to visitors. The rest are reserved for the military. It is a delightful place to spend a few days. Boats do bring tourists here from the mainland, but holidays and weekends are the only really busy times. Isla Larga has a bay which is well protected from the normal winds and swells. The easiest way to approach is by lining up the two beacons which bring you right between the reefs. The reefs are all quite easy to see. There is a conspicuous wreck of an old World War II ship whose mast shows almost before the beacons.

Most of the sand bottom is about 50 feet deep. You need lots of anchoring line and resist the temptation to anchor in any small 35-foot patches, as they are probably coral. An alternative is to anchor bow to the beach, using one anchor in the shallows and a stern anchor to hold you off. This is OK but you have to find a place to do it where your line will not be chewing up the fringing reef which is popular with snorkelers.

The snorkeling here is good, both on the reefs and the wreck. Ashore there are pristine beaches.

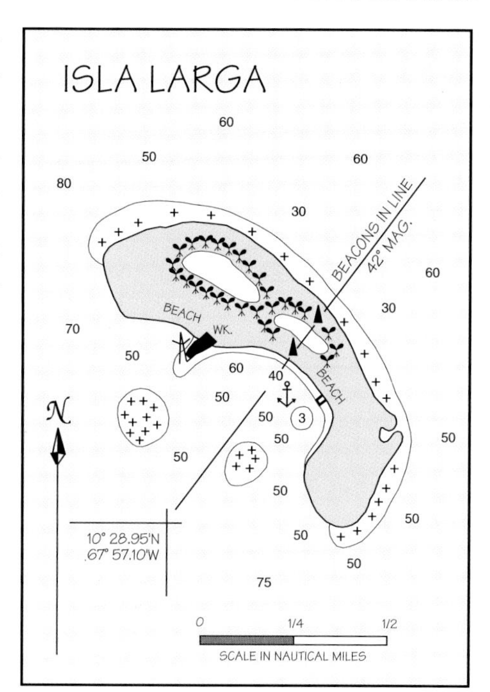

FROM PUERTO CABELLO TO PUERTO AZUL

(See previous sketch chart Pta. San Juan to Puerto Azul)

For those who have sailed from the Windwards or Trinidad and have to return, this is the time you start to pay your dues. However, if you make this trip with plenty of time so you can take breaks and enjoy the anchorages along the way, it is not bad. During the first part of the trip from Puerto Cabello to Carenero the average wind is fairly light and usually comes from an easterly direction. It is often strongest from mid morning to late evening and light and variable from late evening to mid morning. "Often" does not mean "always" and the wind can blow hard against you day and night. It can also be calm day and night and you can even have light westerly winds for some days. The weather is also affected by fronts that come through. In the winter when the winds are stronger and the swells larger, the trip will be rougher than in the spring or summer.

People generally make their way east within a few miles of the coast to keep out of the west setting current. Sometimes you get a weak counter current in your favor. The coast is steep to and if you go by day and keep a lookout you can stay within about half a mile.

Many people prefer to motor when the wind is light. It should be noted that a lack of wind does not mean there is no sea. Sometimes this coast is like a lake, at others it seems that all those seas you saw out there in the outer islands have come home to roost here, resulting in large and confused swells. If you plan your trip using any of the marginal anchorages we describe, you should have a back up plan to push on should the anchorage prove difficult.

For those going the other way, the westwards trip is an easy passage down wind and sea. However, it should be noted that westward sailing is much better by Los Roques and Las Aves.

After Puerto Cabello, Ensa Cata makes a good take off point. If you leave Ensa Cata at first light you probably can make Bahía Puerto Cruz before the wind gets too strong. From here it is also possible to day sail to Caraballeda. If you are getting low on fuel, you can top up in Puerto Calera.

The land from Ensa Cata all the way to Calera is rugged with dramatic mountains and steep valleys rising from the water's edge. There are many beaches and cliffs. Two aerials and a light make Morro Choroní a good landmark . It also has a beach and few houses. About five miles west of Calera civilization begins again with buildings and construction. At his point you begin to get a skirt of flatter land along the coast, while the mountains just behind get even higher and more spectacular. A few miles before Calera there is a large conspicuous power station and half way between that and Calera is Catia La Mar with some big tanks ashore, a long dock and several big buoys. If you are hugging the coast pretty close, both Calera and Caraballeda stand out as distinctive headlands. Puerto Azul is just six miles farther east along the coast.

CÍENAGA DE OCUMARE

Ciénaga de Ocumare is a deep, well protected bay surrounded by mangroves and steep hills. It is the next usable anchorage after Isla Larga and the last really protected anchorage until you get to the marinas near La Guaira. (Puerto Turiamo is military and closed to yachts.)

Ashore you can hear many birds, including cristofues (the Spanish name for the cocrico). At night there are hundreds of mosquitoes. Bats come and try to keep them down, but they do a poor job and it is best to put up nets or plan on burning a coil. Ashore there are several holiday homes. There is no road, only a two and half hour trail to the next village. The people who stay here come by boat. The bay is also used by fishermen from nearby villages. Ciénaga de Ocumare comes under the control of the military, but normally they have no objection to yachts anchoring here.

Although the bay is big, much of it is taken up by a reef and shallows. Enter down the channel, watch out for the reef on the west side of the entrance. The water is 50 feet deep until you get toward the southern end of the bay where you can find anchoring depths of 10-25 feet before running aground.

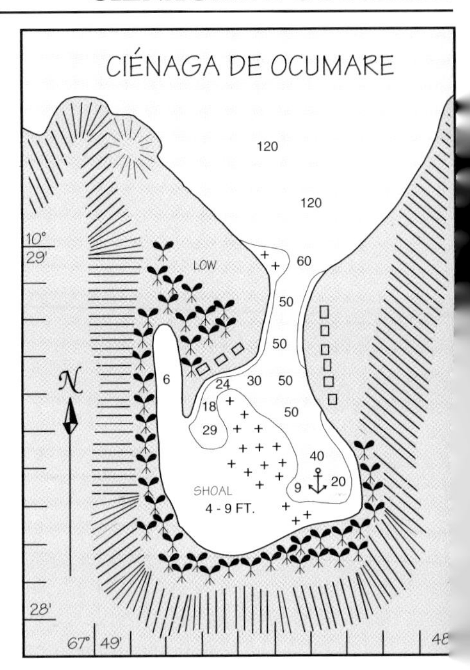

There is a very narrow deep-water passage on the north side of the reef but the area is a bit small for anchoring. Shoal draft boats could get back there and anchor. The whole area makes for good dinghy exploration.

ENSA CATA

Ensa Cata lies about five miles east of Ciénaga de Ocumare. On the way you pass the town of Independencia. There is a protected eastern corner of this bay but it is marginal as an anchorage.

Ensa Cata offers a good, but not totall calm, anchorage up in the eastern corne of the bay behind the protective island an

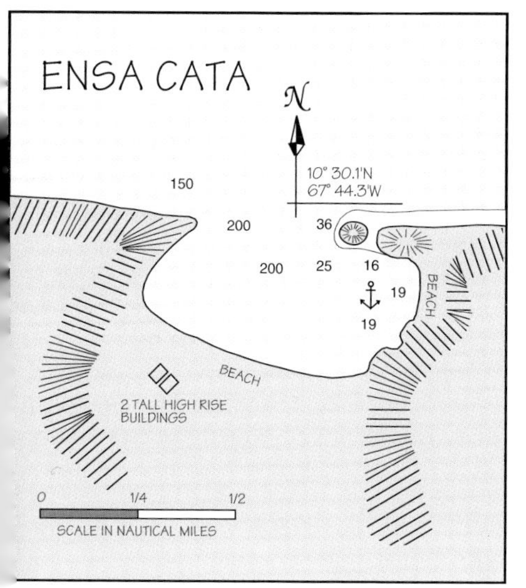

rocks. In heavy northerly winds and swells this anchorage could be untenable. However it is only five miles back to Ciénaga de Ocumare, so if you come with enough time you can decide whether to stay. It is an easy anchorage with plenty of room to anchor in depths of 16-35 feet over sand and weed. If you want to leave at night it is an easy exit. (Ciénaga de Ocumare could be hard to leave at night.)

The main beach is a popular but surgy holiday beach. There are two tall high rise buildings which make it easy to identify the bay. There is also a pretty beach on the east shore right ahead of the anchorage.

BAHÍA PUERTO CRUZ

Bahía Puerto Cruz is a little bay conveniently placed 23 miles east of Ensa Cata. From close to the coast, the entrance stands out as distinctive headland.

It is a beautiful bay with steep hills on both sides and a lush narrow valley leading into peaky hills and mountains behind. At the head of the bay is a white sand beach backed by palm trees.

However, it is a tricky anchorage, usually a bit rolly and untenable much of the winter. If you plan to use this on your way east, have a back up plan in case it doesn't work out. There are crosses on two of the rocks which help identify it, and it is the only bay in this area that looks protected enough to be an anchorage.

The problem with Bahía Puerto Cruz is that the water in the middle of the bay is 240 feet deep and it stays deep almost until the rocks. The only way to anchor is stern to the shore, and the best anchoring area (shown on our sketch chart) is not very large. As you come in, the water shelves abruptly from about 70 feet to about 40 feet. You need to drop your anchor over the deep ledge and take a stern anchor into the shallows by dinghy. Taking a line ashore is probably not feasible as landing a dinghy on the rocks among the waves could be dangerous.

If you come in the rainy season and the

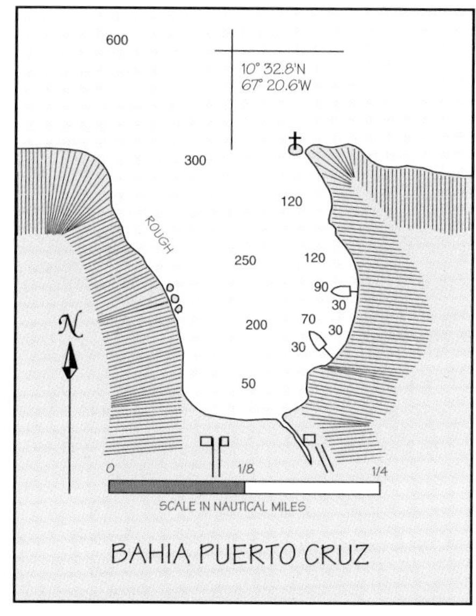

river is running fast it will create a current in the middle of the bay.

Bahía Puerto Cruz was once a coffee estate. There is a stately old road lined with large mahogany trees that leads back to the main village. In the village are a couple of small shops where you can get essentials.

You can return along the other side of the cool looking river. Many fishing boats are anchored off the beach. The large pipes that go over the hills carry water to La Guaira.

Puerto Viejo (T:031 52 40 44), a new marina is about quarter of a mile west of Puerto Calera. It is part of Puerto Viejo Resort, a 5-star hotel. When you are tied up in the marina you are treated like a guest in the hotel and are welcome to use the three swimming pools, along with all the other hotel facilities. Cable TV lines run to the dock along with water and electricity. Should you not be getting along with your companions they have bathrooms for both owners and crew. The marina takes 67 boats and includes a fuel dock with both diesel and gasoline. Foreign flag yachts are welcomed but the price about $2US per foot per day will keep out the riffraff. Puerto Viejo mainly caters to large power yachts, but sailing yachts are welcome. We saw this marina under construction a few years ago, but have not been back so we do not have a plan. The manager told us depths were as much as 10 meters (33 feet) deep. However, since we have not surveyed this one I suggest you approach slowly with your eye on the echo sounder.

PUERTO CALERA

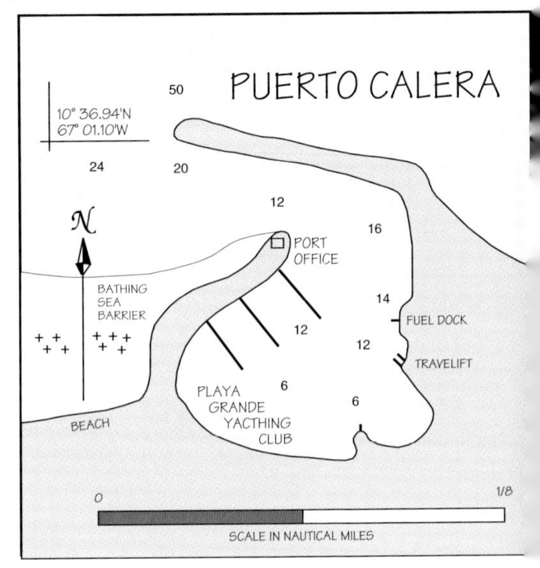

Puerto Calera is the home of Playa Grande Yacthing (sic) Club (T:031-51 50 11, VHF:69/71, SSB 2738). This is a private yacht club. Foreign yachts are not welcome here except to buy fuel. Legally Puerto Calera is a port of refuge, which means a boat can stop here for up to 24 hours if it needs to. You can usually only stay longer if you are invited to by a member. The current price of $3 US per foot per day for non-Venezuelan flagged vessels is designed to discourage foreign visitors. There is room to anchor in the northeast corner. While you would not be given permission to anchor here, if you did so in really bad weather, it is unlikely anyone would stop you. The fuel dock is fine and this is a good place to buy fuel, though it sometimes takes a while to get an attendant.

The port is clean and pleasant and if you decide it is worth the price, you will find restaurant and showers ashore. The restaurant sells ice and the marina office will call a taxi if you wish to go shopping.

LA GUAIRA

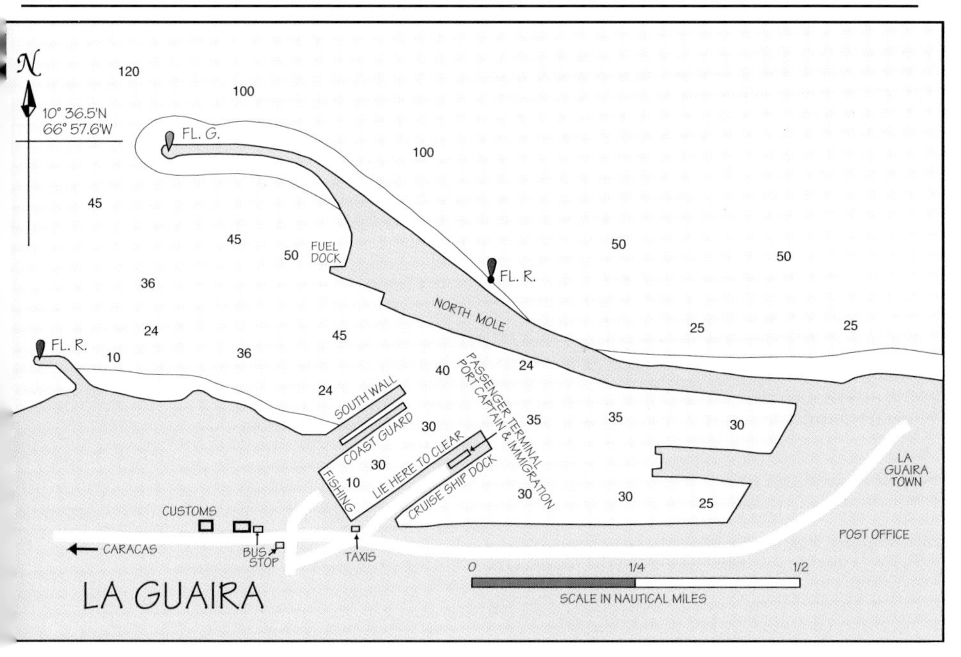

La Guaira is a big commercial port. It has no facilities for yachts, and I can think of no good reason, except inclement weather, for a yachtsman to come in here. We include a rough sketch chart in case you do need to enter. Tie up to the fishing fleet.

MARINA DE CARABALLEDA

Just a few miles east of La Guaira, Marina de Caraballeda is a next logical place to stop when heading east. Marina de Caraballeda (T/F:031 99 27 12, F:031 99 88 77, VHF:16) has now been privatized and is under new management. Much needed renovation has been undertaken. The management speak English and they have a dock reserved for foreign flag vessels. The rates at the time of going to press were around $0.60 per foot per day, which is on a par with Marinas in the Eastern Caribbean. They have a fuel dock attached to the travel lift slip. They sell diesel and gasoline. They have a 40-ton travel lift and are used to hauling power rather than sailing craft, though they can manage the latter. However, advance arrangements would be advisable. There are

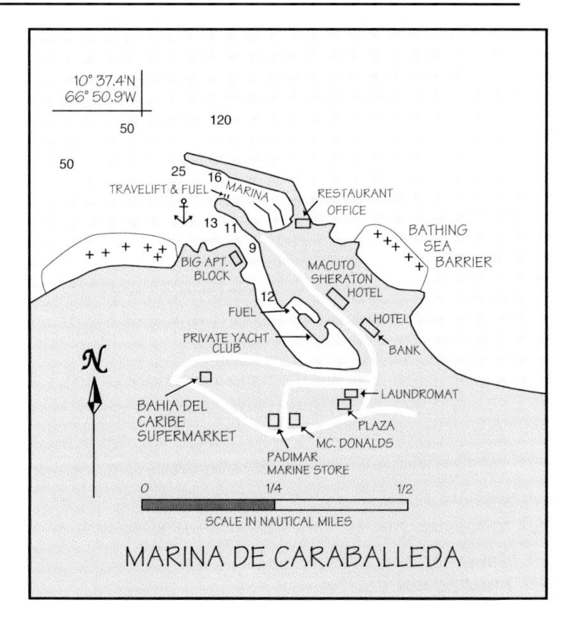

showers, and water and electricity are available on the docks. If there is no room in the marina you can get fair protection anchored just outside with protection from the sea wall.

There is a laundromat on the back road on the far side of the private yacht club lagoon (see our sketch chart).

You can also take fuel from the fuel dock at the private yacht club by the Sherton Hotel which is accessed by a channel just before the marina. If you do this, take care going down the first part of the channel by the big apartment block. There is a shoal on the west side of the channel under the apartment. Stay to the east side until you pass the shoal and then stay in the center. There is about nine feet in the deep part of the channel near the shoal. After that the channel deepens to about 12 feet. This is a very protected bay and there is plenty of room in it. Anchoring is not permitted, but in case of a storm keep it in mind.

Ashore

Before you leave the marina on foot, you need to pick up a pass from the information office just a few steps from the front gate. If you forget and they don't want to let you back in, say you are heading for the restaurant.

A short walk back from the marina takes you to the Macuto Sheraton, a large and luxurious hotel with comfortable seats, air conditioning and a card phone bank. You can also use these phones to get a USA direct operator by dialing 800 11 120. There are a few boutiques here and a quick film developing lab.

In Melia Caribe, the next large hotel down the road, you will find a bank where they will change $US and Canadian but not European currency. The bank starts changing money at 0900.

When you come to the main road, there is a little plaza ahead of you with several handicraft shops and a very small grocery. There are several supermarkets farther down the road. The best is Supermarcado Bahía del Caribe (T:031-94 43 93, cc:V). They open daily 0700-1300 and 1500-2000, except Sunday when they open mornings only. They deliver sizable orders to the marina.

Padimar (T:031-94 46 18) is a marine store a little farther down the road from McDonalds. They have batteries, fittings, bilge pumps, ropes and Racor fuel filters and elements.

A string of restaurants lines the main street from the Plaza to McDonalds, but one of the most pleasant restaurants is right in the marina ($D, cc:A,V). It is run by the marina and has indoor and outdoor dining rooms. On a hot day it is best to hide away in the air-conditioned part, but on a fair evening it is fine to sit outside by the water with a view of the mountains beyond.

If you manage to get a place in the marina, this is a good place from which to visit Caracas if for any reason you have to do so. It is about an hour drive away. Taxis are not exorbitant and buses run from right outside the marina.

PUERTO AZUL

Puerto Azul is about seven miles up the coast from Caraballeda, and makes a good stop for those who are trying to keep their easterly hops as short as possible. Puerto Azul (T:031-72 24 15, VHF:16, SSB 28.37) is a magnificent and very large private club. Foreign flag yachts are not welcome inside but there is a perfectly adequate anchorage just outside. The anchoring limitation line runs from the entrance buoy to the small breakwater on the opposite side. The calmest place is to go right up to the line on the shore side. When you have got your bow anchor holding, put out a stern anchor as the wind switches around. Make sure you do not block the entrance of the small Playa Azul Marina.

There is a light flashing every six seconds on top of an apartment block in Puerto Azul. It is about 100 feet high and the range is over 10 miles.

Services

The fuel dock in Puerto Azul is open to the public and open daily from 0800-1600.

Ashore

While this is a good place to stop for the night, getting ashore presents some difficulties. The only public access is Playa Mansa which is stony and surfy and probably best left to ex-navy Seals.

If you desperately need a new battery or some boat part, there is a good chandlery called Shop Puerto Azul in the marina. Dinghy in and plead your case with a guard. He will probably try to help. Similarly, if you dress up well and ask nicely the guards may let you use one of the restaurants. They also have a sail repair shop and other facilities ashore. However, all facilities belong to the club and are for club members only. Whether they are willing to offer you any assistance depends entirely on the staff. You will meet the patrolling guards first and if you need to talk to anyone else, ask to speak to the harbor master (called the port captain as he is a retired government port captain).

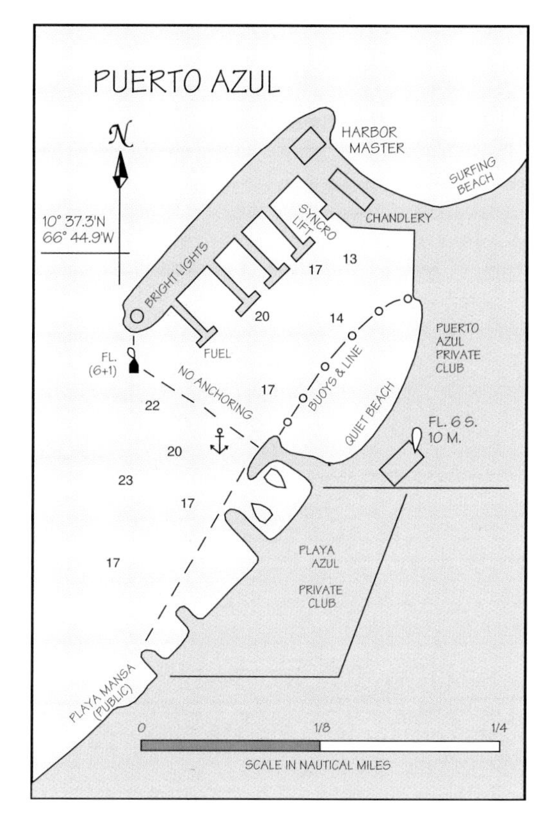

PUERTO AZUL TO PUERTO FRANCÉS

From Puerto Azul it is about 41 miles to Puerto Francés (Ensenada de Corsarios), which is the next good stop and only about five miles from Carenero. It is possible to

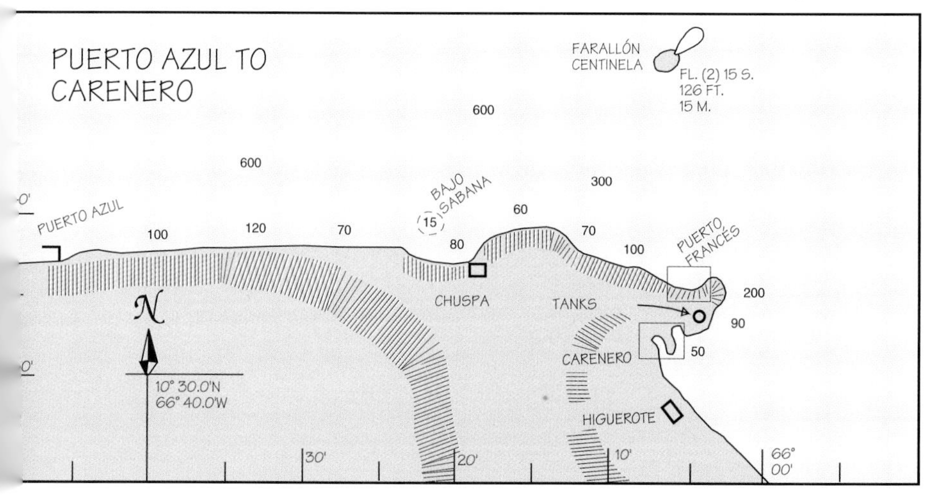

make this in a day sail, though those who want the calmer seas for motoring may want to leave around midnight.

The steep land continues to Bahía Chuspa, where the mountains start to recede behind the coast and there are smaller hills along the water's edge.

Avoid Bajo Sabana in the middle of Bahía Chuspa, even though the charts say it has 15 feet over it. Best stay outside it if you are sailing by night. In good light the adventurous can eyeball their way inside.

Those who hate to power and don't like short tacking in light winds, can try tacking out to Los Roques and then back in again to Puerto Francés. This takes you much farther, but if you are ready for a few extra days in Los Roques, why not?

PUERTO FRANCÉS

Puerto Francés is also known as Ensenada de Corsarios. It was given these names because it was used by French pirates in the olden days.

It is a well protected bay in all normal conditions. If you are approaching from the west you will notice a small island with a house on it about two miles before the headland. Give this a good clearance as rocks come a long way out beyond it. The rest of this coast is also rocky and best given a quarter of a mile clearance.

As you get nearer Cabo Codera you will see two beaches. The main beach is accessible by road and has lifeguard lookout towers. On weekends it is full of visitors. For the rest of the week it is left to a few fishermen. The swells come in around the corner and find their way to this beach, so you want to anchor farther north, any

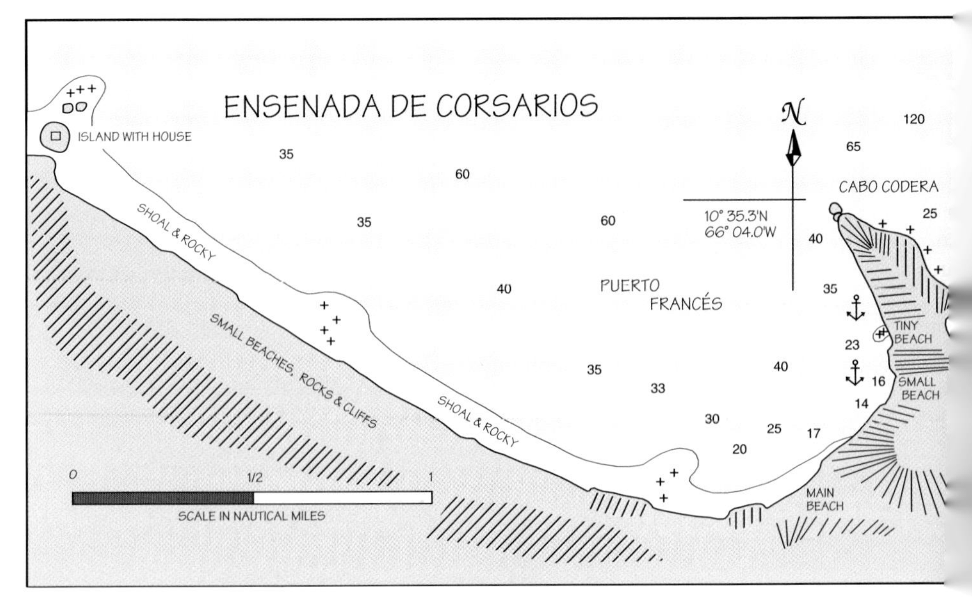

where between the small beach and the headland. You can carry 16 feet fairly close to the beach. There are a few rocks close to shore, especially near the tiny beach, but these are closer to shore than most sane people would anchor. You can find good anchorage 100 yards off the cliffs, between the beach and the headland, in about 25-35 feet of water. Fishermen have huts on the beach and keep boats anchored here. On weekends this anchorage is full of power boats from Carenero. There is a light structure on the hill behind the small beach, but it has not worked for years.

The water here can be refreshingly chilly. The snorkeling is mixed with some good parts and some barren rock and pebbles. The beaches are fine for a visit. The only one with road access is the main beach and there are no restaurants or facilities. The shore between the small beach and Cabo Codera is very attractive with little cliffs and caves and plants artfully arranged by mother nature. At the end of Cabo Codera large rocks make a seabird roosting area. Most are boobies, but you also see frigates, pelicans and terns.

PUERTO FRANCÉS TO CARENERO

As you round Cabo Codera and head south, the first buildings that you see will be those of Higuerote which has several high rises. Southwest of Cabo Codera are some tanks partly hidden in mangroves. Tankers lie off here and there are some moorings. It is best to go outside them all. Carenero looks smaller than Higuerote though it has a couple of high rise buildings and you can see stacked boats from a fair way off. If you head for the white high rise toward the right hand side of the building group on a bearing of 310°, magnetic this will bring you to the edge of Bajo La Crucesita (Small Cross Shoal). Sometimes this bank is marked by a buoy. In good light you can usually see it. When you get near Pta. La Crucesita, go southwest a bit to avoid this bank, then, before you get to Astillero de Higuerote, head back over to the west side of the channel to avoid the four-foot shoal which is harder to see. The area includes two separate harbors, Carenero and Bahía La Buche.

CARENERO

Carenero (The Carenage) is a large well protected harbor with many anchorages and mangrove channels. There is an impressive three-mile dinghy passage all the way through to the town of Higuerote. Bird watching in this passage is always good, but is spectacular at dusk and dawn. You can anchor anywhere you like, but the most convenient anchorage is north of the Club Bahía de los Piratas.

Services

There are three fuel docks where you can also get ice. The deepest is the Carenero Yacht Club. There is about eight feet up to the dock. Unfortunately there is an obstruction very close to the end of the dock. If the wind is blowing strongly from the east, it may be easiest to anchor and come stern to the dock on its east side toward the outer end. It is open Monday 0800 to 1330, other weekdays 0800-1530, weekends 0800-1730.

If you draw less than six feet you can make it into the dock at Club Bahía de Los Piratas. You have to enter almost touching

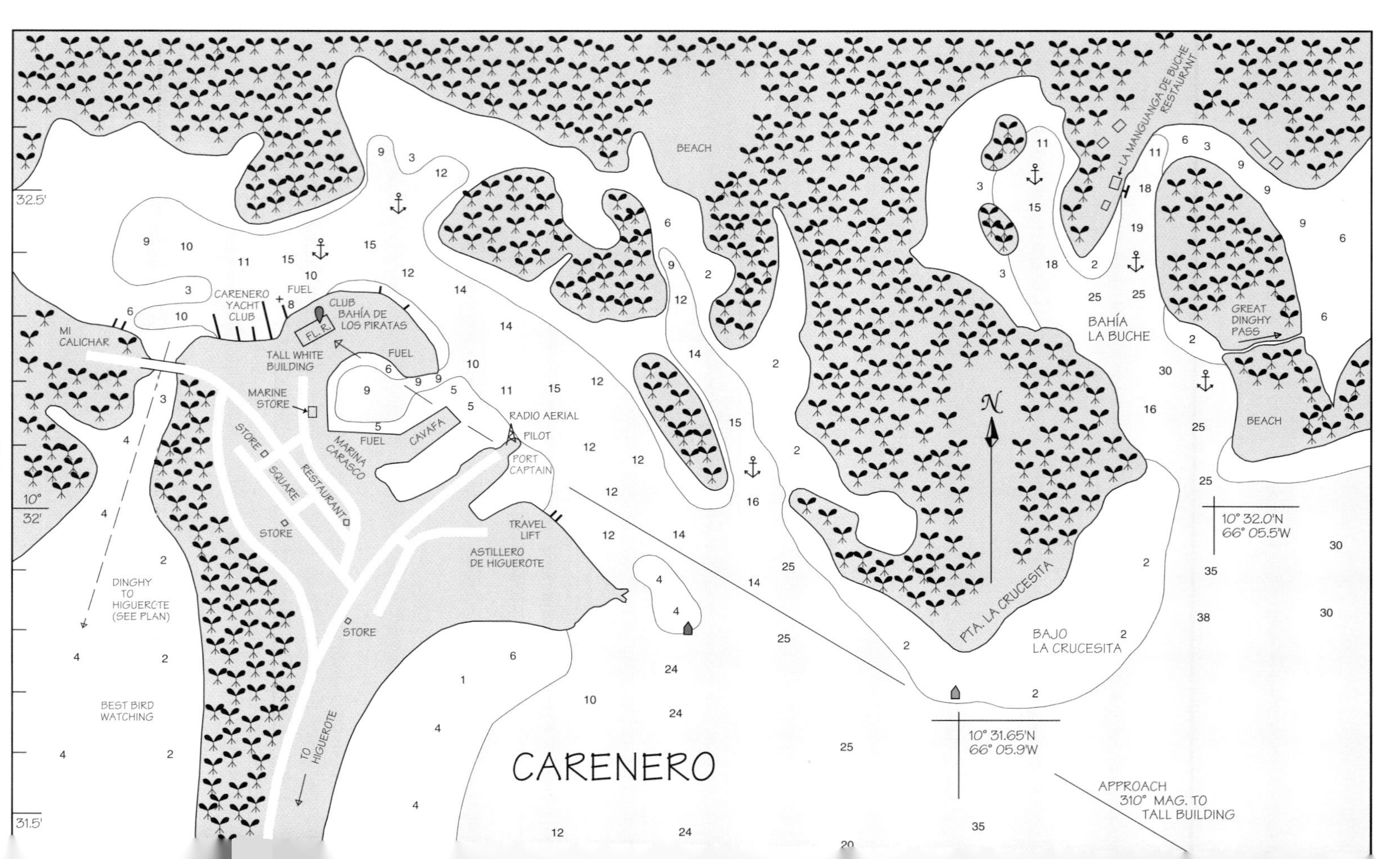
CARENERO
BAHÍA LA BUCHE
GREAT DINGHY PASS
BEACH
10° 32.0'N 66° 05.5'W
LA MANGUANGA DE BUCHE RESTAURANT
BAJO LA CRUCESITA
PTA. LA CRUCESITA
10° 31.65'N 66° 05.9'W
APPROACH 310° MAG. TO TALL BUILDING
RADIO AERIAL
PILOT
PORT CAPTAIN
TRAVEL LIFT
ASTILLERO DE HIGUEROTE
CAVAFA
FUEL
MARINA CARASCO
CLUB BAHÍA DE LOS PIRATAS
FL.R.
TALL WHITE BUILDING
CARENERO YACHT CLUB
MARINE STORE
RESTAURANT
SQUARE
STORE
TO HIGUEROTE
DINGHY TO HIGUEROTE (SEE PLAN)
BEST BIRD WATCHING
MI CALICHAR
32.5'
10° 32'
31.5'

the stones on the north side of the channel. There is about nine feet into the basin, but the fuel dock only has about six feet.

There are two slipping facilities. Mi Calichar (T:02-81 40 81/81 35 65), VHF:16 is a small yard on the west side of the bridge. Their hoist takes 25 tons, and they are happy to fix your boat or let you do the work yourself. They specialize in antifouling jobs and repairing fiberglass. The limiting factor s depth and they can haul a maximum of 6.5 feet at high water. The deepest approach is close by the Carenero Yacht Club.

Astillero de Higuerote (T:02-92 06 38, F:02-64 11 06) is a much bigger ard with a 60-ton travel lift. The head ffice is in Caracas. It is about eight eet deep in the approach dock. The lock is reported to be 22 feet wide but t looks narrower. They are not really sed to working on sailing yachts, so I vould leave this one for an emergency.

Ashore

There is no public access ashore as ll the waterfront is private. However, e guards will let you go ashore at avafa and probably also Club Bahía e Los Piratas if you look smart. Failg that, you can tie to the dock ruins side the pilot boat station. This is so where the port captain works, but u probably will not need to see him cause Carenero is not a port of entry d you have to clear in somewhere se. If you have the correct clearance, u do not need to check with anyone.

In town you will find a square, three nall shops, and a very local laid back staurant.

Club Bahía de Los Piratas (VHF:70, -D, cc:A,V,D) has a good restaurant ith strong air-conditioning for the at of the day. You can tie your diny right outside.

Ashore at Higuerote

For more extensive shopping you ve to visit Higuerote. Buses run fre-

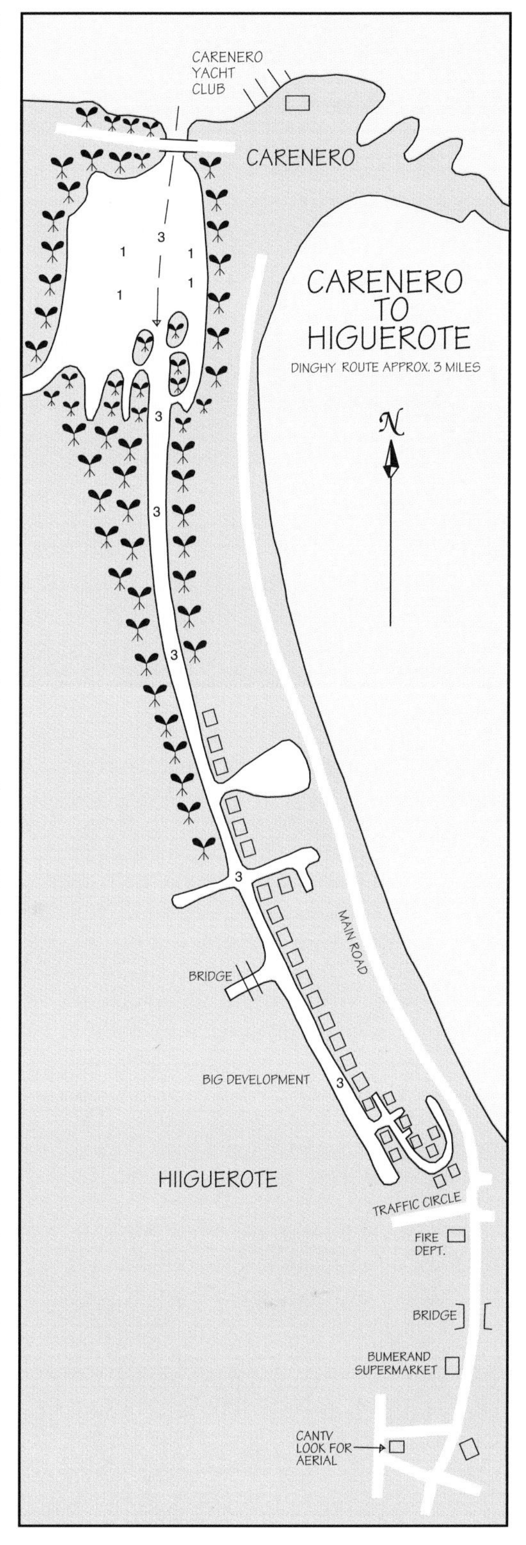

Carenero

quently from near the town square but the dinghy trip is more fun. Access to the canal is under the bridge. The current under the bridge can go either way and is usually strong. You cross the first bay and go straight down the canal. After a while you will start to see lovely homes along the water's edge. To get access to the town take the last turn on the left, just before the end of the canal. Hang a right and follow round into a circular area. Here you will find one or two paths that lead to the road from the water between the houses. The mangrove tree we used to lock our dinghy to may still be there. If you see anyone, you can ask permission.

Any path will bring you to the big main road and a traffic circle. (See our plan.) It is about a quarter of a mile down the road to the beginning of the main drag. Here you will find good bakers, butchers, greengrocers and Bumerand Supermarket which opens daily 0800-1900, except Sunday when it closes at noon. If you need to make a phone call, there is a CANTV which is open daily 0800-1930. They d not have a USA direct phone.

While in Carenero, don't miss th evening bird show under the bridge in th first lagoon. For the evening performanc go about an hour before sunset and anch toward the east side about half way dow (If you go too close to the mangroves, th birds will avoid your spot.) Take cushion bug spray, binoculars, cocktails an snacks and wait for all the birds to come i All manner of herons, cormorants, pel cans and parrots are the supporting cast f the scarlet ibis, prima donna of the ma grove. If you are a parrot fan, the ear morning show may be better. Hundreds parrots wake up and squawk to each oth before they take off for the day's foragin When a big flock clears out of a tree it almost like a parrot explosion.

BAHÍA LA BUCHE

The entrance to this harbor is about half a mile to the east of the entrance to Carenero. If you are coming from Carenero you have to pass outside the Bajo la Crucesita.

There are shoals both sides of the entrance to Bahía La Buche, but in between the water is 25 feet deep. The breeziest and most pleasant anchorage is right off the beach as you enter. In really bad weather you might want to go deeper into the mangroves up either channel.

Ashore

This is a lovely and safe bay in which to anchor and relax. There is great dinghy exploration through all the mangrove channels. The narrow dinghy pass just north of the beach is overhung with mangrove trees. Follow it down until it comes out in a bay almost a mile wide on the other side. The inland lagoons heat up during the day and make good warm bathing in the afternoon. Fishing is good, as is the evening bird show with many herons, parrots, doves, various land birds, cormorants, frigates, pelicans and a few scarlet ibis flying over. While not as spectacular as in the Carenero dinghy passage, here you can sit and enjoy it from the comfort of your yacht.

On the north central part of the bay there is a landing ramp, some campers, smart holiday houses, a small first aid station and La Manguangua de Buche Restaurant ($D, cc:V,D). This pleasant and friendly place is open every day from 0900 to dinner. They serve excellent calamares rebozados and paella. There are also several huts on the beach that serve food on the weekends or whenever there are enough people.

CARENERO TO ISLAS DE PÍRITU

It is a 70-mile haul from Carenero to Islas de Píritu and it is usually pleasant. The winds in the morning are often south through to west. By mid afternoon they are often northeast and blow at their hardest. After dark they tend to drop.

If your boat is good in light airs you can make it under sail. Otherwise, if you motor-sail well, you can probably do the 70-mile haul as a long day trip.

Islas de Píritu are very low lying and you cannot see them until you are about five miles away. Isla La Borracha will usually appear long before.

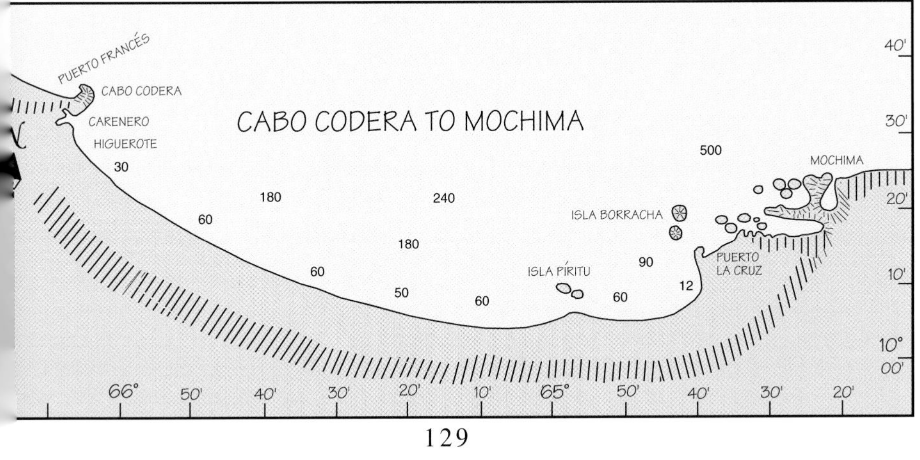

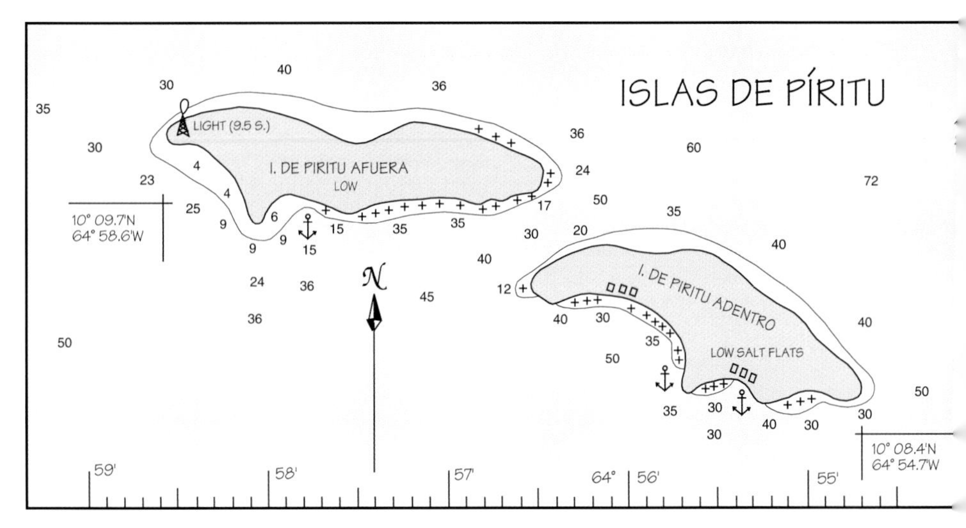

These islands make a perfect overnight stop on your route eastwards, and are also good for a day away from it all on the beach. They are very low and scrubby with beaches that look delightful in bright sunlight. The islands are surrounded by reefs which make for acceptable snorkeling.

The easiest anchorage is in Isla de Píritu Afuera in the area shown on our sketch chart. Approach from the south toward the eastern end of the bay where the water is deepest. You will find a good anchoring area in 15 feet of water.

Anchoring in Isla de Píritu Adentro is more of a problem. The water is usually too deep or too shallow for anchoring. There is an anchoring area in the southwestern bay in 30-40 feet of water, but getting the anchor to hold can be a problem.

A scenic alternative is to anchor bow or stern to the sand spit at the eastern end of this bay taking an anchor ashore. It is possible to do the same at the eastern end of the next bay.

PUERTO LA CRU

Puerto La Cruz is the center of yachting in Venezuela. There are over six marinas in operation or nearing completion. You can find good haul out facilities, excellent chandleries, a sailmaker and several people who are happy to help you get things done. Nearly everyone in the marine industry speaks English. The coast and offshore islands from Puerto La Cruz to Mochima constitute the Mochima National Park and offer outstanding cruising, starting just a couple of miles outside the city.

Puerto La Cruz is an excellent place to leave your yacht and make a trip inland. It is well located, there are plenty of places to leave your boat and there are excellent travel agents, an airplane pilot and taxi drivers.

Police checks are rare, but keep at least photocopy of your green entry paper and your inside passport page with you just in case. When traveling out of the city, take your passport.

Communications (except mail) are good. There are several places to send and receive faxes and you can get a USA direct line on most phones by dialing 800-111-20/1. And Canada direct 800-111-00.

There is a yachting net which provides an informal exchange of information on VHF:77 at 0745. VHF:77 is the general calling channel for businesses, except marinas (look for marina details). The net

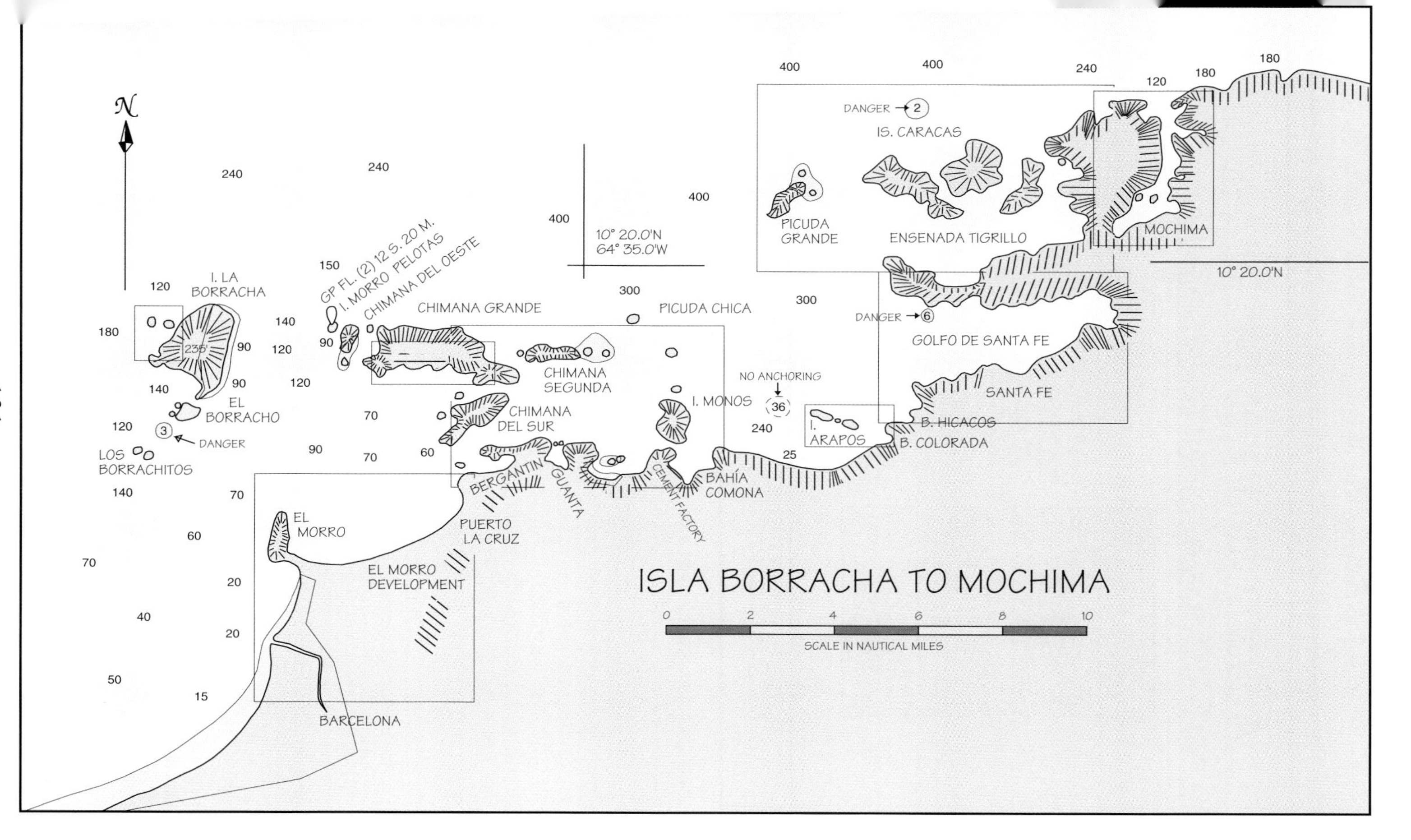

ISLA BORRACHA TO MOCHIMA
0
2
4
6
8
10
SCALE IN NAUTICAL MILES
N
DANGER → 2
IS. CARACAS
PICUDA GRANDE
ENSENADA TIGRILLO
MOCHIMA
10° 20.0'N
10° 20.0'N
64° 35.0'W
I. LA BORRACHA
235'
GP FL. (2) 12 S. 20 M.
I. MORRO PELOTAS
CHIMANA DEL OESTE
CHIMANA GRANDE
PICUDA CHICA
DANGER → 6
GOLFO DE SANTA FE
CHIMANA SEGUNDA
NO ANCHORING
36
I. MONOS
SANTA FE
CHIMANA DEL SUR
EL BORRACHO
I. ARAPOS
B. HICACOS
B. COLORADA
3
DANGER
LOS BORRACHITOS
BERGANTIN
GUANTA
CEMENT FACTORY
BAHÍA COMONA
EL MORRO
PUERTO LA CRUZ
EL MORRO DEVELOPMENT
BARCELONA

usually announced on VHF:77 just before it starts.

Navigation

You can approach Puerto La Cruz from any of the passages between islands. Avoid sailing between Borracho and Los Borrachitos and avoid the eastern end of Isla Chimana Segunda. The other passages are very straightforward.

The anchoring area is just west of Marina Puerto La Cruz (Marina Paseo Colón) off the Fuente de Mar restaurant. There is currently no convenient dinghy dock and you have to haul yours up the beach, an independent dinghy watching service has been in place for a nominal fee, observe where the other dinghies are tied. You can load and unload at the small docks used by the lanceros. At night it is recommended that you hoist your dinghy on board.

Regulations

When you come into Puerto La Cruz you are going to have to clear in. The authorities here are pretty straightforward but the process, while costing very little, is tim consuming. In the past you could do yourself but new regulations allow onl registered agents to do the clearing in an out of vessels. Marisol Nuñez of Wind located in town, clears lots of boats, speal perfect English and is fast and efficie Carmen at Dockside will check you in you come in to Bahia Redonda. Likewi at CMO they have an agent. You can al contact Dolphin Services who can cle you in or out.

Servic

Servinauti also known as Marina Pas Colón or Marina Puerto la Cruz (T:081- 24 67/65 25 63, F:081-68 63 16, VHF:7 SSB 2738) is right in the center of tow The security here is very good. They do r have many slips for cruisers and do r take advance bookings, but as they wc on a first-come-first-served basis, you c usually get in if you wait a few da Facilities include showers and toile There is water and electricity (110/1 volt 60 cycle) on the dock. Their fuel dc

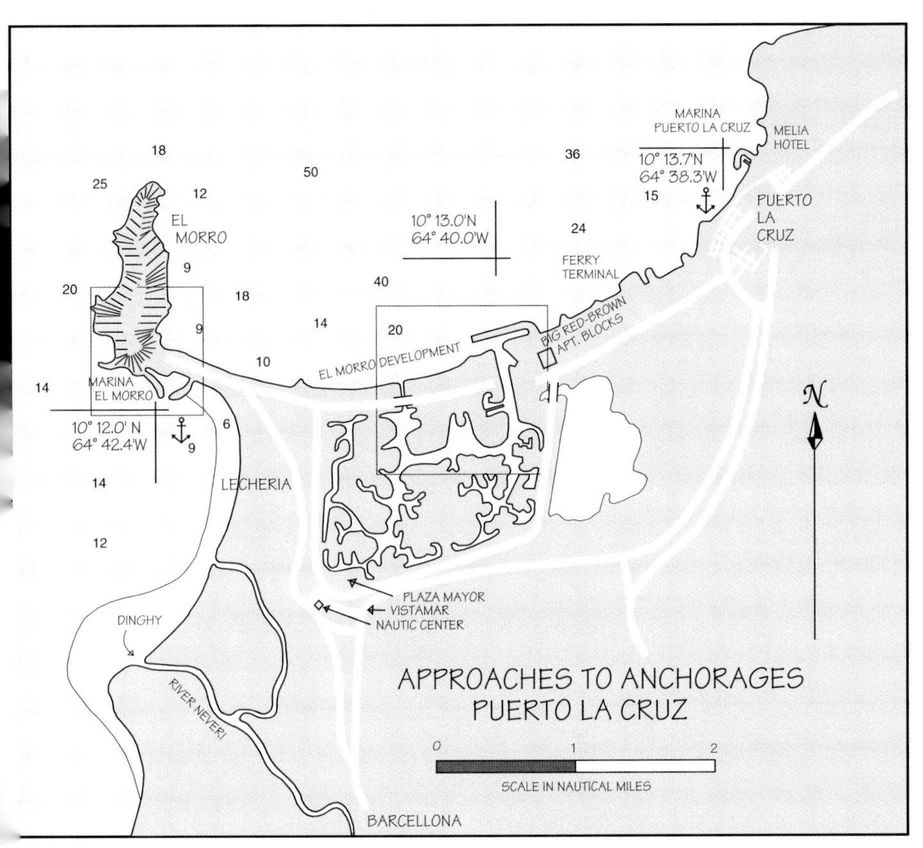

s open daily 0800-1200 and 1400-1700. Before you come in with your boat, dinghy over and make sure there is enough depth for your boat. The high speed ferry to Margarita has created such a wake that the channel as well as the inside has silted up, reducing the depth to about 6 feet, and it is unlikely that it would be dredged to it's former depth. Also bear in mind that due to an antiquated law, marinas and shoreside facilities pay ten times the cost that others pay for water, so check with them before you take water. The dockmaster, David Burroughs, speaks excellent English. Ice, beer and soft drinks are available during working hours. Marina Puerto la Cruz only takes local currency.

The other marinas are to the west of town, most are part of the huge new El Morro development. The entrance to El Morro is easy for boats with up to 10 foot draft. Those of 11 or 12 foot should check out first or go in gently on high tide. Once inside the wall the deeper draft boats will have to turn east immediately, into the new Bahía Redonda Marina. The reason for this is a rock in the main channel. The shallow part of the rock is not always marked. Stay in the eastern side of the channel where the maximum depth is nine feet at low tide. Yachts with a draft of 10 feet can squeeze through by working the tides. Once over the rock there is 12 feet through much of the complex. A smaller rock lies in the channel beyond CMO between the red and green markers. Hug the green (see our sketch chart).

The fuel dock is on the inside of the main wall just before the Bahía Redonda Marina.

Bahía Redonda Marina (T:081 67 74 12, F:081 67 78 10, VHF: 71, SSB 8291.1) is the newest and largest docking facility to date. It has a capacity for 120 boats up to 90 ft. long with all the amenities to make you feel relaxed and secure. Several shower and toilet facilities are scattered around so one is always close to your boat. There are a couple of swimming pools, a restaurant, laundry, phones, a small store, and a gym. Cable T.V. and telephone hook-ups are planned as well as a 40 ton travelift for dry storing your boat. By the time this book is in circulation there should be a grocery store with easy dinghy access. Also planned are hotel rooms so you can house your guests or get off the boat yourself for a few days. On Monday evenings they fire up the B.B.Q. pit and invite yachties from all over Puerto La Cruz to come cook their dinner and intermingle. This is a perfect place to leave your boat in the care of Manuel, the dockmaster, and head into the interior of Venezuela for a few days.

Dockside (T: 081-67 76 92, T/F: 081-67 76 92, VHF:77) run by Carmen is the yacht and travel agent in Bahía Redonda Marina. She will clear you in or out as well as providing travel arrangements and tours. She is a fountain of services, from procurement of provisions to medical help, car rentals, pet services or arranging ready meals delivered directly to your boat. Carmen arranges mini-tours that take you into the city for a day of shopping or a night of entertainment. Or instead of moving your boat, get a group together and take a speedboat out to the nearby islands for a day in the sun without the responsibility.

In the same building towards the back is the La Cruz Nautic Shop (T:081-63 17 36, F:081-63 04 19, VHF:71 e-mail: omcca@telcel.net.ve) Operated by Helios and Terry who speaks English. For your dinghy needs they are both Caribe dealers and agents for OMC Evinrude outboards offering sales, spares and service. If your hypalon dinghy is getting old but you don't want to part with it, they can send it to the Caribe factory for expert repairs. La Cruz Nautic also represent Magellan GPS's and Shakespeare VHF's, if they don't have what you need, they can catalogue order it in a few days. They have a book, magazine

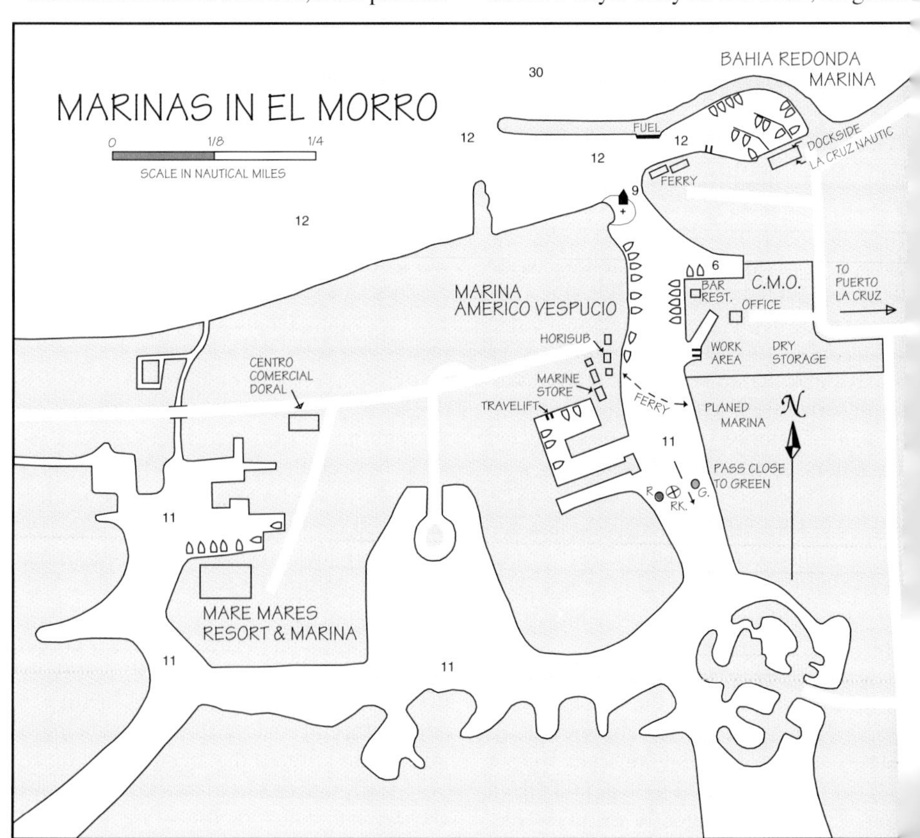

nd video exchange for marina guests as ell as a fast letter system from the U.S.

Centro Marino de Oriente (T:081-69 22 4/67 70 11, F:081-67 85 50/69 20 21, HF:80/71, SSB:6215) is more often nown as CMO. This is an impressive arina: it has about 62 berths, dry storage r 155, and every kind of workshop. They ven build boats here, in modern wood/ poxy laminates, traditional planking and berglass. Jimmy Capriles, the manager, president of ASONAUTICA the asso-ation of marine services. Their offices e in CMO and they are interested in your npressions and suggestions.

Docking is mainly stern to, with a few ongside berths. If you draw six feet or ore, berth along the main canal wall as e cut to the east is shallow. There is water ongside and electricity (110 and 220 lt, 60 cycles). Ashore you will find good curity, showers, toilets, laundry, and a ack bar where you can watch cable TV in Spanish or English. In the office they sell charts and guides and rent videos. If you call on the telephone the operator speaks English. Every Sunday they hold a barbe-cue supplying the fire, ice and some com-plimentary rum, you bring your own food. Once a month is yachties "treasures of the bilge bazaar day" and there is also piñata bashing for those with birthdays.

CMO has a 70-ton travel lift which can take up to 22-foot beam and a special trailer for hauling multihulls of almost any size. Boats left in dry storage are fenced off with closed circuit TV, and guard dogs are let loose. Each time an owner comes down the dogs are fed, so the owners can get the boat out. A separate storage area is set aside for do-it-yourselfers and sandblast-ing is done under cover to contain the flying sand. For refitting boats they have a machine shop and paint, mechanical, electrical, refrigeration and upholstery workshops.

Right next to the dock is Communications Center (T\F:081-63 05 51, 63 06 66, VHF:71) Here you can send and receive faxes, mail, packages via courier, buy the Daily Journal, have film developed, make copies, and even rent a cellular phone and a car. They can also tell you where to get what at the best price.

Those with a yen for a touch of luxury will opt for Marina Maremares (T:081-81 30 22/81 10 11, F:081-81 30 28/81 44 94, VHF:71, SSB 2738, cc:A,V,D). Marina Maremares is part of a large hotel complex with restaurants and an exotic pool. There is room for 47 boats stern-to and four alongside. Electricity (220/120 volt 60 cycle), phone and cable TV, are all supplied to the boat. If you do not have a TV, you can rent one.

When you check in it is like checking into the hotel, and you are treated just like a guest. You sign your credit card slip and the register and after that you can order anything and just have it put on your bill. Room service is available to the yacht, as is a cleaning service. They will watch your boat if you want to go on a trip or wa your kids if you want a night on the tov Tennis and golf are right there too. T emphasis is on service. This starts wh you call them on the radio before you co in. They will send out a boat to guide y in and to help you get correctly hooked the mooring for stern-to berthing. Ma ager Victoria Vasquez speaks English a is assisted by Luis the dockmaster. F those of you that enjoy deep sea fishi they hold two annual fishing tourname in October and November.

Marina Americo Vespucio (T:081-81 78/81 67 55, F:081-81 48 29, Cel:016 38 00 VHF:71) is opposite CMO. T marina is almost in two parts. The insi part is for Venezuelans and stern-to outside wall is for visiting yachts. T outside is the more pleasant place to li as is more breezy. There is water, electr ity (220/110 volts, 60 cycles) toilets a showers. Arturo Barrios, who ru Horisub dive shop on the wall, looks af the arrangements for visiting yach Horisub is a PADI dive shop that will f hydrotest and maintain scuba bottles as well instruct and do excursions. They will receive faxes and mail. Arturo speaks excellent English and will help in any way he can.

Marina Americo Vespucio also has a 50-ton travel lift. They do excellent repair and paint jobs of all types, but they do not have room for long term storage. Victor, the yard manager, supervises everything and can also be contracted to do surveys. He speaks English and you can sometimes get him on VHF:77 "Varamar."

There is also a complete chandlery at Marina Americo Vespucio which is convenient to those in that area. It is called Rich (T:081-81 16 30, F:81 15 64, VHF:71, cc:V). They have a complete tock of yachting accessories and fishing gear.

From any of the marinas in the El Morro omplex you can get to Plaza Mayor by dinghy. This newly opened super-mall is worth a visit just to see it, and you might ust spend the day there and never have to ake a taxi again. A restaurant called the Albatros faces the dinghy dock, and beond, every and any kind of store, shop or ffice exists. Ampitheatres, Banks, booktores, boutiques, bakeries, clothing hops, travel agents, family centers, opometrists, perfume shops - you name it, ey've got it and it is all beautifully laid ut and landscaped.

Just outside this complex are a couple of marine stores. Nautic Center (T:081-86 19 1, F:081-86 38 29, VHF:71, cc:V, Av. rincipal de Lecherias, C.C. Classic Center), are the agents for Mariner outboards as well as carrying AB and Caribe dinghies. In stock are Uniden VHF's, GPS and other electronics, a good stock of fishing and diving equipment as well as fastenings and some sports clothing.

The Marine Collection (T:081-86 50 34, 86 42 69, VHF:71, cc:V,M) is close to the Vistamar shopping center. They are the Mercury dealers. Not only do they have a good selection of parts, they will come out to your boat for repairs to your outboard. They carry Caribe dinghies, Delco batteries, S.S. fastenings, fishing and diving gear and will catalogue order items that you may need with a 3-day delivery.

Marina Club Nautico El Morro (T:081 81 88 80, 81 71 17, Cel. 016 21 26, VHF:23,) is sometimes known as Marina El Morro. It is not in the El Morro complex, but over on the south side of the El Morro headland. It is quiet, pleasant, open to the breeze and well protected with good security. The only drawback is that it is rather a long way from town, and while you can make it in a por puesto, you will have to change at the Vistamar shopping center. You can get most of your shopping needs at Vistamar which is not far away. It is an excellent place for anyone renting a car, for those who want to leave their boats while going off into the interior, and for those working on their boats.

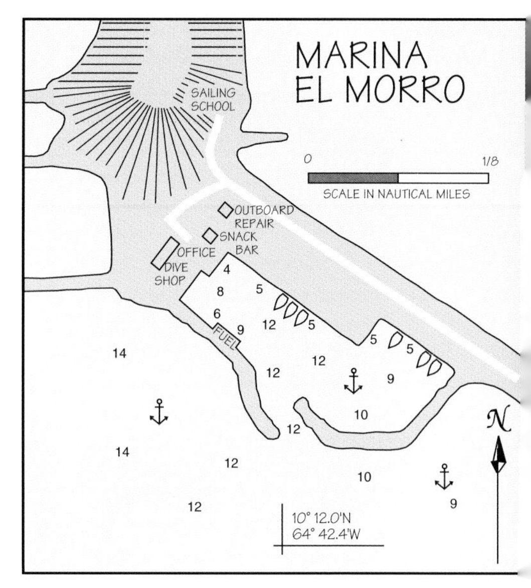

There is about 12 feet into the marina. Along the edges of the wall where boats come bow- or stern-to, it shelves to five or six feet, depending on the spot you choose. Floating docks into the main marina area are planned. Meanwhile there is anchoring room for anyone too deep to come to the dock. They have a fuel dock with about nine feet at the deeper end, shelving rapidly toward the marina offices to about six feet. The office offers full communications (they can get you a USA direct line), showers, toilets, water, electricity at 110-220 volts, 60 cycles.

Fransisco Pando, better known as Paco, the proprietor, is the best paint spray man in Puerto La Cruz. The slipping facility is inadequate for hauling yachts here, so Paco usually works on them over at CMO or at Americo Vespucio. Analy in the office speaks English, as does Paco.

In the same complex is a restaurant, outboard repair facilities, a dive shop and reputedly the biggest disco in the state.

North of this marina is the Americo Vespucio sailing school founded 14 years ago by Umberto Constanzo. He has been teaching youngsters not only how to sail race and maintain their boats, but how tc do it exceptionally well. In 1996 one of hi pupils, 22 year old Eduardo Cordero re took the title of World Sunfish Champio that he had won 3 years before in 1993 And 17 year old Hector Vidal in 199 brought home both the World Junior Sun fish as well as the North American Junio Sunfish title. This enthusiastic group i also the heart of the annual yachting even called the SCOR (South Caribbean Ocea Regatta) a three week event in June tha races in Margarita then moves on to Puert La Cruz for more racing. This event is nc only for serious racers but special classe accommodate live-aboards and one c the big benefits is free dockage for a participants during the whole event. S think about intermingling with your Venezuelan hosts and learn to make that tub go a little faster while you wait out the hurricane season.

There is another marina, Yacht Club Marina de Guanta (T:081-68 28 34, VHF: 71) which is over in Guanta, the big commercial port a couple of miles east of Puerto La Cruz. A few boats are in the marina, though it is only partly finished. This is a little out of town for easy access. But they do have a fuel dock, a small mini-market and a restaurant.

Changing money is no problem at the Casa De Cambio at the Hotel Riviera on Paseo Colón. (T:081-67 31 11, 67 56 59, 67 47 34) or at the Asecambio in the Hotel Gaeta, also on paseo Colón (T:081-67 33 02/68 78 51) and Oficambio at the Hotel Rasil (081-67 56 71/67 98 87, F:081-67 44 98) These last two give a better exchange rate. To get money from a Visa card you will have to go to Banco Union.

Winds C.A. - Calle Honduras #11, between Maneiro and Freites (T:081-67 16 07, F:081-69 68 98, Cel:016-81 96 57, VHF:77) is run by Marisol Nuñez and her husband who have a yacht clearing service for national and international clearance, a travel agency and a mail drop. She will also receive (but not send) faxes. Marisol is Venezuelan, very helpful and she speaks perfect English. She is a good person to go to for general advice. Her main business is as a travel agent and she has been selling tours to yachtspeople for many years and understands their needs. She organizes tours to Angel falls, La Gran Sabana, Merida, Orinoco delta, Guacharo caves and more. Also, if you want to do it on your own, she can get you tickets and make suggestions.

If you are thinking of flying anywhere in this area, you should know about Steve Patterson. He is an ex-USA airline pilot, and engineer, certified as a pilot both in the USA and Venezuela. Steve is reliable and his rates are unbeatable. He has his own plane and several others are at his disposal, both single and twin engine, and he can take any size group. Steve is an excellent person to talk to about a trip to the interior, including Angel Falls and Canaima. He often takes people to other islands such as Los Roques or to Grenada or Trinidad, and he can be invaluable in a medical emergency. You can call him at (T:081-65 33 71, Cel. 014-80 01 15). He has an answering machine (wait for the English message after the Spanish).

Chaser Tours (T:016-80 20 79, F:081-68 45 82/74 49 03, VHF: 77) is operated by Jim and Linda Chase who came here to retire and after traveling through Venezuela extensively for two years they wanted to help others share the same great experiences. They have a couple of vans that can take groups as big as twenty or as small as four. You can go on one of their planned tours or rent one of them and their van and head off on your own personalized adventure. Tours can be for just a few hours, like the one to Los Altos de Santa Fe. Half an hour away but a world apart, this is a village of traditional artisans that have been producing arts and crafts for generations. Or you can go for days. Try the Guri

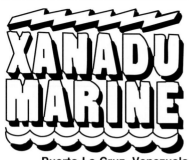

Dam for several days of fishing for Venezuela's national fish, Pavon - peacock bass that get up to 20 lbs. give a great fight and make a great meal served up that night. The dam itself is a wonder of human engineering, having taken 20 years to build and supplying electricity to just about all of Venezuela's neighboring countries.

Xanadu Marine (T:081-65 38 44, F:081-65 24 48, VHF:77, SSB 6215 0800 to 0900) is an excellent chandlery. It is run by John and Patti from the USA who cruised the Caribbean for 20 years in their Tayana 37 called Xanadu. They found themselves coming back to the beauty and culture of Venezuela year after year. John started an electronics repair business out of his boat. When the cabin was crammed full of circuit boards and testing gear they decided it was time for a move ashore and they opened a chandlery. It contains a wide range of gear from boat alarms to the popular AB and Caribe dinghies. John understands all his products from a GPS to antifouling. He will help you choose the right gear and if it is electronic his technicians will come and install it. He will save you much pain by making sure you have the product you need. In addition, if you have any problems, he will help you sort them out. This is the first place to come for paints and antifoulings as Venezuelan paints are excellent, but the names can be confusing and John knows what works best for this area. They carry a good selection of charts, guides and books. And if it's the weather you want, this is the place to come for an updated picture since he gets them direct from a couple of satellites via his own earth station. He also receives weather updates from The National Weather Service in Miami and the Barbados met office. Children's Service League cards are sold here for a very small price but a big cause.

Patti designed the most used map of Puerto La Cruz (you can get them free all over the place), and she runs a weekly ladies lunch, where boat parts, engine problems and water-makers are never discussed. Girlfriends, wives, and female

Puerto La Cruz with the anchorage and Marina Puerto La Cruz in the foreground. El Morro headland is in the background.

;kippers meet at Xanadu Marine at noon ɔn Tuesdays and they visit a different 'estaurant each week. If you want a custom nade bathing suit or wedding wear she :an steer you in the right direction.

Caribbean Sport (T:081-66 84 30/66 72 ›4, F:081-67 24 86, VHF:77, cc:A,V) is .nother complete and excellent chandlery. t is on Av. Municipal, not too far from ⁄Iarina Paseo Colón. They have a good upply of marine hardware, ss fastenings nd accessories. They also carry Mercury ›utboards, VHF's, Rule pumps, inflatable inghies, resin, fiberglass and ropes.

Mauricio Costanzo runs a first rate sail ɔft right in the center of town. It is called ;ostan Sails (T&F: 081-81-68 82 66, 'HF:77). Mauricio speaks perfect En- lish and Italian. He can build good sails ɔr yachts up to about 56 feet and if you refer you can order North sails through im from the USA, as well as Shore Sails. ı addition to making and repairing sails, Iauricio does awnings, biminis and ɔdgers complete with frames which he ıstom makes. He is also an agent for Norseman and Stalok. You can get a new mast and rig or just a new stay or roller furling (Harken, Profurl and Furlex). His rigging stock is not all that large, so with some jobs you may have to wait a week or two for parts to arrive. If you call him on VHF:77 he will come to your boat to collect your torn sail or to measure up for that new one.

Venezuela is a good place to recover cabin cushions or make new awnings, for upholstery work check Tapimar (T:081-68 88 24) Calle Freites # 108, El Pensil, Puerto La Cruz. Luis Marcano and his wife can make and repair awnings, biminis and dodgers, though they don't do the metal frames they have Sumbrella and other materials in stock. For covering cushions they have access to a large selection of materials including local or imported leathers. They will pick up and deliver.

For quality metal work see Serviboat (T:081-68 62 84, 65 64 05, Cel. 014-80 33 31, Fax:081-65 64 05, VHF:77) Calle los Cocos #48, Puerto La Cruz, Near the Rasil

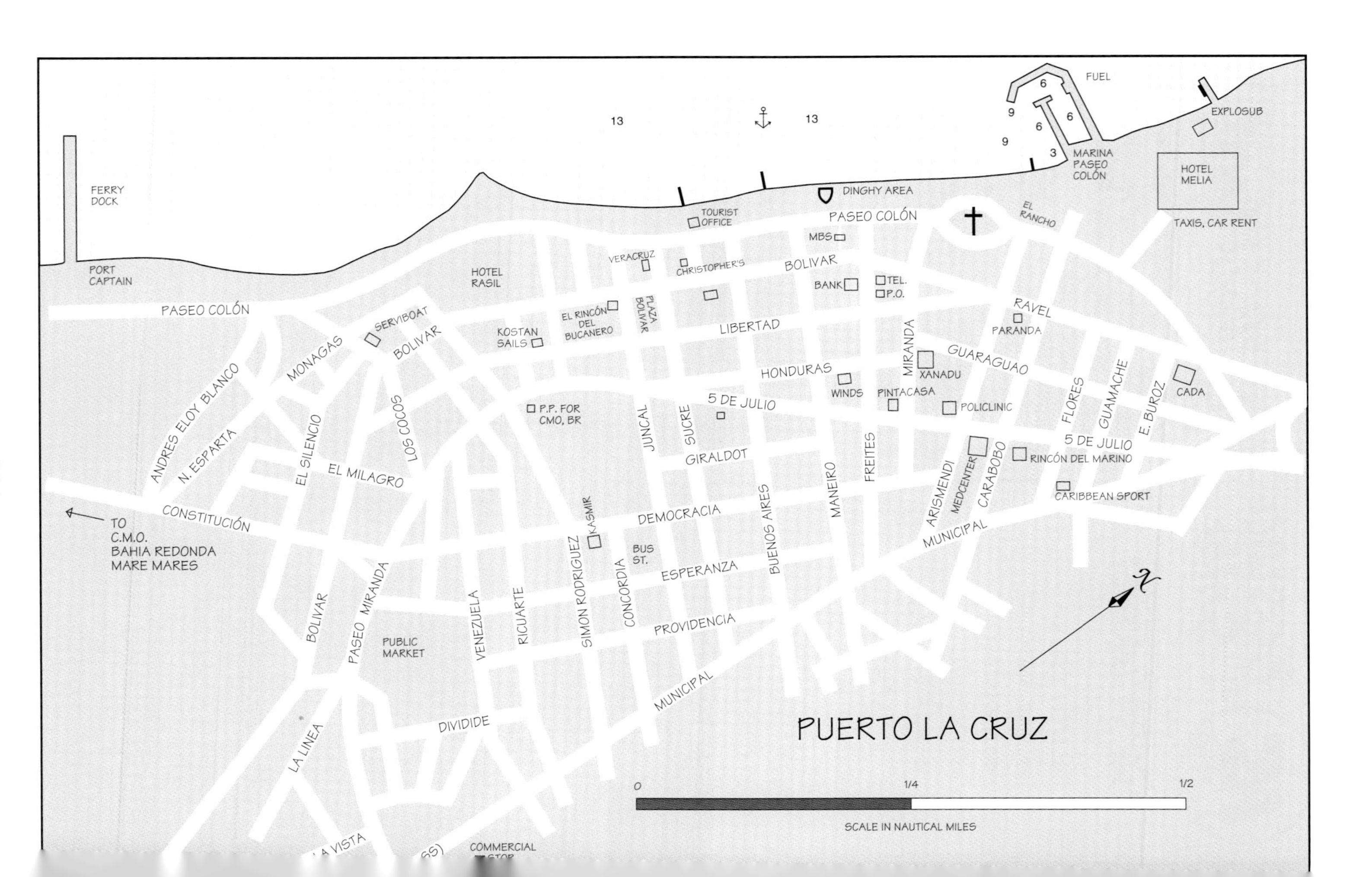
PUERTO LA CRUZ
FERRY DOCK
PORT CAPTAIN
13
13
FUEL
6
6
6
9
9
3
EXPLOSUB
MARINA PASEO COLÓN
HOTEL MELIA
TAXIS, CAR RENT
DINGHY AREA
TOURIST OFFICE
PASEO COLÓN
EL RANCHO
MBS
VERACRUZ
CHRISTOPHER'S
BOLIVAR
HOTEL RASIL
BANK
TEL.
P.O.
PASEO COLÓN
EL RINCÓN DEL BUCANERO
PLAZA BOLIVAR
LIBERTAD
RAVEL
PARANDA
SERVIBOAT
KOSTAN SAILS
BOLIVAR
MONAGAS
MIRANDA
GUARAGUAO
XANADU
HONDURAS
CADA
ANDRES ELOY BLANCO
P.P. FOR CMO, BR
5 DE JULIO
WINDS
PINTACASA
POLICLINIC
FLORES
GUAMACHE
E. BUROZ
N. ESPARTA
EL SILENCIO
LOS COCOS
JUNCAL
SUCRE
GIRALDOT
FREITES
5 DE JULIO
RINCÓN DEL MARINO
EL MILAGRO
MANEIRO
ARISMENDI
MEDCENTER
CARABOBO
CARIBBEAN SPORT
CONSTITUCIÓN
DEMOCRACIA
BUENOS AIRES
KASMIR
MUNICIPAL
TO C.M.O. BAHIA REDONDA MARE MARES
SIMON RODRIGUEZ
BUS ST.
ESPERANZA
CONCORDIA
BOLIVAR
PASEO MIRANDA
PUBLIC MARKET
VENEZUELA
RICUARTE
PROVIDENCIA
MUNICIPAL
DIVIDIDE
LA LINEA
0
1/4
1/2
SCALE IN NAUTICAL MILES

Hotel. Jose Luis de Veer, the owner, speaks English. His machine shop can do all types of work with SS 316, aluminium, steel and bronze. He often does tubing for dodgers, biminis, stanchions etc. He can build davits, solar panel frames and repair water pumps, or turn new parts for bearings, shafts, motors or fabricate a new cleat or fairlead to match the rest on your boat. He can work on your boat or move the work to his shop.

MBS - Manuel Boat Service (T:081-65 00 12, F:081-68 82 43, Cel. 014-80 18 18, VHF:77, Compuserve:102213,1634, e-mail: mdeb@telcel.net.ve) is run by Manuel and his wife, Yvonne. Both speak English and Italian and, in addition, Manuel speaks French. They are charming, helpful and straightforward. They bring in equipment or parts from anywhere in the world and get it delivered "hassle free" from various catalogues. They help with communications and send, receive faxes and e-mail service. They also are the agents for Village Marine desalinators, Siemens solar panels, Airmarine wind generators, as well as Newmar, Simpson Lawrence, Adler Barbour and Kenyon Galley. They also book people on tours and help with taxi and travel arrangements. Manuel and Yvonne are the publishers of a monthly paper called Mar y Tierra written in English with the visiting yachtperson in mind. Pick up a free copy to keep you informed of regional events and local information.

Jose is a cheerful and friendly soul who has a van and runs errands for yachts (VHF:77 "Jose"). He is half Trinidadian and half Venezuelan and speaks both languages. He will collect your laundry, bring you cases of beer and soda and run general errands.

Leslie has been helping yachtsmen for a long time. He used to live in Canada and speaks English as well as German, French and Hungarian. Leslie has a big bus taxi (up to ll people) and takes people both around town and on sightseeing tours to the waterfalls, Caracas, Cumaná or any-

where in taxi range. Call Leslie's Limo (VHF:77) to make arrangements.

Armando Cordova (081-86 36 69, VHF:77 "Armando") speaks English and Italian, worked on boats and has an engineering background so he understands the boater's needs. He will act as a taxi, run errands and help with communications, is honest, reliable and organized and he keeps an appointment book so you can book him in advance without fear of being disappointed.

Pintacasa (T/F:081-68 70 45/68 79 95 cc:A,V,D) is the International, Sherwin Williams and Sika paint store in town, with a good range of paints and accessories. You can get many types of antifouling and hull paint here.

Distribuidora Colorama (T:081-66 48 04) is the Imron paint shop. Imron is an excellent buy in Venezuela and a good choice for redoing your hull. Here the paints are usually used for cars. It is on Calle La Fe # 6, off our town map, but you can take a cab there.

Right outside Marina Paseo Colón is the local Yamaha sales and service agent (T:081-66 43 85, F:081-65 76 08) where they will happily fix your old outboard or sell you a new Yamaha.

Thomas Winfield (Cel:016-81 24 12) offers a refrigeration repair service, as well as diesel and general boat mechanics.

Commercial Stop (T/F:081-66 82 08) is a good photocopy shop near the big Cada. They carry a large stock of charts and are willing to sell photocopies of these. The charts they have are US Defence Mapping Agency charts which are currently in the public domain so you can legally copy them. If you want Imray Iolaire charts you can buy them at CMO (copying them is illegal).

The CANTV is open daily 0800-1930 and accepts major credit cards for calls and is a good place for sending faxes. You can get a ATT USA direct operator on most pay phones by dialing 800-111-20/1. For MCI Direct 800 124 30, SPRINT 800-111 10, For Bell Canada direct 800 111 00.

Most por puestos travel along Av. 5 de Julio. We have marked the most important por puesto stops. Buses to all destinations, including Caracas and Cumaná, leave from the bus station. You can also take a por puesto from there, they are signs indicating the destinations, under each sign is a car that leaves when 5 people sign up, you tell them where you want to get off when you get there and they will usually drop you there as long as it is not outside of the destination city.

For your laundry cleaning take it to Altagracia (T:081-65 22 01) drop it off in the morning after 0700 and pick up before 1830. They pride themselves in using good quality detergents and being careful with not mixing colors with whites, and at a good price.

The Tourist Information Service indicated on the map is open everyday from 0800 to 2100.

You can rent a car from Budget at the Melia Hotel (081-65 31 55, 65 36 11). Alternatively, Amigo Car Rental (081-6? 27 59) are one block inland, open every

ıremares marina and surrounding area

day, and are less expensive (about US$ 50.00 , 250 free kilometers per day)

To charter a yacht, go to Orizzontiblu (T/F:081-67 77 50, VHF:77, SSB 6215.0) They are at CMO and have sailboats from 40' to 52' that you can charter bareboat or with a skipper and/or cook.

If you chain needs re-galvanizing or your propane tanks refilled, call King's Service. (081-67 83 54, Cel:016 80 25 98, VHF:77)

For mechanical help with diesels, generators and hydraulic systems talk to AC Marine Mechanics (014-81 11 58, VHF:77), they fix all these systems.

Ashore

The main shopping area is the town of Puerto la Cruz. The local market is the cheapest and best place to get fresh produce. You can also get meat and fish. It is open seven days a week from 0700 and the earlier you get there the better. It is all over by noon.

Enrique Cordenons Automercado Veracruz (T:081-65 24 98, T/F:081-68 78 80, VHF:77) offers a good stock of the usual supermarket items, including wine, beer and liquor, as well as European cheeses, deli goods, imported caviar and grade-A meat cuts. They will deliver to your boat and both English and Italian are spoken.

For more good meats check out Comercial Las Flores (T:081-65 13 63, 65 78 94, cc:V) They have a wide selection of meat cuts packaged to order. Orlando the butcher has a beef chart that is easy to understand and point to for selecting cuts. They also stock vegetables and other foodstuffs.

There are two Cada supermarkets good for a big provisioning, but the one that is furthest away on Municipal is the biggest.

Vistamar Shopping Center, is almost indispensable if you are in Marina El Morro or Americo Vespucio. You can get there by por puesto from either marina. This shopping center and the area surrounding it contain almost everything you might want: Dandy's Supermarket, a laundrette, a bakery, an hardware store, a pharmacy, restaurants, a pizzeria and a coffee shop.

In Puerto La Cruz the main street is Paseo Colón, an attractive broad street with a large walkway by the water. It becomes lively in the evenings when people wander up and down and street sellers, artisans and entertainers set up along the walkway, westwards from the big roundabout.

There is a news stand in the middle of Paseo Colón which stocks the Daily Journal, an English language Venezuelan newspaper with much international news, and a wide selection of magazines in both Spanish and English

If you have prints to process, then Fotolisto is one of the quickest and best places. For slides, there is a Kodak lab at the Rasil Hotel that can develop all brands provided they are the E-6 process.

If there is an American movie you want to see, check out the cinema, they are in the original language with subtitles in Spanish, only the animated cartoon type movies are dubbed in Spanish.

Eating out is no problem. There are countless restaurants, many of them along Paseo Colón. The wide variety includes Chinese, Japanese, a lot of Italian, and Arabian, (try their main dish served wrapped in a tortilla like patty rolled up with a variety of meats with vegetables). Christopher's Bar (T:081-65 39 95, $D, closed Sunday) is the most popular yachty and expat. hangout. It is run by Chris and Karen Johnston from Canada. They open at 1630 and keep going to whenever. It is a friendly place where you can meet both English and Spanish speaking people, play darts, listen to rock music and relax. Little snacks keep getting put down near your drink so you may not feel too hungry, but if you do they have a good selection of food. They have live music Friday and Saturday nights.

The first place you should try for a good meal out is El Parador del Puerto (T:081-65 03 91, $C-D, cc:A,V,D). They have been consistently good for many years, with excellent food and smart, attentive service.

El Rincón Del Bucanero (Pirate's Corner) (T:081-67 07 65, $C-D, cc:A,V,D) is a good traditional Spanish style restaurant with snappy service and good food at reasonable prices.

When you want a change from the usual menus, try El Faraón (The Pharo) (T:081-66 23 68, $C-D, cc:A,V,D). It is a great place when you want a change of diet. They serve good Arabian food in an exotic and gaudy atmosphere.

Hotel Melia has an expensive restaurant on the outside, but there is a good and less expensive restaurant inside and if you walk into the hotel and go upstairs, there is a fancy looking bar and next door a coffee shop/restaurant ($D, cc:A,V,D) where you can get a good meal at a reasonable price. They tend to close a bit on the early side, so don't expect to get a meal at 2100

Restaurant El Rancho del Tío (T:081-65 36 77, $C-D, cc:A,V,D) is particularly convenient if you are in the Marina Paseo Colón. It is said to be built out of a typical old farm house, though quite what they were farming, sandwiched between the sea and Paseo Colón, I am not sure. The interior is airy and pleasant and the food is good.

Riccardo's (T:081-65 06 29, $D, cc:A) small but with very attentive service, specializes in pizza but also has a varied menu including a giant salad. Owned and operated by Ricardo, a Brazilian and his Canadian wife Carol.

For those on a smaller budget who want a more typical meal try Rincon Del Marino on 5 De Julio, the owner Enrique speaks English and will help you make a choice.

After dinner you can head to one of the popular local bars. We have already mentioned Christopher's Bar. After that you may want to try Cafe Rose or if you are a gambler casinos can be found all around, and if you are in the mood for dancing, try Parranda.

If you happen to be in or near Marina El Morro, there is a super dinghy trip you can take a long way up the River Neveri. Enter where we indicate on the sketch chart and explore. You can go all the way to Barcelona on the river and be treated to views of wildlife, including alligators, egrets, cormorants, herons and parakeets. Arboleda, a restaurant on the river, makes a good destination. It is not signposted, but it has a thatched roof and a big tree and is on the left side as you go up. When you visit Barcelona check out the old church and museum. For more information consult Patti at Xanadu.

Trips in ultralight aircraft are available on the west side of El Morro. Other points of interest around Puerto La Cruz include the remaining big lagoon on the east side of the new El Morro development. This is not a particularly beautiful lagoon, but the bird life here around sunset can be spectacular. La Sirena waterfalls are set in a park about 40 minutes east of Puerto La Cruz. The park closes at 1600. The bus ride to Cumaná is delightfully scenic.

Barcelona is worth a visit for it's historic value, one of the oldest towns in the area, founded in 1671, is the capital of the state of Anzoategui. Plaza Boyoca has on one side the Cathedral where the glass encased remains of Saint Celestino and other venerated objects are to be found. The Museo de Anzoategui is housed in the restored and oldest building remaining in the town, which also borders the square. A couple of blocks away is the Ataneo de Barcelona with a collection of Venezuelan paintings from the early 1900's. For more arts and crafts check out the Galeria de Arte and Gunda Arte Popular.

Centeno, Roth and Asociados (T/F:081-68 55 74, VHF:86) are major language instructors. They often need native English speaking people for conversation sessions with Venezuelans. Yachtsmen are welcome as conversationalists. If you have a little time and want to get more into the local culture it is a good way to make friends and even get paid for it. You could also take a Spanish course with them.

Water Sports

Diving here is rather special as the rock formations around Puerto La Cruz are exceptionally dramatic. Some more interesting dives include: Cathedral Rock which is located just outside the western headland of the anchorage in La Borracha. It is a cave with an entrance like a cathedral, some 40 feet tall. Inside are three chambers. In one of them there is a hole in the roof. If you time it to be there between noon and 1300, a shaft of sunlight comes through the hole and shines on the bottom of the cave. This gives the illusion that the bottom of the cave is actually the surface. This fools the fish and they all swim upside down. If you shine a flashlight on the wall of the cave, the quartz in the rocks gives brilliant reflections. However, for the best reflections go to the Manhattan Cave in Los Borrachitos. This is a dive for a maximum of three experienced divers. You step out of the boat over a rock wall and drop into a pool. You go straight down a well-like hole about 30 feet until a chamber opens out on one side. Inside the chamber you must attach a chemical light to the wall so you can find your way out again. In the chamber you turn on your light and the reflections from the quartz rocks are both beautiful and dazzling. There are lots of sharp pinnacles which stick up from the bottom and down from the top, so you have to proceed with caution.

Those who have a horror of caves will prefer the Manta Wall Dive around the corner from the Cathedral. This is a vertical wall some 90 feet deep with lots of soft corals and brightly colored Christmas tree and feather duster worms. There are many arrow crabs and small reef fish. At the bottom of the wall is a cavern which is used by thousands of baby fish which hang out in a huge group. You can come up a slope beyond the wall if the current is not too strong. Here you see a profusion of hard and soft corals and angelfish. There is always a chance of seeing a manta ray.

The Twin Tunnels is a dive that starts between two rocks near the southwest corner of El Borracho. You can see the tunnel going into the rock on the left. Swim through it (it is only about eight feet long). As you come to the far end there is a great view of thousands of small fish clustered in the entrance. Follow the reef around to the right at 40 feet deep. There is an abundance of hard and soft corals and colorful reef fish. You finish by passing through another tunnel through the other rock and this brings you back to the boat.

Lolo's Diving Center (T:081-68 30 52, F:081-68 28 85, Cel. 014-80 15 43, VHF:71) is at the Yacht Club Marina de Guanta. It is a good dive shop offering all kinds of dives and courses. They have a retail shop and repair facilities. The owner, Eddy Relevant, speaks English and Italian and is keen to work with yachts. If you call them on the telephone or VHF, they will come by your boat to collect you for a dive.

Explosub (081-65 36 11, 65 05 74 ext. 3347, F: 081-67 32 56) is on the beach in front of the Melia Hotel and has it's own dock. Vinicio Albanese is Venezuela's first instructor whose number is 001 and probably one of the most experienced. He speaks English, Italian and French, fills bottles and will take you on dives to a dozen locations between Puerto La Cruz and Mochima.

Horisub (T:081-81 48 78/81 48 29, F:081-8148 29, VHF:71, cc:A,V) is owned and run by Arturo Barrios, a welcoming Venezuelan who speaks English like an American which he learned while he taught diving at Texas University. It is a full Padi shop and they have two 30-foot dive boats. You can go diving, take resort or certification courses, and they sell dive gear and fill tanks.

Scuba Sport (T:081-81 15 79, cc:V), based in Marina El Morro, is the obvious choice for anyone with a boat in this marina. There is an instructor who speaks good English, and in addition to dives and courses they will help get equipment checked and tested.

Scuba Divers Club (T:081-65 57 03, Cel. 014-80 03 70, VHF:71) is in a mall that is across the street from the Hotel Melia. They are PADI instructors and also offer tours to the neighboring islands for snorkeling and beaching for those that just want to stay above water. Or if you want to go to the other extreme the same office is shared with Hato Nuevo, a five star hotel about an hour from Puerto la Cruz which lies in a natural environment of 1000 acres of vegetation with five lakes, horseback riding, fishing or just lying in a hammock

(See previous sketch chart Isla La Borracha to Mochima.)

The area from Isla La Borracha, just off Puerto La Cruz, to Mochima is a wonderful national park. There are dozens of anchorages in secluded bays, by beaches and among tiny islands. Development is restricted and wildlife is protected. Dolphins, seabirds, small green parrots and hawks are abundant. Fishermen are allowed to use existing camps, but cannot build new ones.

Yachts are allowed to visit and anchor in the park. Spearfishing is not allowed, nor is the collecting of coral or shells, dead or alive. The park is still preparing regulations so other restrictions may come into force. There have been robberies at night in this area. Some form of policing was started. Enquire in Puerto la Cruz about the current situation.

The abundant rainfall in the mountains south of the park reaches as far as the coast. It rarely makes it to the outer islands, and you can see the abrupt transition from rainforest to desert.

Much of the rocky terrain is soft and unstable limestone. Landslides and erosion are reshaping the area little by little. Consequently there may be changes in depths close to land. There are rocks and shoals close to shore and some of them are missing from the charts. The water is generally clear and it is prudent to approach in good light and not to cut corners. Some of our charts are small scale. Rocks within a hundred feet of shore do not show on this scale, and where anchorages are small, we have often put the anchor outside the anchorage so we can include depth data within. The sketch charts should be used with the text.

When walking on cactus covered islands hefty shoes are essential.

ISLA LA BORRACHA

Isla La Borracha (The Drunk Woman) is a dramatic and prominent island just over 1200 feet high. South of Borracha is El Borracho (The Drunk Man) and southwest of him are Los Borrachitos (The Little Drunks). If you are sailing between El Borracho and Los Borrachitos watch out for the elusive three foot shoal that is said to lurk somewhere in the middle. The anchorage at Isla La Borracha is scenic with dramatic cliffs on the eastern side. The anchorage is rather small and you need to get out of the deep water on to the 9-20 foot shelf in front of the village. To the northeast of the village is a clearly visible rock. The anchorage is west of this in the middle of the bay. There are reefs extending out on all sides but the water is usually clear enough to make them visible.

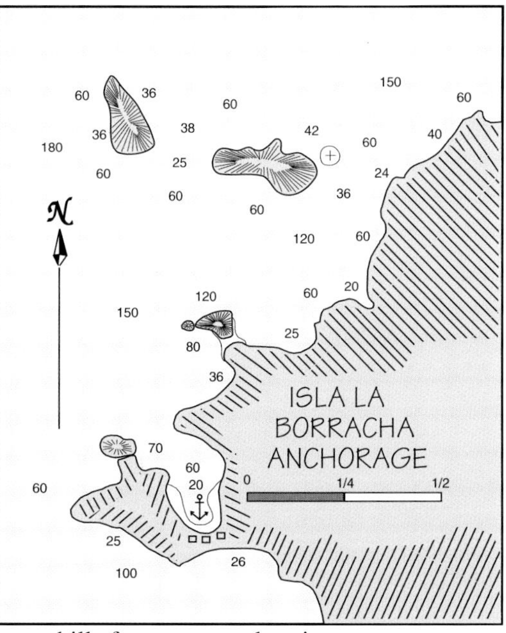

Diving is excellent around the western ntrance to the harbor and snorkeling is worth a go anywhere. Climb the cactusy hills for a spectacular view.

Over the years many people have anchored in Isla La Borracha, most of them without a problem. But about three have been attacked by bats (see "Dangers" at the beginning of this book). The villagers also mention occasional bat attacks. To be on the safe side, use screens.

CHIMANA GRANDE

Chimana Grande is just four miles from Puerto La Cruz but it is a thousand miles away in atmosphere, with peaceful bays, pretty red-brown hills, mangroves, parrots and seabirds.

It is so dry here that bugs are not usually a problem and the water is clear so you can find some fair snorkeling.

The two best anchorages are Ciénaga (Mangrove Lined Bay) and Ciéneguita (Small Mangrove Lined Bay). These are both well protected bays with easy anchoring areas that are breezy enough to keep them cool.

Ciénaga

This large bay has mangroves at both ends and a small beach in the middle. Fishermen camp in the western half. A large coral bank extends from the southern shore of the eastern part (see our sketch plan). Occasional coral heads on this shoal rise within a foot or two of the surface, so it is best avoided. Anchorage is off the northern shore close to the mangroves in 12-18 feet of water.

There is plenty of room is this bay and you should check out the mangrove passage to Ciéneguita (see Ciéneguita).

Ciéneguita

Ciéneguita is a splendid hideaway. You enter down a narrow channel with steep hills on both sides. This gives way at its head to a larger mangrove lined bay with an excellent anchoring area 9-16 feet deep. There is room for just a few boats who are friends. At night, Puerto la Cruz glows between the hills guarding the bay, providing the ideal background for your after-dinner drink.

There is an intriguing mangrove channel between Ciéneguita and Ciénaga. It is a tiny, pull-yourself through affair that will not take a dinghy with a beam much over four feet. It takes faith to find it, because it is so hidden you have to turn the first bend before you are sure you are in it.

Those with a taste for a prickly, dangerous climb on loose rock and soft earth can try to make it to the top of the southwest hill for the view.

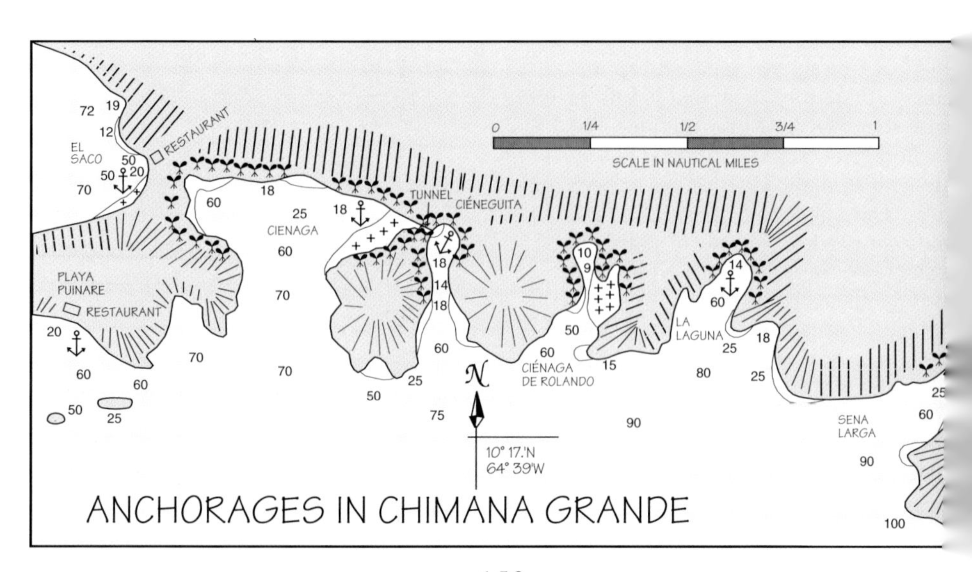

Overlooking Ciéneguita and Ciénega

Anchorage in Chimana Segunda

Playa el Saco

On the western side of Chimana Grande, Playa el Saco is protected from the west by Chimana del Oeste. The beach is divided in two. The northern part has a concession with a restaurant which is open on weekends and busy times. The southern part is in a more natural state. Anchoring is not easy as the water is deep close to shore. With two anchors you can get yourself safely anchored off the southern part of the beach where there is a shelf about 20-30 feet deep. You may need to snorkel to get your anchors laid in such a way they are not damaging the coral heads. This is a popular spot on weekends and holidays.

Playa Puinare

This popular weekend spot is good as a day stop. There is a shelf about 20-30 feet deep to anchor on. You may need to set two anchors. Be careful of the swimming buoys. Ashore is a weekend restaurant where you can get seafood.

Ciénaga de Rolando

Ciénaga de Rolando is a great place to explore by dinghy. There is a secluded anchorage in the western tongue suitable for shallow draft boats. The channel is close to the mangroves on the western shore and is about seven feet deep, but there are so many shallow coral heads that you need to check it out with a dinghy first.

La Laguna

There is an anchorage at the head of La Laguna Bay in about 25 feet of water. The swinging room is limited so you may need two anchors or a line ashore. This bay is sometimes buggy.

Sena Larga

The island's most dramatic cliff and rock formations can be found at Sena Larga. The water is deep close to shore, so it is best to drop one anchor and take another into the shallows or up on the beach.

ISLA CHIMANA SEGUNDA

There is a delightful anchorage on the western end of the south coast of Isla Chimana Segunda called Playa El Faro. The bay is surrounded by soft multicolored cliffs that have been sculpted by the elements into attractive shapes. At the head is a broad beach. Ashore Kike's Chimana Segunda restaurant (T:014-886 1185, 081-814 816, VHF:71, $D) is open daily till 1800, though if not much is happening they sometimes go early. Kike encourages the local iguanas and tree boas to come for food and they are easily seen. He serves good seafood and paella. Kike commutes daily from Puerto La Cruz and he is willing to bring good customers the odd necessity or sell them a little gasoline or diesel. He will also take well wrapped garbage for a small fee.

The park rules say that you are not supposed to stay here more than 24 hours, but if things are quiet you probably can stay an extra day.

The red and white lighthouse up the hill flashes every nine seconds and the walk up will get you a bird's eye view of the bay.

This bay is quiet and peaceful during the week, jolly and busy on weekends and holidays.

Isla Cachicamo, two miles east of Isla Chimana Segunda is under special protection of the park and anchoring is not allowed anywhere around it.

BAHÍA BERGANTÍN TO BAHÍA PERTIGALETE

Heading east along the coast from Puerto La Cruz, the first bay is Bahía Bergantín. This is owned by an oil company and is private. Bahía Guanta is the next bay heading east and it is the main commercial port for the area. A small marina is under construction on the western side and part of it is in operation. However, it is beyond walking distance of Puerto la Cruz, and so is more suitable for those with cars.

One mile east from Bahía Guanta, around Punta Guanta, is Bahía Pertigalete. A large cement factory dominates the eastern side. In the middle are two little islands called Islas de Plata. Because they are close to shore, the ferry ride is cheap, and on weekends they become packed with people, making them lively and colorful. In the old days yachts used to anchor here because there was a marine railway on the southern island. This has been cleared as part of the conversion to a park and now the only reason to come is to check out a popular beach scene.

You can edge toward the gap between the islands from the southwest and anchor in about 30 feet of water. You can also anchor stern to the southern island or off the reef.

There is a passage between the western end of the reef and the shore which is marked by three red buoys, two on the west side and one on the east side.

BAHÍA COMONA

Bahía Comona is a quiet bay with pretty beaches. Some mining has been done on the surrounding hills, but you can anchor out of sight of the scars. There is a neat anchorage behind Isla Comona. A large shoal extends from the middle of the island to the shore and northwards, so you must enter on the south side where the water is 0-40 foot deep. It gets busy at around 0700 when boats land people who are working in the factory.

Playa Cominita is a lovely beach backed by jungle from which one can hear the strident sounds of exotic birds. At odds with this untamed atmosphere are the trash cans and don't litter signs. Playa Cominita is a public beach, but it is often deserted on weekdays and not too crowded

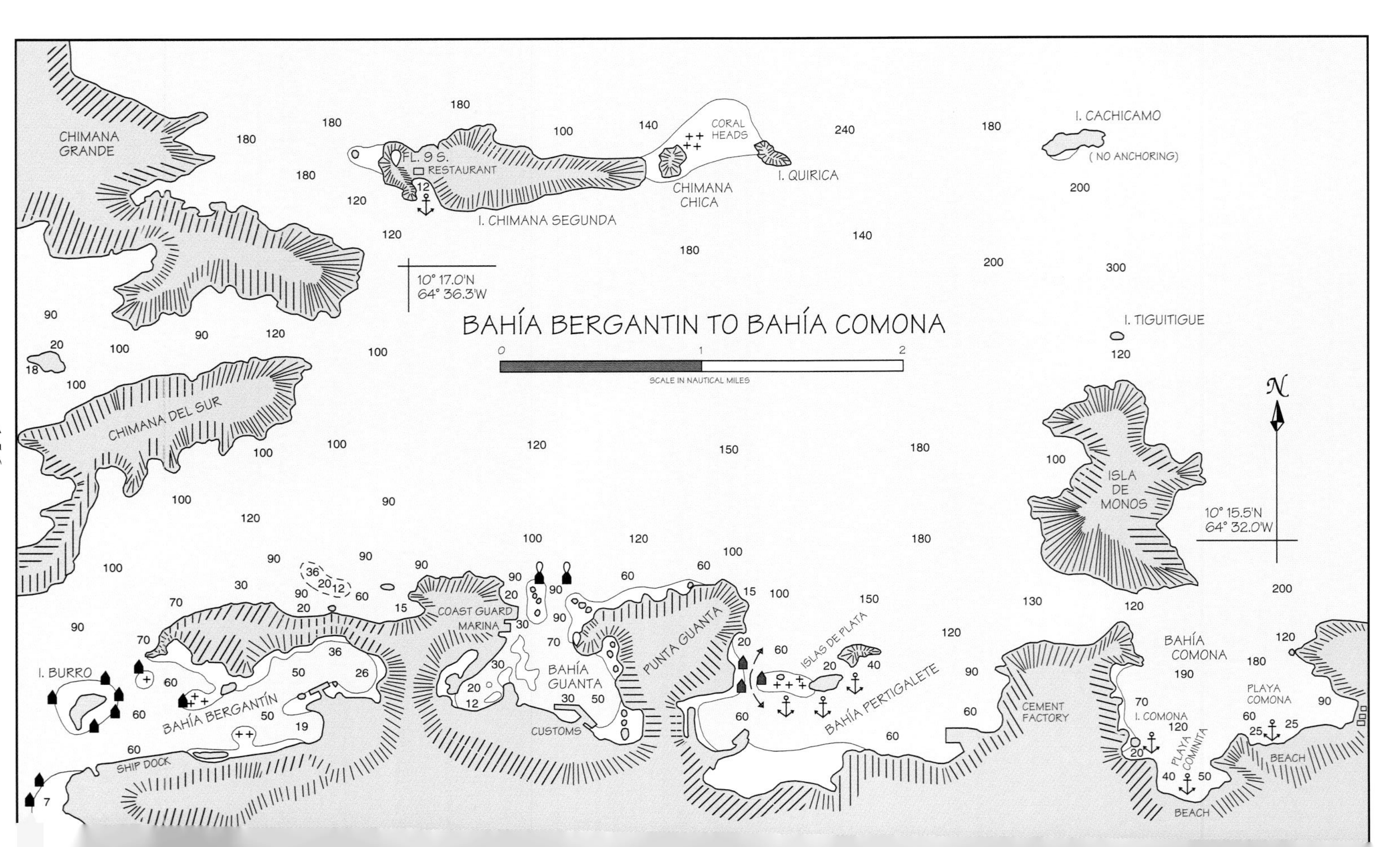
BAHÍA BERGANTIN TO BAHÍA COMONA
SCALE IN NAUTICAL MILES
10° 17.0'N
64° 36.3'W
10° 15.5'N
64° 32.0'W
CHIMANA GRANDE
CHIMANA DEL SUR
I. CHIMANA SEGUNDA
FL. 9 S.
RESTAURANT
CORAL HEADS
CHIMANA CHICA
I. QUIRICA
I. CACHICAMO
(NO ANCHORING)
I. TIGUITIGUE
ISLA DE MONOS
I. BURRO
BAHÍA BERGANTÍN
SHIP DOCK
COAST GUARD
MARINA
BAHÍA GUANTA
CUSTOMS
PUNTA GUANTA
ISLAS DE PLATA
BAHÍA PERTIGALETE
CEMENT FACTORY
BAHÍA COMONA
I. COMONA
PLAYA COMINITA
PLAYA COMONA
BEACH
BEACH

on weekends. The water is deep close to shore so a second anchor in the shallows is required. If you edge right up into the eastern corner and tie stern to the mangroves north of the beach you have an excellent anchorage even in northerly swells when the rest of the bay is untenable.

ISLAS ARAPOS AND PLAYA COLORADA

Anchorage between Islas Arapos

Islas Arapos are two delightful little islands, well populated with holiday houses. At the western end of the western island there are some conspicuous white rocks. This is a bird sanctuary and anchoring is not allowed from the western end of the island to well beyond the rocks.

The easiest anchorage is in the big bay on the south side of the western island. The water is deep so you will need a stern line. You can also use a mooring if one is free. Ashore you will find a good dinghy dock and a restaurant.

The area between the two islands and well beyond to the north and south is dotted with reefs. Approach on the south side where the water is very deep between the southern reefs. Eyeball your way between the reefs to find a delightful anchoring area either side of the small island with a house on it that separates the two larger islands. The water here is from 12-25 feet deep and anchoring room is tight, so if you are staying long you will need two anchors.

These anchorages offer some of the most colorful snorkeling I have seen. There is a superabundance of Christmas tree and

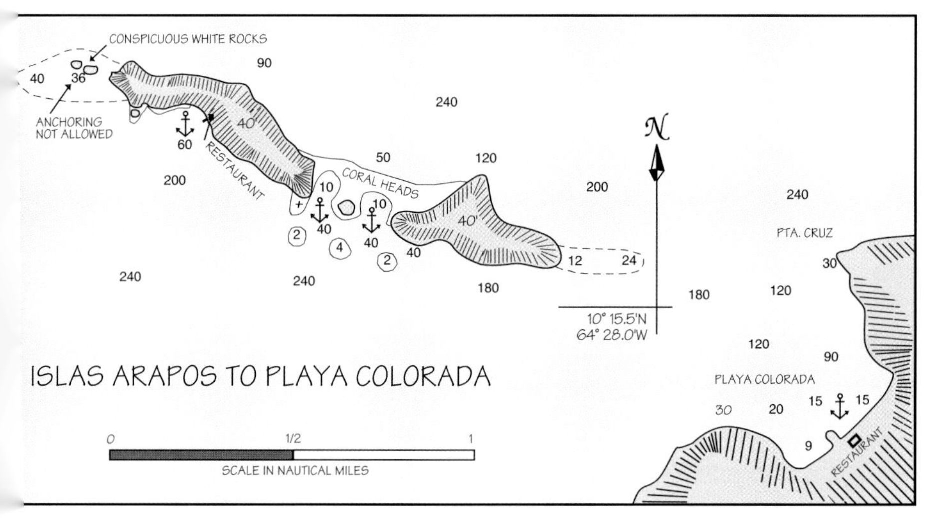

feather duster worms which cover all the coral and glow like precious gems. There are some reef fish, including baby barracudas, pufferfish and moray eels.

Playa Colorada is on the mainland about a mile from Islas Arapos. There is an ample anchoring shelf in 15 feet of water. The beach is attractive and very popular, so the restaurant here is nearly always open. A main road runs right behind the beach.

Islas Arapos from the southwest. The shoals show clearly

GOLFO DE SANTA FE

Golfo de Santa Fe is about five miles long and from one to two miles wide. You often see dolphins swimming here. Many excellent anchorages lie along its shores. A road runs all along the southern shore, so the most secluded anchorages are in the northern part. Most anchorages offer peace, interesting animal and insect sounds, fair snorkeling and small beaches. After heavy rains the water can be murky.

Distances between anchorages are short, so you can poke around until you find one you like. There are so many that you will find one to yourself, even on the busiest weekend. We mention the anchorages that seemed the easiest and most attractive. However, the weather is often calm, the area is sheltered, and adventurous sailors can anchor wherever they choose.

Navigation

There is one hidden danger called Coralie Rock (10° 18.47'N, 64° 26.46'W) about 300 yards south of a conspicuous point (see our sketch chart). This is a very nasty rock with a double point, one about seven feet deep, the other about six feet. It is not marked on current charts. It claimed a significant part of the bottom of the steel S.Y. Coralie in 1989. If you snorkel, you can still see signs of the impact on the rock.

Bahía Valle Seco

In the northeastern corner of Bahía Valle Seco there is a small bay with a beach at the head which has been planted with coconut trees. The water is deep but you can find anchorage close to the beach in about 20 30 feet of water.

Chapín

Chapín has a very clean well maintained beach with a couple of houses in the western corner. Anchoring is very close to the beach in 20-30 feet of water. The area is narrow so you will need two anchors. You might prefer to anchor a little farther out and take a line in to the rocky part of the shore.

La Petaca

The eastern part of this bay is shoal with lots of coral heads and long seaweeds that sometimes rise 20 feet to the surface. This makes for excellent snorkeling. Anchor in the western part of the bay where there is 20-30 feet of water off the beach with no weed. It is narrow so two anchors will be necessary.

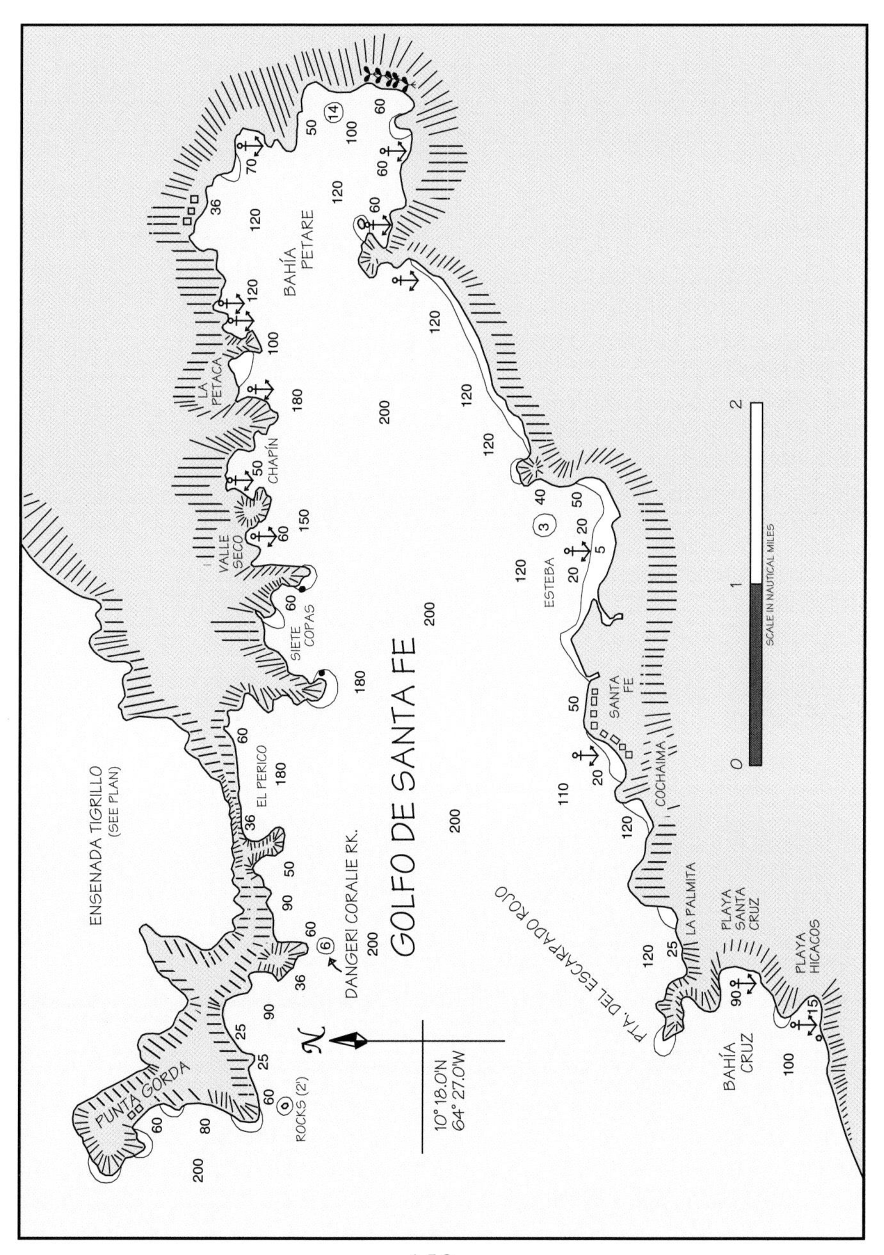

Bahía Petare

This is the large bay at the head of Golfo Santa Fe. It has several excellent anchorages. Right up in the northwest corner are two lovely little coves next door to each other with fair snorkeling between them. The westernmost one has a beach and you can anchor close to shore in 20-30 feet of water. The other does not have a beach but it is still charming with rocks and hills. It has an anchoring area about 30 feet deep and is large enough for one anchor to suffice.

As you proceed eastwards up the bay there are two beaches, one with a sizeable village and the next with several houses. Beyond that, as far east as you can go in the northern part of Bahía Petare, is a gorgeous, long, wild beach, backed by palms and heavy vegetation. The water is very deep close to, so you will need to go bow to the beach or use an anchor in the deep and one in the shallows.

In the southern part of the bay there is a private beach, the water is shallow in the eastern part and deep in the western part, so anchoring with two anchors, one in the shallows would be essential.

In the southwestern corner of the bay there is a delightful anchorage in the little cove south of the small island. There is room to anchor in the head of the bay in about 26 feet of water. It is very jungly and wild. The road and human habitation are just far away enough not to intrude.

The coastline between Bahía Petara and Esteba is alluring with many luxurious private homes and pretty beaches. You can feel your way into an anchorage on the beach at the easternmost part of this coast. The rest of this shore is unsuitable for anchoring as the water is either very deep or shoal with lots of coral heads.

Esteba

Esteba is just round the corner east of the village of Santa Fe. There is a very wide shoal off the southern part of this bay. The shoal comes up slowly, allowing you to find a large anchoring area in 10-25 feet, well offshore. This makes a pleasant contrast from the other anchorages in the area where you are usually nose into the beach. Here you get a feeling of space, with pretty views of beaches, palms and hill lines.

Santa Fe

When the peace gets too much, try anchoring off the little village of Santa Fe. The eastern part is a fishing village and the water is very deep close to shore. The western part is a cheerful area of brightly painted holiday homes and restaurants. You can find a good wide anchoring area in 16 to 20 feet off the western part of the town.

Playa Santa Cruz and Playa Hicacos

Playa Santa Cruz is a popular public beach lined by a fleet of fishing boats. There is a village ashore with a restaurant. It is well protected, but is at least 30-40 feet deep close to shore, so you need a stern line to the beach or a second anchor in the shallows.

Playa Hicacos is a delightful secluded little bay edged with coconut and mango trees. A little spring sometimes provides fresh water out of a pipe that has been rigged up. There is an excellent and ample anchoring area right in front of the beach 15 to 25 feet deep. Do not anchor north of the beach as there is a shoal there. If there is a slight swell running, you may need to hold yourself bow out to sea. In a bad swell you may prefer to be farther up in Golfo Santa Fe.

The beach is part of a private club. There is a restaurant which is sometimes open.

PICUDA GRANDE TO PUNTA TIGRILLO

This area is made up of a series of islands and bays with many delightful away-from-it-all anchorages that you can have to yourself. Observe a couple of park restrictions here; Anchoring is forbidden anywhere around Picuda Grande, though you are welcome to sail by it. There is a coral reef about 25-40 feet deep right in the middle of the channel between Caracas del Sur and I. Venados. Anchoring is forbidden on this reef.

Navigation

Bajo Caracas, just over a mile north of Caracas del Oeste, has several rocks just below the surface. Since this is out in the middle of nowhere it is a serious navigational hazard and should be avoided. It is often used as a dive site by the local dive groups, though the boat watcher usually gets seasick. Apart from this, the water is steep-to close to shore almost everywhere.

Underwater rocks often extend about 150 feet from the shore, so when coast hugging or coming into anchor, keep a good lookout.

The wind is constantly shifting in this area and you will probably point every which way. Danforth style anchors often trip themselves in these conditions, so better set two.

Snorkeling is often excellent, with lots of coral brightly decorated with Christmas tree and feather duster worms. Try snorkeling wherever you anchor and if it is not good, take the dinghy round the next corner and try again.

Bugs are only an occasional problem. If they get to you, move to the next bay. It is just round the corner and probably bug free.

SOUTHERN ENSENADA TIGRILLO

From Punta Gorda to La Costa del Pauviz, the shoreline is a bit exposed to the northeast and it is deep close to shore. About halfway along La Costa del Pauviz there is a fairly deeply indented bay (10° 19.93'N, 64° 23.92'W). It is a peaceful place surrounded by green hills and has a little beach. There is an anchoring shelf off

Looking east over Caracas del Oeste. Carenero in foreground

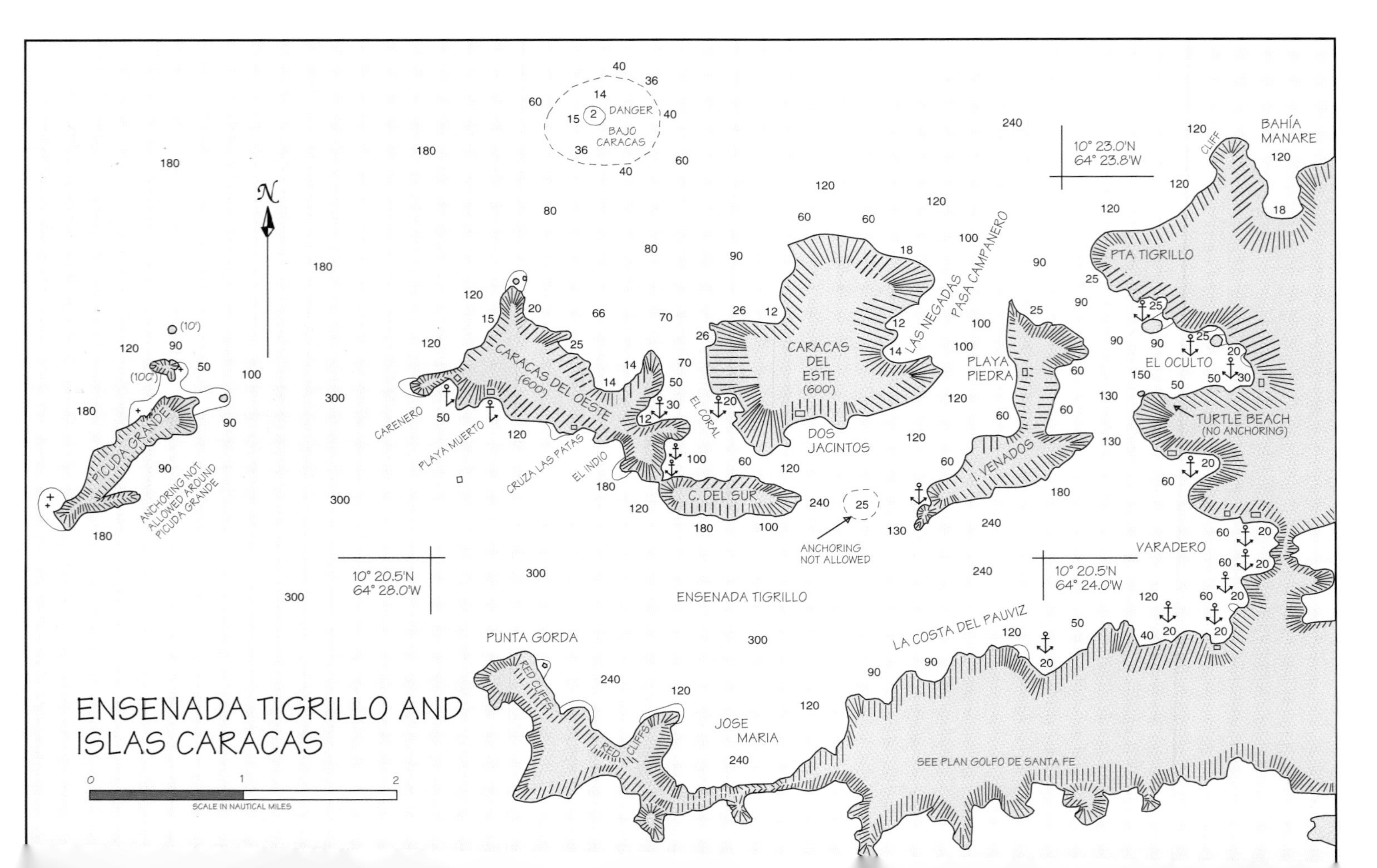

ENSENADA TIGRILLO AND
ISLAS CARACAS
BAHÍA MANARE
CLIFF
PTA TIGRILLO
EL OCULTO
TURTLE BEACH (NO ANCHORING)
VARADERO
10° 23.0'N 64° 23.8'W
10° 20.5'N 64° 24.0'W
10° 20.5'N 64° 28.0'W
PLAYA PIEDRA
I. VENADOS
PASA CAMPANERO
LAS NEGADAS
LA COSTA DEL PAUVIZ
SEE PLAN GOLFO DE SANTA FE
CARACAS DEL ESTE (600')
DOS JACINTOS
ANCHORING NOT ALLOWED
ENSENADA TIGRILLO
EL CORAL
C. DEL SUR
JOSE MARIA
DANGER
BAJO CARACAS
EL INDIO
CRUZA LAS PATAS
CARACAS DEL OESTE (600')
PLAYA MUERTO
CARENERO
RED CLIFFS
PUNTA GORDA
ANCHORING NOT ALLOWED AROUND PICUDA GRANDE
PICUDA GRANDE
SCALE IN NAUTICAL MILES
0
1
2

the beach, 20 to 30 feet deep. It is fairly narrow, so anchoring stern toward the beach with the bow facing out to sea is probably sensible. This bay is exposed if it really blows from the northeast.

If you keep heading east around the next headland, you come to a long bay (10° 20.20'N, 64° 23.13'W). There is an excellent anchorage in the eastern half of this bay with ample room to anchor in 20-25 feet of water. Ashore there are green hills and a tiny beach. The next bay to the east is the southeastern most bay in Ensenada Tigrillo and it is quite delightful (10° 20.23'N, 64° 22.78'W). The area is well covered in vegetation with some good sized trees close to the little beach. On the shore to the west of the beach is an area of colorful rocks. This anchorage is well protected with a large shelf on which to anchor in 20-30 feet without getting too close to shore. North of this bay is a small fishing camp, and a shoal sticks out from the headland. Beyond the shoal is a one boat anchorage amid pretty rocks in 20 feet of water.

Varadero (Boatyard Bay) is a big double bay and Mochima is only a few hundred yards away on the other side of the hill. There are anchoring areas in 20 feet of water in both the northern and southern part of this bay.

NORTHEASTERN ENSENADA TIGRILLO

Between Varadero and El Oculto there is a large deep bay surrounded by hills (10° 21.32'N, 64° 22.85'W). There is a small fishing camp on the north side and few small mangroves along the shore. This is an easy and good anchorage as there is a large shelf at the head of the bay with 20 feet over it. Eyeball your way in to a spot that suits you, or if the water is murky, feel your way in toward the middle of the bay and anchor in 25-30 feet of water.

El Oculto (Hidden Bay) is a delightful, well protected bay. The eastern end of the bay has a wide shelf with 20-30 feet of water over it, though you have to watch for few shoals close in. You can anchor anywhere on this shelf and have plenty of swinging room.

On the north side of El Oculto are two islands. One is sizeable, the other is not much more than a rock about 12 feet high which almost touches the shore. Both have good anchorages.

There is a good 25-foot shelf just off the smaller island. Those willing to use a bow and stern anchor can find room between the island and the shore in front of the beach. The anchorage here is unbeatable for one or two boats. You cannot see the sea at all, just pretty hill lines in every direction giving the impression you are landlocked. The pink beach is perfect for a barbecue and the little red island makes it picture perfect. To top it off, snorkeling is bright and colorful.

The larger island is just one bay to the northwest. Between this island and the shore is a good sized bay with an ample 25-30 foot anchoring shelf off the little beach at the head of the bay. The only problem you may run into here is that the fishermen may want to net and if so, they may ask you to move. You would probably not be in the way in the other anchorage in this bay which is close to the island. From the northwest you approach the gap between the island and the shore, edging in until you get water shoal enough to anchor. This is a pretty spot right close to the island but the space is limited so you will need two anchors.

ISLAS CARACAS

Carenero, in the southeast corner of Caracas del Oeste, is a picturesque bay surrounded by dramatic red hills and rocks on which a few green shrubs manage to eke out an existence. There is a good anchoring area at the head of the bay in 25 feet of water, though the bay is very narrow so two anchors may be necessary. There are two fishing camps in this bay and anchored yachts are in the way when fishermen are netting. Therefore, it is probably best to treat this as a lunchtime stop. If there are no fishermen about, or if you talk to them and they say it is OK to stay, it makes a good overnight anchorage. Fine snorkeling can be found all around. There is also room to anchor in Playa Muerto and Cruza La Patas, but these are also used by fishermen.

The best overnight anchorages are between Caracas del Este and Caracas del Oeste in an area known as El Coral. The most protected of these is on the southwest side of Caracas del Este. Here you have a large bay with two small beaches. There is an adequate anchoring shelf in 20-30 feet of water off either beach. Watch out for rocks close to shore. The snorkeling here and throughout this area is delightfully bright and colorful, though the water can be cold.

West of this anchorage, over on Caracas del Oeste, is a deeply indented bay where anchoring is very easy as there is a large area of water that shelves gently from 30 to 12 feet. It is generally well protected, though it could be exposed to northerly swells or strong northeasterly winds.

Another lovely and well protected anchoring area is off the eastern side of Caracas del Oeste just where Caracas del Oeste is joined to Caracas del Sur. You get protection here from the northeast from Caracas del Este. The water here is very deep so you have to anchor off and find something on shore for a stern line.

There is a tiny anchorage in the southwestern corner of Isla Venados with room for just one boat to anchor, bow facing ou and the stern facing the beach. Since there is a fishing camp here, you should check with the fishermen to see that you are no in their way.

BAHÍA MANARE

Bahía Manare is just west of Mochima. It is a big bay with two deep indentations. There is a delightful anchorage in the eastern corner of this bay. A spectacular reddish cliff dominates the northern shore and you can anchor close enough to admire the rich textures and the little swallows which nest in the caves.

Anchoring is easy in a broad expanse of water from 15-30 feet deep with a sand bottom. This bay would not be tenable in bad northwesterly swells.

Ashore, a fishing camp has been bui and the fishermen have trails up to variou fish watching posts. These make for varie walks.

The sea has undercut the cliff some 6-1 feet and the snorkeling is fair all along thi cliff. It is best to go in the afternoon whe the sun lights up the undercut area beneat the cliff.

MOCHIMA

It is thought that Mochima is a sunken valley, making it long and deep like the fiords. It extends four miles into the surrounding hills. It is a magnificent natural harbor of green hills and red rocks. Sailing in and out is much of the pleasure, watching the ever changing hill contours.

Inside, the southwest part is deeply wooded and during the rainy season there are frequent afternoon thunder showers. The entrance is much drier with red rocks and cactus-covered hills. Apparently several hundred years ago there was anoth exit into Ensenada Tigrillo. This made an ideal hideaway for pirates and rum has it that one or two stashes of treasu have been found. There is abundant bi life, including flocks of small green pa rots.

Mochima itself is a pleasant small tow that thrives on a combination of fishi and tourism. Visitors arrive by coach a car and along the waterfront long op boats line up, ready to take them to

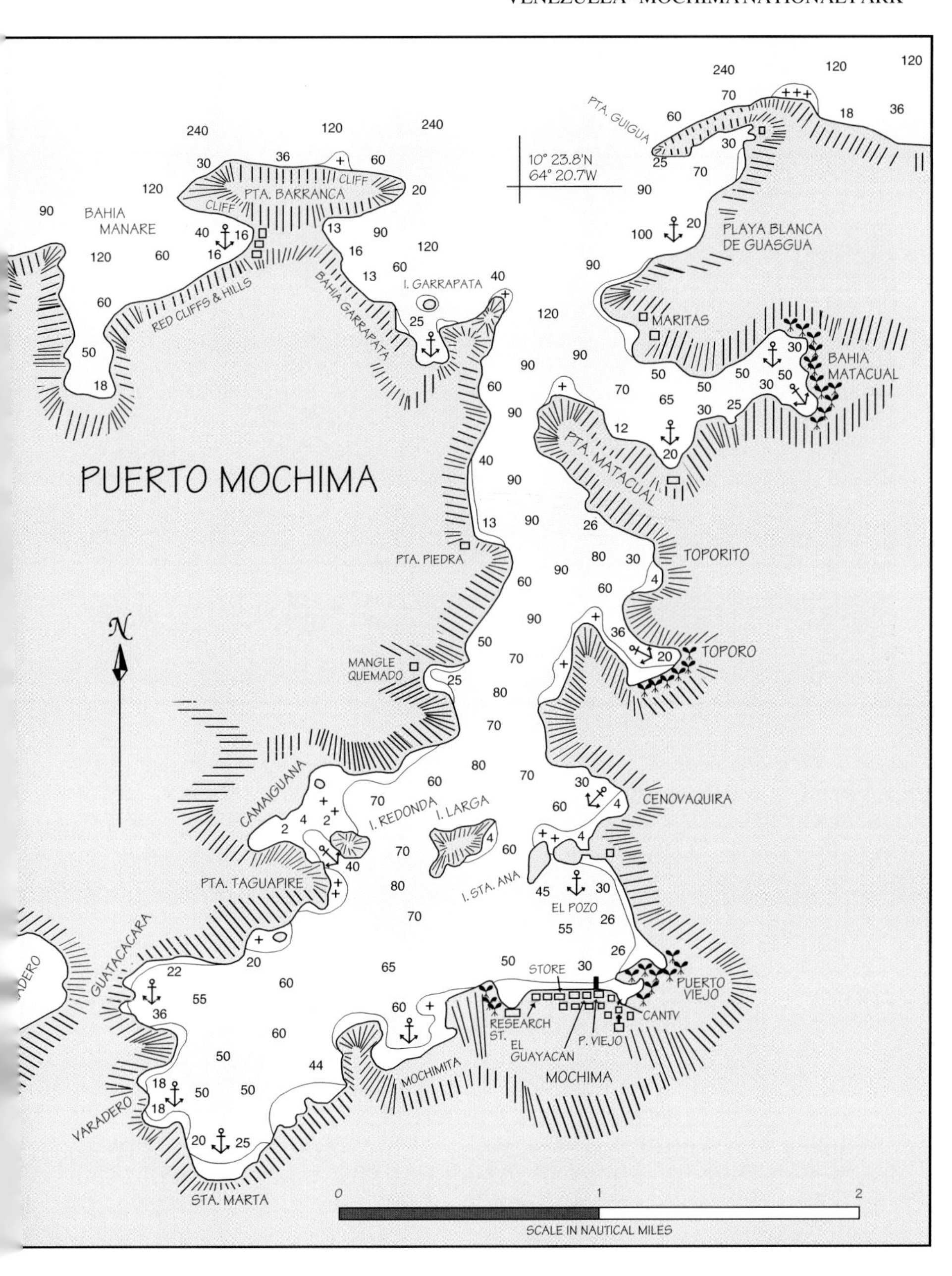

earby beach.

Bugs are not generally a problem but if ou get bothered, just move away a bay or vo.

Mochima is attractive to yachtspeople nd a few years ago yachting got totally out hand, with some 80 boats anchored in e bay off the village. Some were just left ere, others were owned by people who seemed to have moved in permanently. Toilets pumped into the bay were affecting water quality at the research station.

The park authority stepped in, chased the boats out and instituted, at various times, a 3-day rule and a 24-hour rule. This seems to have worked well.

The present situation is ambiguous. The head of the parks told me four years ago

Looking south into Mochima. Punta Guigua just shows front left. Isla Garrapata shows clearl

that yachts are banned from anchoring anywhere in Mochima except in the area off Playa Blanca de Guasgua, which is open to northerly swells. He claimed that this ban was made at the request of the inhabitants in Mochima. No printed rule was available and yachts have been happily anchoring in Mochima ever since. The locals we spoke to liked the yachts and the business they brought and said that we were welcome to stay. I would be inclined to stop for no more than three days in Mochima. Go have a meal or two, buy some supplies and if half a dozen yachts are in town, anchor in one of the other lovely bays. Move if the park authorities or locals tell you to. One thing is sure, if lots of yachts start hanging out semi-permanently in Mochima again, the ban will be enforced. Should this happen I still recommend a sailing tour round Mochima to see it.

Navigation

The water in Mochima is generally deep and the problem is to find somewhere shallow enough to anchor. In some places you may need an anchor and a line ashore Be prepared to anchor in 40 feet of wate The holding is generally good. You ca anchor almost anywhere and always find place to yourself.

If you are gunkholing, do so in good ligh as there are often small shoals close t shore.

The best anchorage close to the village i in El Pozo off Isla Santa Ana on the far sid of the bay from town. To the southwest th next bay is Mochimita. A shoal extend from its eastern headland and there a quite a few reefs inside, but it is possible t feel your way into an anchorage off th beach. Santa Marta is a quiet bay wi some palms and you can anchor fair close to shore, in about 25 feet of wate Varadero (The Boatyard) is a boatyard n longer, but a thickly wooded bay wi vegetation to the water's edge. You ca anchor where it shelves to 18 feet, but you go in closer it shoals very abruptly.

Guatacacara is a handy bay for those wh want to explore ashore and climb over th small hill to Ensenada Tigrillo. Most Camaiguana is shallow, but there is

ıhía Matacual in Puerto Mochima

delightful anchorage at the southern entrance between Pta. Taguapire and Isla Redonda in about 40 feet of water. Flocks of small green parrots are often in residence on Isla Redonda.

Toporo is a real hideaway. Avoid going too close to either shore and anchor in the southeast corner. You can also find good anchorage in Cenovaquira and Toporito.

Bahía Matacual is possibly the prettiest anchorage. If you anchor right up at the head of the bay in about 35 feet of water, it is like being anchored in a landlocked lake. There is another anchorage off the beach, half way along the southern shore in about 20 feet of water. Maritas and Playa Blanca de Guasgua are both white sand beaches used by visiting tourists. Facilities for tourists have been built with little thatch huts and restaurants that open when there is enough demand. You can feel your way into an anchorage off either but you may need a second anchor. There is a sheltered area northeast of Playa Blanca with lovely cliffs all along the shore. The water here is deep till you get close in. Unfortunately, the fishermen will usually ask you to leave.

There is an enchanting anchorage in Bahía Garrapata, tucked down in the southern corner inside Isla Garrapata. You often get a few gnats at dawn and dusk and you would need to leave in a northerly swell. Here you are surrounded by red hills, a red sand beach and fair snorkeling close to shore.

Ashore

Mochima has several very inexpensive and friendly restaurants. Some are open only on holidays. Restaurant Puerto Viejo ($D, cc:A,V) and El Guayacán ($D cc:A,V) are open most days. There is a local cooperative store with a limited stock. Since it is right on the waterfront loading supplies is no problem. Close to shore is a fuel pump which sells gasoline (no diesel) and the depth is only good for a dinghy. There is a little one-telephone office with flexible hours. You cannot make overseas calls. Por puestos run to Cumaná.

From time to time a local boat operator takes people diving and has a compressor that works. Snorkeling is interesting inside of Punta Barranca, but try snorkeling wherever you anchor. There are many little reefs close to shore.

CUMANÁ

Cumaná is a handsome town set on a river about three quarters of a mile inland. There are pleasant plazas, colorful streets and a walkway along the river. Cumaná is the capital of the state of Sucre and its main commercial center. The waterfront area is called Puerto Sucre. It is less alluring than the town, but compensates with some good haul out facilities and a first class marina.

Cumaná is a conveniently placed gateway to the Golfo de Cariaco, and it is only about 10 miles from the Mochima National Park.

Cumaná was an important Indian town before Europeans arrived and derives its name from the Cumanagoto tribe who lived there. The Cumanagotos were great seafarers and known as the owners of the sea throughout the islands.

Franciscan missionaries were here in 1506, but the town didn't become a European stronghold until pearls and gold were found. The town was officially claimed by the Spanish in 1521 and Indians were taken from Cumaná to dive in the pearl beds at Cubagua.

Gold and pearls passing through Cumaná made it an attractive target for pirates, who would pass by for a little looting and mayhem. This led to building of the fort called Castillo de San Antonio de la Eminencia. Construction started in 1660 and was completed nine years later, just in time to repulse Henry Morgan who was passing by on his way from sacking

Maracaibo.

Cumaná is in an active earthquake zone and the fort was destroyed repeatedly by tremors, once in 1684 and again in 1853. It was rebuilt by 1906 only to be destroyed by a disastrous earthquake in 1929 which was accompanied by a tidal wave 20 feet high. The fort is now repaired as a tourist attraction. At some point there were tunnels leading from the fort into town, but these were blocked by the earthquakes.

Regulations

Cumaná is a port of entry and if you are already cleared in to Venezuela, you will have to check in again here if you are going to stay long. Marina Cumanagoto or Navimca will do all the paperwork for you. Varadero Caribe also do paperwork for their customers.

Navigation.

The approaches to Cumaná from the north and west are clear. You can anchor either side of the big ship dock (see sketch chart, p.226). The southern side is bigger and has a much wider anchoring shelf; the northern side is a little more central. Both anchorages get rolly during the afternoon when the winds reach their peak strength.

In both anchorages you have to find a beach and pull your dinghy ashore where the wharf urchins will play havoc with it. One way to avoid this is to dinghy up the river into town. There is usually enough water to get all the way up to the river walkway in town. It is an adventurous way to go, though probably slower than walking. If you can get up near the third bridge you can find plenty of riverside trees to tie your dinghy to and it will probably not be molested. There is one dinghy hazard, just after the first bridge, there are two metal posts sticking up almost to the surface right in the middle of the stream. It should be mentioned that if you follow the river walkway away from town too far it goes through some exceptionally seedy and probably dangerous areas.

Most people opt to go into the marina and it is sometimes full. Advance booking is possible, but you will probably get in if you are prepared to wait a few days. You can anchor in town while you wait for a slip, or you can spend time on the northern shore in one of the pretty bays such as Laguna Grande. You can stay in touch with the marina on the VHF. The anchorage right outside the marina is uncomfortable. The entrance to the marina is down a narrow channel that is currently well marked by buoys (red right returning). Optimally it has a minimum depth of 8.5 feet at low tide and you can come in with nine feet of draft or more at high tide. But the channel does from time to time silt up due to the currents, the marina is pretty good about keeping it dredged, so if you draw more than six feet or so, call the marina to find out the present state of the channel. The berths immediately in front of the entrance bounce a bit when the wind is strong.

Services

Marina Cumanagoto (T/F:093-31 14 23, VHF:16, 71, cc:V) is pleasant and secure

Cumaná - the marina shows clearly. Península de Araya can be seen across the channel

and many people leave their boats here while they adventure inland. Manager Gaston Fortoui speaks English and Swiss, if your Spanish is poor, ask for him when you call on the radio. They have proved over the years to be a good mail drop: c/o Cumanagoto Marina, Av., Perimetral, Al Lado de Ensal, Cumaná, Edo. Sucr There are card phones in the marina wi a USA direct line. You can send an receive faxes at the marina office. There water and electricity (110/220 volt, (cycles) on the dock and the marina has fuel dock with diesel and gasoline. Asho

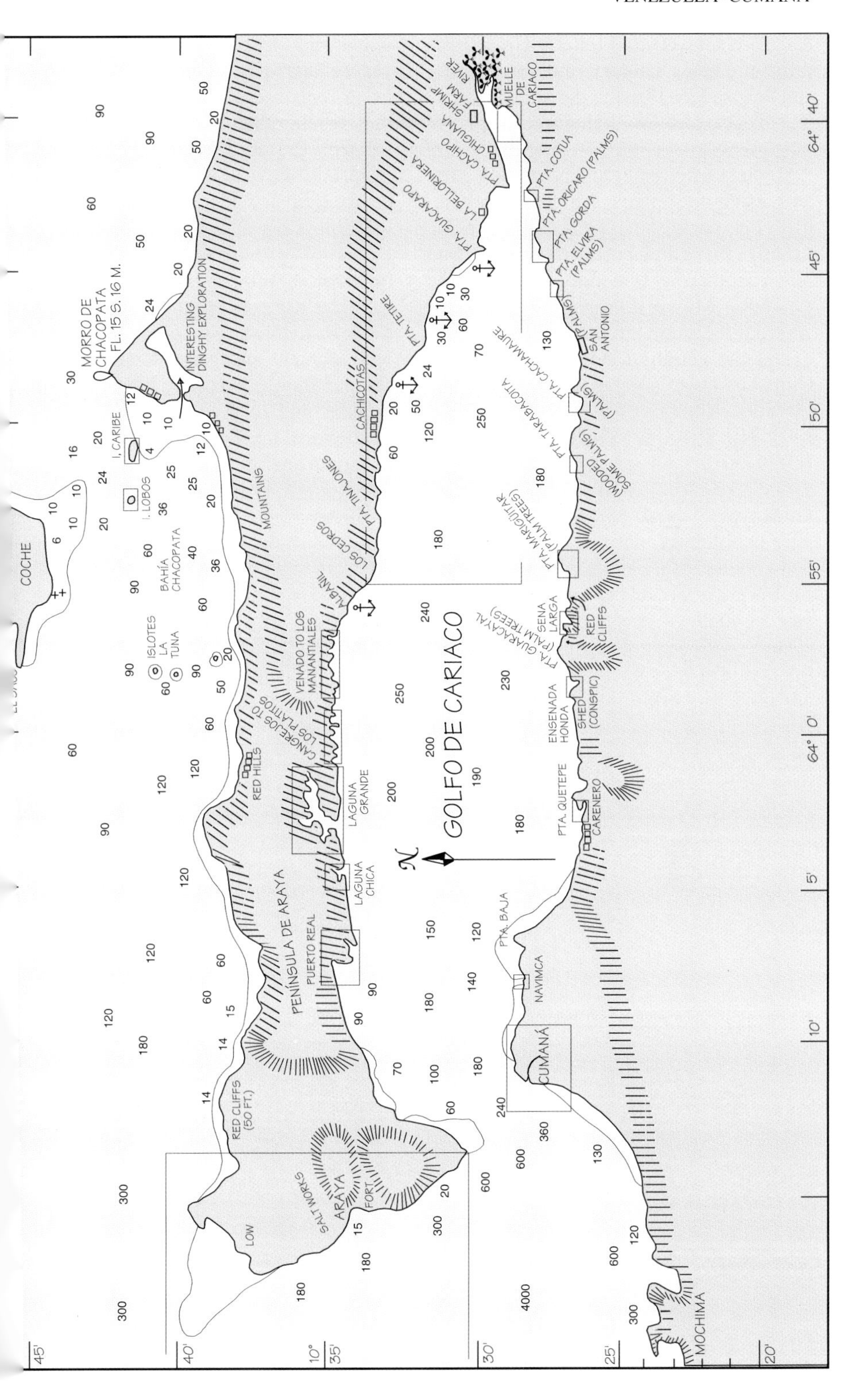
GOLFO DE CARIACO
PENÍNSULA DE ARAYA
MORRO DE CHACOPATA
FL. 15 S. 16 M.
INTERESTING DINGHY EXPLORATION
COCHE
I. CARIBE
I. LOBOS
BAHÍA CHACOPATA
ISLOTES LA TUNA
MOUNTAINS
RED HILLS
RED CLIFFS (50 FT.)
LOW
SALT WORKS
ARAYA
FORT
PUERTO REAL
LAGUNA CHICA
LAGUNA GRANDE
CANGREJOS TO LOS PLATITOS
VENADO TO LOS MANANTIALES
ALBANIL
LOS CEDROS
PTA. TINAJONES
CACHICOTAS
PTA. IETIRE
PTA. GUACARAPO
LA BELLORINERA
PTA. CACHIPO
CHIGUANA
SHRIMP FARM
RIVER
MUELLE DE CARIACO
PTA. COTUA
PTA. ORICARO (PALMS)
PTA. GORDA
PTA. ELVIRA (PALMS)
(PALMS)
SAN ANTONIO
PTA. CACHAMAURE
PTA. TARABACOITA
(PALMS)
(WOODED SOME PALMS)
PTA. MARIGÜITAR (PALM TREES)
SENA LARGA
RED CLIFFS
PTA. GUARACAYAL (PALM TREES)
ENSENADA HONDA
SHED (CONSPIC)
PTA. QUETEPE
CARENERO
PTA. BAJA
NAVIMCA
CUMANÁ
MOCHIMA
64° 40'
45'
50'
55'
64° 0'
5'
10'
10° 35'
40'
45'
30'
25'
20'

there are showers and toilets. The marina drugstore does laundry and boat caring can be arranged through the manager. The marina also has restaurants and shops (see our "Ashore" section).

Miguel makes his living by getting parts and arranging repairs. He speaks no English but manages with sign language. He usually comes down in the morning to find out what there is to do and returns in the afternoon. Miguel is the son of Old Bolívar who did the same job before him.

You can get any kind of work done in Cumaná. There are several good hauling facilities. The busiest is Varadero Caribe (093 310 804/310 837/310 908/663 156 F:093-66 25 64 compuserve 102213, 3340, VHF: 13). It is run by the Plaut family who speak perfect English. The yard is big, busy, very reasonably priced, and you nearly always know exactly what a job is going to cost before you start. They use a couple of massive marine railway systems with ways of easily shunting boats to the side. It is a commercial yard and they are used to working on fishing boats of wood and steel. It is also excellent for yachts built of steel, wood and concrete. Long keeled glass yachts are fine, too, but they would rather not see anything with a fin keel. Bottom jobs are first-rate for all materials, they can do an excellent Imron or Awlgrip topside spray finish. A full machine shop allows them to undertake large repairs to shafts, rudders and rigging in stainless, bronze and aluminum. They can treat osmosis problems and do major refits in traditional wood construction as well as steel and glass. Consistent high standards and good prices have made them popular and for years there has been a waiting list. It is best to call them a couple of months before you want to haul.

Next door Astilleros de Oriente (T:093-32 10 59, 32 41 19, T/F:093-66 49 29,) has a hundred-ton travel lift and can haul boats up to a nine foot draft and 24.5-foot beam. They are more expensive than Varadero Caribe, but they can usually haul immediately.

If you want to get off your boat while the work is done, there are several inexpen-

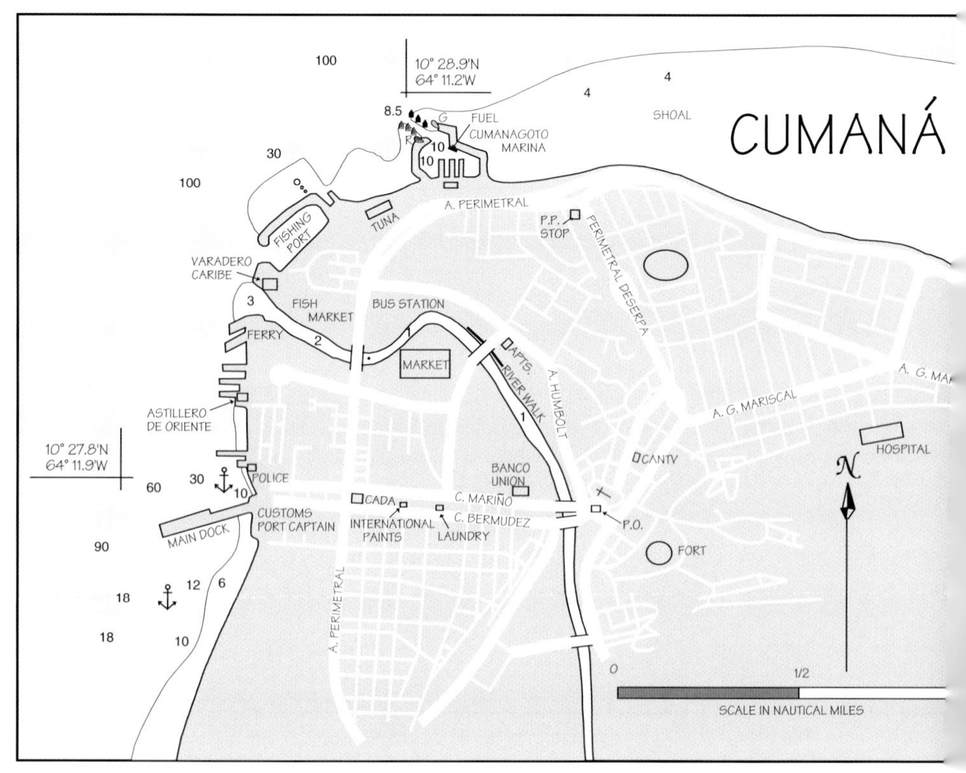

sive hotels nearby where you can be a lot more comfortable.

Ashore

Ashore at the marina there is a great mini market called El Bodegón which will deliver your orders to your boat at no extra cost. If they don't have it in stock they will get it, including meats and vegetables, so you can fully provision without any hassle. They carry a fair stock and always have beer, liquor and ice.

The Drugstore (T:93-31 50 23, cc:A,M,V) is versatile. They have a great gift shop, will help with tours and laundry. They sell newspapers and magazines, including the Daily Journal.

There are two good restaurants. El Navegante (T:93-31 50 23, $C-D, cc:V) is the fancy one, air conditioned with original nautical decor (notice how they have done the air-conditioning ducts) and a picture window view of the marina. The Coffee Shop (T:93-31 50 23, $D) is open to the breeze and is open for breakfast, lunch and dinner and serves snack type food as well as a varied menu of traditional and seafood dishes. Both will prepare take out meals.

There is also a branch of Nauti Hogar (T:93-66 35 18, F:93-66 38 04, VHF:18) in the marina. They can supply rubber dinghies and outboards and carry a stock of nautical accessories.

The main roads in town are the two that run from CADA to the river. The area between the river and CANTV has lots of appealing small shops. Avenue Mariscal also has many shops.

You can quickly get currency changed at the money change in town. If you need to get cash from your Visa card, go to Banco Union. CANTV in town has a USA direct phone. There is a big CADA for supermarket shopping and nearby are two chandleries. Casa Mar (T:093 31 38 51) offers a good price on all the Venezuelan inflatables. They also stock Yamaha outboards, sigma paints and a good supply of nautical hardware. Nearby is the main branch of the Nauti Hogar chandlery (T:093 66 35 18/66 38 04, F:093-31 33 09, VHF:18, cc:V,A). Here you will find a complete range of boat gear including Yamaha and Evinrude outboards and spares, Jabsco pumps and parts, fishing gear, Yamaha gen. sets and some electronics.

You can buy fish at the fish market near Varadero Caribe and the tuna plant just west of the marina sometimes sells off large boxes of frozen tuna at excellent prices.

The big central bus station for out of town buses is marked on our sketch chart.

While visiting Cumaná it is worth making time to visit the guácharo cave near Caripe. (See our section on sightseeing). If you go by bus make sure you take one that follows the waterfront of the Golfo de Cariaco.

THE NAVIMCA HAUL OUT FACILITY

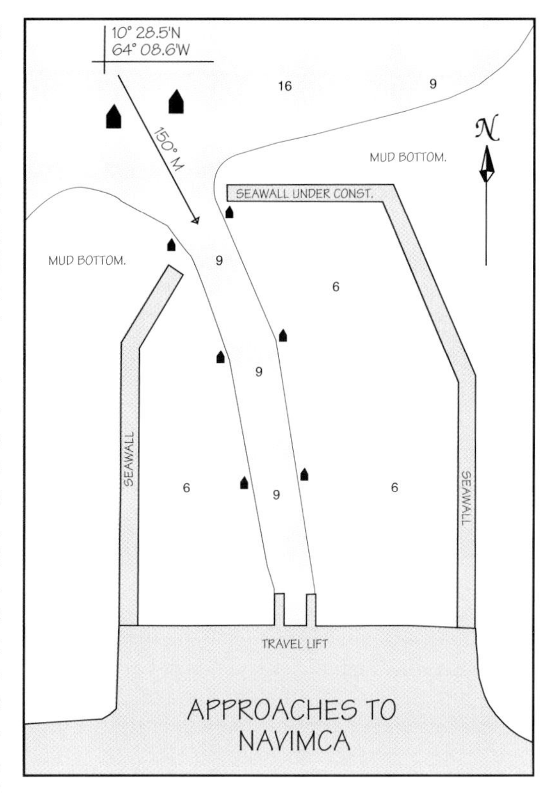

On the eastern edge of Cumaná is the Navimca haul-out facility (T:093 31 90 64, F:093 31 71 62, VHF:16). This was for many years a boat-building company that produced seaworthy fishing boats, about 120 feet long. When demand dwindled they went into the yacht repair business and put in a travel lift. The travel lift dock lies in an enclosed basin of about 800 feet by 600 feet.

It is both very good and inexpensive, perhaps the best price in Venezuela. Many people take their boats out for dry storage. They can handle Imron spray painting, osmosis jobs and anything else you might need. They have all the equipment left over from the shipbuilding days. They have separate areas for storage and working so your boat does not get covered in someone else's sandblast. For those living on their boats there are showers, toilets and a coffee shop/restaurant. The president, Giorgio Neri, speaks English. They offer a free check in service for their customers.

The approach is easier than it was. If you have any doubts call them on the radio and they will probably send someone out to guide you in. From Cumaná stay well offshore as shoals extend about half a mile out to sea. If you have an echo sounder with an alarm, set it to 50 feet and follow the shoal around. When it shoals, it does so fast. The shoal gets narrower and there is deep water a few hundred yards from the shore before it broadens and becomes shoal almost a mile offshore. Navimca is to be found at the beginning of this second shoal. If you have a GPS, a setting of 10° 28.52'N, 64° 08.67'W should get you close enough to see the first two big channel buoys. From there a route of 150° takes you to the next buoys which are at the entrance of the basin. You then follow the buoys up to the dock. At the moment most of this basin is only 6 feet deep, so deeper draft boats must follow the channel all the way to the haul out slip.

The large basin will eventually be a big marina and when this happens it will be a first rate place to stay. In the meantime There is one wall with water and electricity (maximum draft 6') and endless room without facilities for boats drawing less than 6 feet. Security is excellent and this is a very calm and secure place to leave your yacht while you travel. It will probably be a while before they finish the whole project.

The Golfo de Cariaco is 35 miles long and never more than about eight miles wide. While you can get a nasty chop, it is completely protected from ocean swells and you are never far from an anchorage. It contains a range of different environments, from dense green hills and palm-fringed beaches in the southeast to desert areas of pretty rocks in the northwest.

It is typically calm at night and the wind is light and often easterly in the early morning. By mid-morning the wind starts picking up from between east and northeast and by mid-afternoon it is often blowing about 25 knots with short steep seas. The wind drops again after dark. While this pattern holds throughout the gulf, it is far more intense in the western half. This area seems to be subject to a wind funnel which sweeps down across the islands of Coche and Cubagua, across the Península de Araya and right over Cumaná, to die in the mountains behind. The winds are also more intense in winter than in summer. At the eastern end of the gulf the winds start later, blow weaker and die earlier. As anywhere in Venezuela, a wind of about 20 knots, associated with rain and squalls, will blow from the southwest every few months. It usually only lasts a few hours, but it makes most of the anchorages along the northern coast unpleasant. In normal conditions, the north coast gets some lee from the mountains and the seas are much less than on the south side of the gulf. In some anchorages the wind manages to come through the valleys.

If you enjoy sailing, the best way to see the gulf is to make large close reaches from side to side, stopping at anchorages as the mood takes you. This is not hard because there are many anchorages. In our review of the anchorages in Golfo de Cariaco, we go around in an anti-clockwise direction starting eastwards down the south coast and returning westwards along the northern shore.

It should be noted that the Golfo de Cariaco is a big area and the charts are not very detailed. There is not much to worry about out in the middle, but close to shore keep a good lookout. There may be shoals that we did not spot.

Los Platitos

CUMANÁ TO CARENERO

There are extensive shoals off the coast to the east of Cumaná as far as Punta Baja. Toward Punta Baja they extend nearly a mile offshore. Stay well out or skirt the bank carefully, paying close attention to your echo sounder. Best stay in at least 35 feet of water. Once you have rounded Punta Baja and cleared the bank you can head directly toward Punta Quetepe.

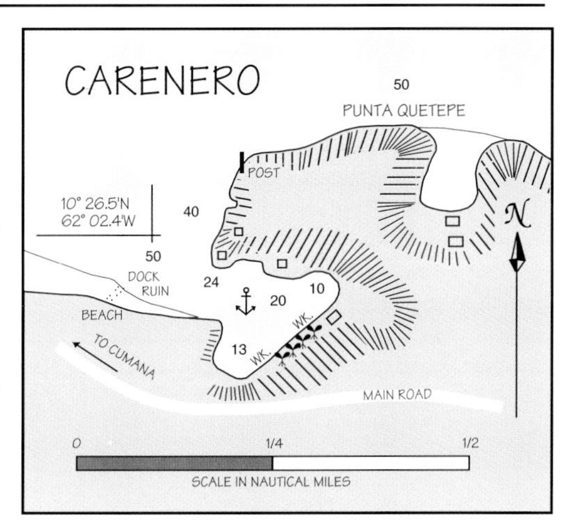

Carenero is a superb little harbor that cuts its way into the west side of Punta Quetepe. Inside there is a sizeable anchoring area in 10-20 feet. The bay is pleasant with little beaches, small mangroves, a couple of wrecks and a few houses belonging to fishing families. The main road runs close by and you do hear the traffic.

The fishermen do not mind yachts coming in for a night or two, but they would not like boats to start hanging out in the bay. Fish do occasionally come in and when this happens they close off the whole bay with a net and yachts would be in the way.

ENSENADA HONDA

As you sail east from Carenero the water is deep close to shore for two miles, then there are a few shoals less than a quarter of a mile offshore. You will see a headland on which there is a very large shed, a boat building enterprise that seems to have stalled. About a third of mile beyond this headland is a tiny but well protected bay called Ensenada Honda (Deep Water Bay). This is a lovely spot with some well-to-do homes and a small beach. The main road is some way away so it is peaceful. It lives up to its name, the water is a good 60 feet deep in the middle of the bay. To anchor here you need to drop an anchor almost on the beach, then put a stern one out to hold you from going ashore.

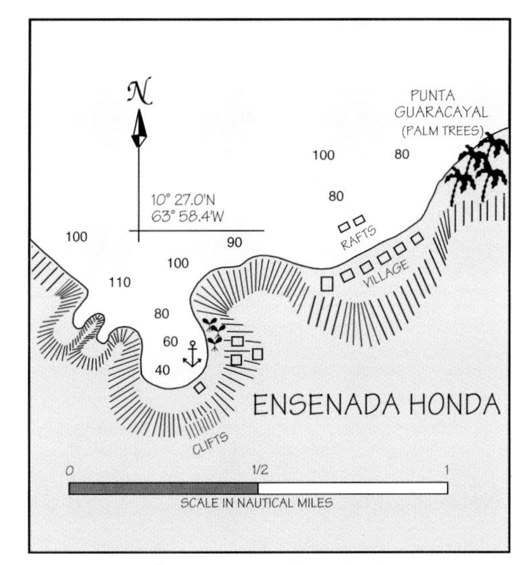

As you head east from this bay, watch out for oyster floats off the village before Punta Guaracayal. The bay after Punta Guaracayal is shoal, so give the coast a reasonable clearance, but don't stay so far offshore that you miss the next bay, Sena Larga. If you are approaching from the north coast there are some conspicuous red cliffs on the coast either side of the harbor.

Sena Larga (Deeply Indented Bay) cuts well back into the land. The only danger we could see was a rock very close to shore on eastern headland just outside the bay. Inside, the water is all 18-25 feet deep with plenty of swinging room. No houses, just colorful red rocks, a few mangroves and a public beach at the head. The main road does follow the bay right round. You can follow the coast pretty closely from here down to Punta Marigüitar. If you sail within quarter of a mile of the shore, look out for shoals.

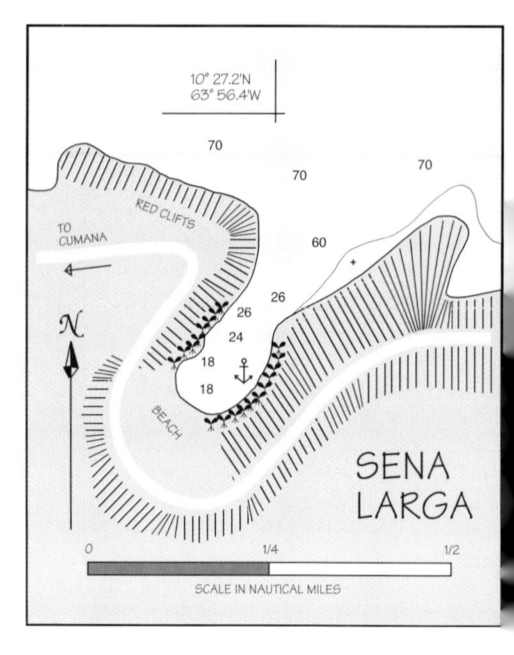

MARIGÜITAR

Puntar Marigüitar is a prominent headland magnificently decorated with palm trees and beaches. It provides shelter from both the seas and the prevailing wind which gets broken up by the trees. There are often some boats anchored here associated with the Club Maigualida ashore. There is a mud bank which extends up to two hundred yards from Punta Marigüitar, but you can see this in reasonable light. Anchor right up in the head of the bay off the dock. The water is deep so you may want to edge close to the shore and use second anchor. You may also tie up to the Club Maigualida dock where water is available.

If you leave the anchorage to head east early in the morning, remember that the mud bank comes out a long way. Do not follow the headland right round into the next bay as it is shoal though the fish factory has reclaimed some of the shoal area. Apart from this you can follow the coast fairly closely to the next anchorage off Punta Tarabacoita.

Ashore

Club Maigualida ($D, cc:V) is a great place to stop for a meal. It has a pleasant open air bar and dining room, the atmosphere is friendly and the prices are reasonable. They have a mini zoo in cage with cristofues, an agouti, a monkey and a parrot. They have a card phone which is not very reliable.

About three quarters of a mile dinghy ride round the headland, there is a large and conspicuous building which is a fish canning plant for sardines and tuna. (Occasionally you get a whiff of the operation from the anchorage.) Just before you get to the factory there is a dock with a public market at its head which is active in the mornings. You can also walk back to the village where you will find a few shops with most necessities. It seems that nearly everyone in the village is employed by the fish factory and many of them walk around in matching work clothes. They also appear to get around by bicycle as there are enough here to run a Tour de France.

PUNTA TARABACOITA

The anchorage to the west of Punta Tarabacoita gives good shelter from easterly winds. In a northeasterly you would be better off in Marigüitar to the west or Punta Cachamaure to the east. The headland is wooded with some palms and small beaches between the beach greenery. The most sheltered anchorage is tucked in to the head of the bay as far as you dare go. You can anchor close to the shore in about 20 feet of water. You get a little protection from the shallow mud bank which extends from the shore to the north of the anchorage. A dock comes out to the edge of this bank. Ashore there are several houses. If you are leaving this anchorage to head east, note that the mud bank continues right round the headland and can be nearly 100 yards wide in places.

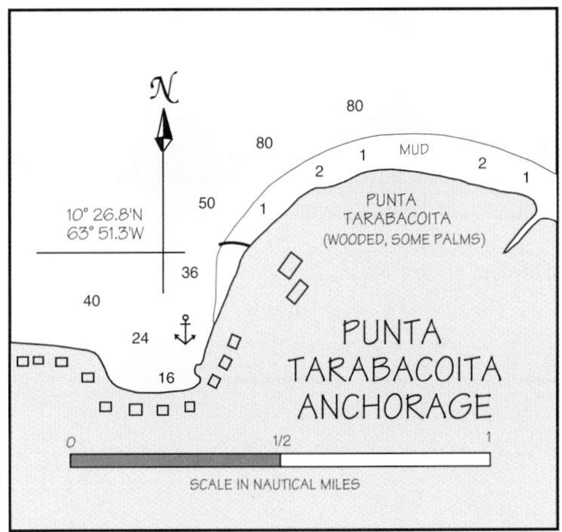

PUNTA CACHAMAURE

Punta Cachamaure is two miles east of Punta Tarabacoita and the anchorage west of Cachamaure is perfectly delightful and much more protected. The bay is quite wide and very deep. Punta Cachamaure is picture-perfect with sandy beaches, tall palms and banana plants behind. The hills are bright green and along the shore are several simple fishing huts with thatched roofs. The main road is a bit set back so it is not too obtrusive. You have to head right over to the eastern shore where you will find bottom close to the beach, about 30-35 deep. You will need two anchors, one deep and one shallow, or one anchor and a line ashore. You can anchor alongside the

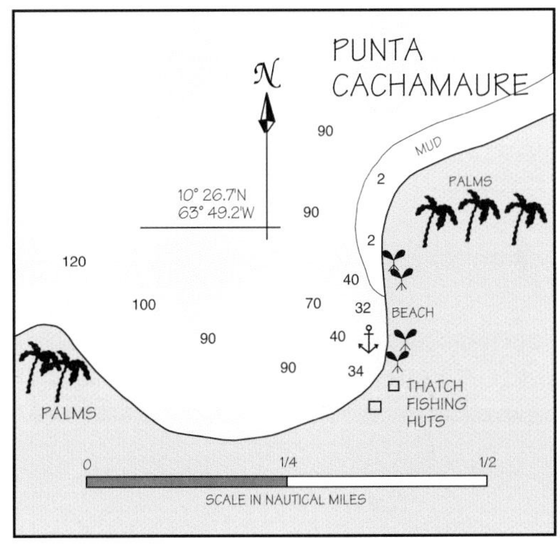

fleet of open fishing boats or a little farther up off the next beach. Be prepared to cooperate with the fishermen if they need to net.

When heading east from this anchorage, give Punta Cachamaure good clearance as there is a mud bank around the head and down into the bay to its east. The next sheltered anchorage is Pericantal, nearly four miles east in the lee of Punta La Elvira. Along the way you will pass the town of San Antonio. Watch out for mussel platforms which are sometimes put out here.

PUNTA LA ELVIRA/PERICANTAL

Pericantal is a super little bay, well protected from the regular trade winds and far enough away from the road that any traffic is well muffled. Punta La Elvira is a magnificent, palm-fringed headland with lots of small beaches. The water in the bay is 16-25 feet deep, perfect for anchoring. There is one house on the western headland. The beach at the head of the bay is used by fishing boats. The prettiest anchorage is off the beach just north of this bay. Fishermen do not usually set nets here, so you can relax and enjoy the peace.

A mud bank extends round Punta La Elvira, so give it a reasonable clearance.

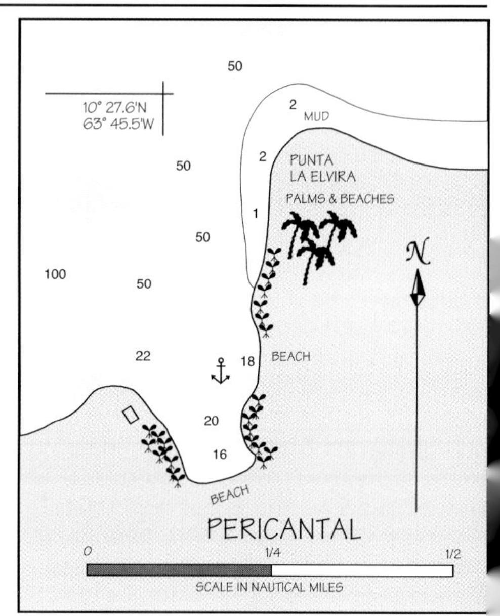

PUNTA GORDA AND PUNTA ORICARO

There are anchorages to the west of both these headlands. They are very peaceful as the main road has gone back inland. The bay west of Punta Gorda is a quiet, mangrove lined bay. There is a large shoal that takes up the southeast corner of the bay. North of this shoal is a little red-colored stone beach. You can approach this beach from the northwest and find plenty of anchoring room in 20-30 feet of water. However, you may well prefer to anchor in the bay to the west of Punta Oricaro (Punta Gorda is surrounded by a mud bank, so do not hug it tightly). This is a charming bay. The shore all around is wooded with some lovely beaches. Anchoring depth is an ideal 17-20 feet. The best spot is off the beach, on the eastern side of the headland.

If leaving this anchorage to go east give Punta Oricaro a couple of hundred yards clearance.

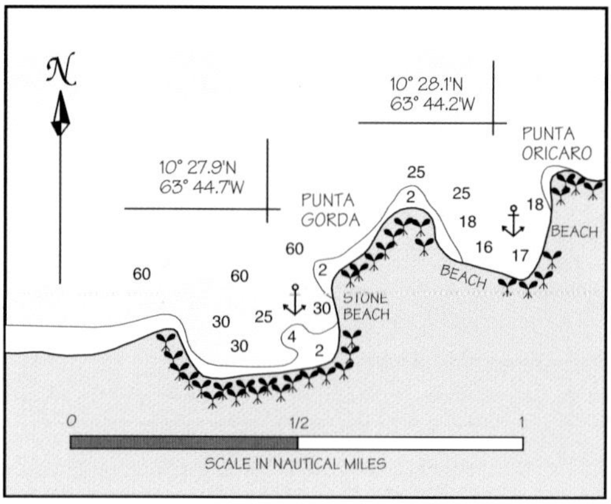

PUNTA COTUA

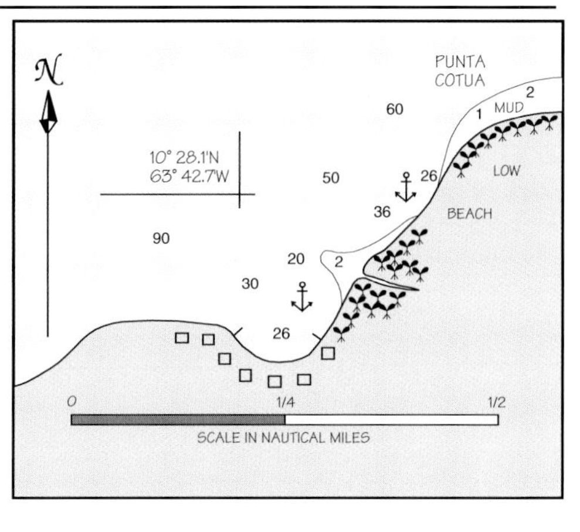

The anchorage west of Punta Cotua is really not very well sheltered, but you are getting so far up in the bay that the winds and seas are not quite as bad as they are farther west. In normal winds you will get some little waves creeping round the corner. It makes a very pleasant lunch spot and if it is calm enough you can spend the night. The nicest anchorage is off the beach toward the point. The bottom shelves to a suitable 26-30 feet before you run aground. The best way to anchor would be bow to the beach with a line ashore and a stern anchor to hold you from going aground.

MUELLE DE CARIACO

As you proceed east from Punta Cotua there are some shoals which extend out several hundred yards and can take the coast hugger unawares. The problem here is that the water becomes murky and unreadable. Stay closer to the middle of the channel than to the shore. Don't go way over the north side as it is even shallower there. As long as you stay somewhere near the middle there is plenty of water and it gets deeper toward the south side as you approach Muelle de Caraico, the town at the head of the bay. You can feel your way into anchorage anywhere in this large and protected bay which is about a mile wide. I suggest anchoring about quarter of a mile off town and well back from the mangroves as the best bet for a bug free night. The big building at the entrance to Laguna Cariaco on the north side is a shrimp farm. You can pay a visit and see if you can persuade them to sell you some shrimps.

Ashore

Muelle de Cariaco (The Dock of Cariaco) was an important little trading town where ships were always loading cargo. When a good road was built to Cumaná, ships no longer came, and now it is charming in a sleepy sort of way.

You can leave your dinghy on the dock while it lasts, which will not be too long unless some repairs are done. Close to the dock is a picturesque tree-lined stretch of road with old houses. The old upper road is well worth exploring for charming views to the east, west and south.

The main drag in town is from the dock eastwards toward the gas station. You will find several basic stores. One sells ice and you can often find bread. Las Brisas is a bar right on the waterfront. They only open on the weekends and improvements are planned. The seawall is under repair and a kitchen should be going soon. On weekends their loud music rocks the night, so you may want to consider this when choosing an anchoring spot.

The hub of travel has left the sea and retreated up the road to the main crossroads by the gas station. The gas station has a small snack bar where you can get a simple meal and be entertained by watching the comings and goings from the different buses and por puestos.

If the travel bug gets you, you can get a por puesto to the village of Cariaco just a few minutes away which has more shops. You can also carry on to Carúpano or go back to Cumaná. Better yet, take a day trip to Caripe to see the guácharo birds (see our sightseeing section for more details). It is only about a 45-minute ride away and if you start early in the morning you can easily do the round trip and the caves in a day.

While at the eastern end of the Golfo de Cariaco, you should take a dinghy trip up into Laguna de Cariaco in the head of the bay. This is great for exploring and bird watching. There are plenty of herons, cormorants, pelicans and parrots. Don't miss exploring up the river on the north side of the Laguna. You can make it all the way till the water is fresh (about one and half miles). If you happen to be here on a moonlit night, come back down the river as darkness falls and you will be surrounded by a host of fish eating bats.

PUERTO NUEVO

Puerto Nuevo is a large bay between Punta Cachipo and the village of Guacarapo. This is a lovely spot, with some excellent bird watching. If you are coming from the east, take a very wide swing around Punta Cachipo as there is a shoal off the eastern shore. If you are approaching from the west pass the Bellorinera Restaurant before heading in, as there is a shoal that extends southwest of the restaurant. You can anchor just east of the restaurant in 12 feet of water or feel your way eastwards to a more secluded spot.

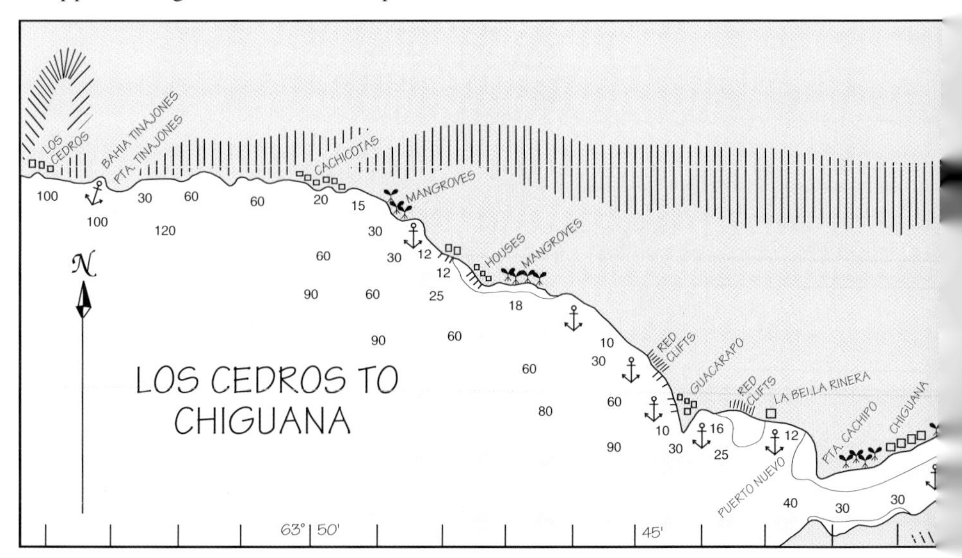

Ashore

La Bellorinera Bar and Restaurant ($D, cc:V) is open daily 0800-2000. It is informal and friendly, owned and run by Atilano and Paulina Bellorin. They specialize in fish, clams, shrimps and chicken. If you need to go shopping, you can get a por puesto from Guacarapo.

The shoal at the eastern end of the bay is a fabulous bird watching spot. Best take binoculars and dinghy right out around the Punta Cachipo, go ashore on the eastern side and make your way back closer on foot. You can see flamingos and many kinds of wading birds feeding together here.

Scarlet ibis also frequent this area and are often seen flying or in the trees between La Bellorinera and Chiguana. Some people have also reported seeing them up in Laguna de Cariaco.

GUACARAPO TO CACHICOTAS

A small road runs behind the coast linking these villages and other houses. The people here live by fishing and cattle ranching.

When the wind starts to blow hard down the gulf, this part of the coast is protected from the worst of both wind and sea. However, small wavelets do turn the corner and follow the coast down, building in size the farther they go. This whole stretch of coast has a wide rather shallow shelf, making anchoring anywhere very easy. The water is often too shallow within a couple of hundred yards of the shore. In many places there are fancy docks built out to the edge of the shallows with roofs and sitting areas.

It is a peaceful area with a thin strip of beach miles long which you can have to yourself. Even so, it is not especially exciting. There is one anchorage that is more alluring than the rest. There is a small bay about two miles southeast of Cachicotas (10° 32.42N, 63° 48.39W). What makes this special is the view. The sandy beach of the bay forms the foreground and the eye gets led back up the green slope to the dramatic mountain range behind.

The bay is quite shoal but you can feel your way in to the outer edge and this seems to get you out of the little waves.

Medregal village (T:014 93 07 00/93 33 11/F:014 93 07 12) is a new resort close to this bay. The manager Pierro is a Dutch-Italian, and the PR man, Mr. Albaladego is an American, despite his name. You can anchor in front of the hotel and use their dinghy dock. They have day and night security and offer showers, laundry, a restaurant with French food, pool, kindergarten, excursions, small sailing boats, an ultra light plane and customs clearing services. If you need a night ashore they have 15 rooms with plans to expand.

Once you pass Cachicotas the small waves are big enough to make some kind of shelter desirable. The next place you can find this is in Bahía Tinajones (10° 33.18N, 63° 53.32W) which is sheltered by the punta of the same name. This is a congenial small bay with a beach, a green valley and interesting rocky ledges. You can find anchorage close to the beach in about 25 feet of water. About a mile beyond Tinajones is the small village of Los Cedros.

ALBAÑIL

Shortly after Los Cedros the coast takes a turn to the northwest to a small bay called Albañil. This shift in direction of the coastline gives fair protection from the seas and almost too much protection from the wind. For the most part it is very deep close to shore and you need two anchors. Not an especially exciting area but it is worth knowing anchoring is possible.

This two and half mile stretch of coast is rugged with many indentations. The coast is mainly steep-to until you tuck into the little bays where there is usually good anchoring depth. Some bays are so small that the only way to be out of the seas is to anchor bow or stern to the beach. Always proceed in good light when close to shore, though the only potentially dangerous shoal we found extended southwest off the eastern headland of La Marita. All our old charts showed a rock or shoal a hundred yards or so off this headland. We spent some time gingerly powering up and down looking for it, without success. The fishing family who live in La Marita say it does not exist and I think they would know. Proceed with caution.

Los Manantiales (Spring Bay) is just west of Albañil. You can find protection by going bow or stern to the small beach in the eastern corner.

La Marita is a fine bay with mangroves and colorful little cliffs round the shore. A beach fronts a lush verdant valley which ascends to peaky green mountains behind.

The bay gives outstanding protection with plenty of room to anchor in 16-25 feet in the eastern bay. A single fishing family lives on the beach here. You can also anchor comfortably in the western tongue off the mangroves.

Sena Larga is also quite delightful with three little beaches separated by rocky headlands. There are cactus-covered cliffs, open valleys and small mangroves. The biggest bay with the largest anchoring room is the eastern one, but this has a fishing shed and it is much prettier to be anchored just off the middle bay in about 22 feet of water.

You can also find a small protected spot for one boat west of Sena Larga's western headland. You have to anchor stern to the beach with your bow facing out. There are lots of pelicans for company.

Toldo (The Awning) is a small bay with colorful cliffs and a single fishing camp at its head. If no one is fishing here, you can get fair shelter close to the beach in about 30 feet of water.

Sena Venado (Deer Bay) is half a mile westwards. The only way to get complete protection is to anchor with your stern to the tiny eastern beach and your bow out to sea.

The next bay about half a mile farther west is so small the local fishermen have not even given it a name. It is an attractive, wild little bay with rocky outcroppings sticking through the green vegetation. You have to anchor in the eastern side of the bay to keep out of the swells, going stern to the beach.

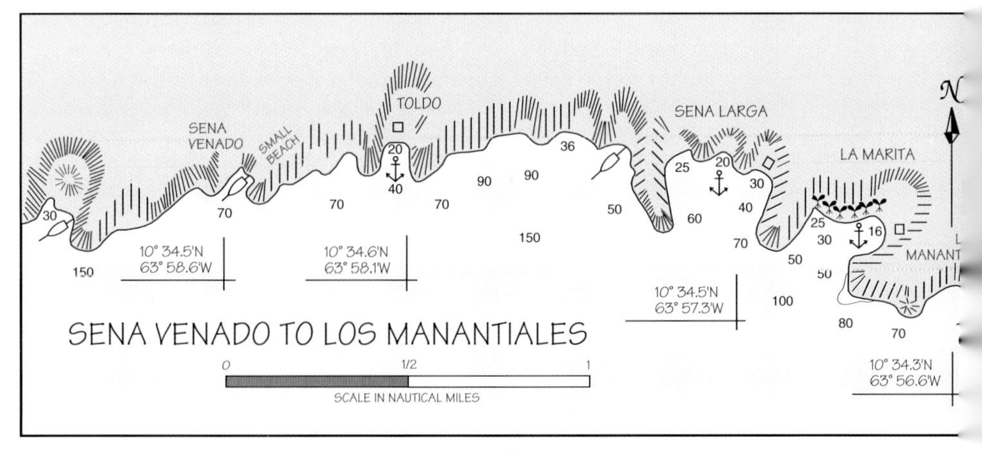

LOS PLATITOS TO CANGREJO

This short stretch of coast is very deeply indented with the added attraction of some small islands. There are three excellent anchorages here, all perfect hideaways. Don't bring the fleet, but they are large enough for a couple of boats.

Los Platitos (The Small Plates) is a romantic little anchorage in the lee of a small cactus-covered island where you can see mockingbirds, woodpeckers and little green parakeets that flash by like bright emeralds. The protected part of the bay is west of the island. You can pass between the north of the island and the shore in about 12 feet of water but watch out for shoals on either side. You can anchor in the middle of the bay in about 25 feet of water. Better still, drop hook in the shallows between the island and the shore, drop back and use a stern anchor to hold you in position. The snorkeling is good around parts of the island with lots of brightly colored worms covering the coral and making a colorful display.

Juanacuña is just over the headland. You can walk between the two. It is a charming secluded bay with a fine thatch-roofed open shelter on the western headland. There is a small shoal patch in the northwestern corner of the bay. It is easy to see and you have room to anchor to its east.

Between Juanacuña and Cangrejo is a distinctive white island. You can pass inside the island with about 30 feet of water under you, but shoals come from both sides so do it in good light.

Cangrejo (Crab Bay) is deeply indented and well protected. A large dry valley heads the bay and plenty of interesting rocks and cliffs line the shores. The few mangroves that have gotten a toehold are well used by roosting pelicans and cormorants. There is plenty of room to anchor anywhere at the head of the bay in 18-30 feet.

The coast from here to Laguna Grande is rugged and mainly steep to. There is really nothing by way of a decent anchorage.

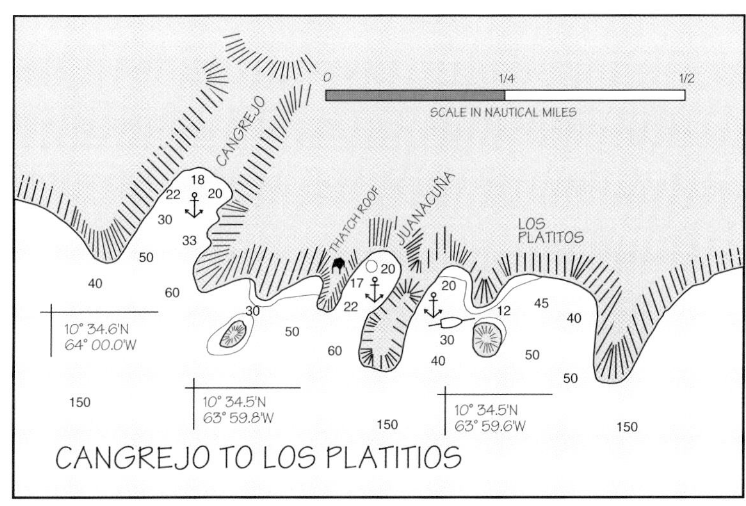

This colossal bay is breathtakingly beautiful with an endless variety of contrasting hills in whites and glowing reds. Small islands have beards of dense green mangroves and wear cactuses like some scraggly Afro. It is a timeless desert landscape, outstandingly colorful and decorative. It must rate high among the Caribbean's hidden treasures and only a few people stop by. There are a few fishermen's houses up in the western corner of the lagoon, otherwise it is deserted. Nothing happens here and the bay will only appeal to those who like desert landscapes.

We noticed a couple of shoals that might give trouble which we have marked on our chart. However, there may be others, so keep a good lookout. When you enter the bay, do not cut fine round the western headland as a shoal extends a long way off. We have put a few anchors on our plan but you can anchor anywhere that takes your fancy. If you follow the bay in around the eastern headland there is a small bay and then a mangrove island. Both these anchorages afford spectacular views. The entire bay is ideal for contemplating the view and for dinghy exploration. Those with sailing dinghies can take advantage of the afternoon breeze which sweeps through the hills. The energetic can hike in the hills.

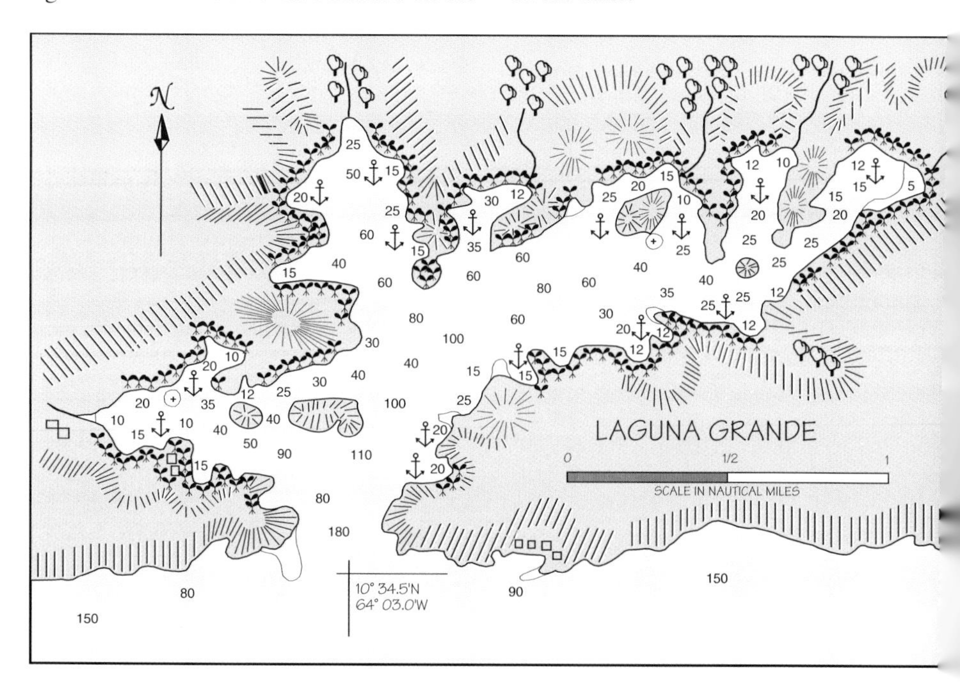

LAGUNA CHICA

When the rarefied atmosphere of Laguna Grande becomes too much, Laguna Chica makes a cheerful change. It is inhabited by fishermen and boat builders. The colors are festive; red hills, bright green trees, white and blue fishing boats. There is always a little activity with boats coming and going without the pace getting hectic. There is a bar/dance hall in the eastern corner of the bay and it has a shower outside. Late afternoon, when it is cool, is the best time for taking a walk.

We have marked several good places to anchor. The most intriguing is in the little

ooking north over Puerto Real and Los Cañónes to the other side of Golfo de Araya. Note the shoals round the southern headland of Puerto Real.

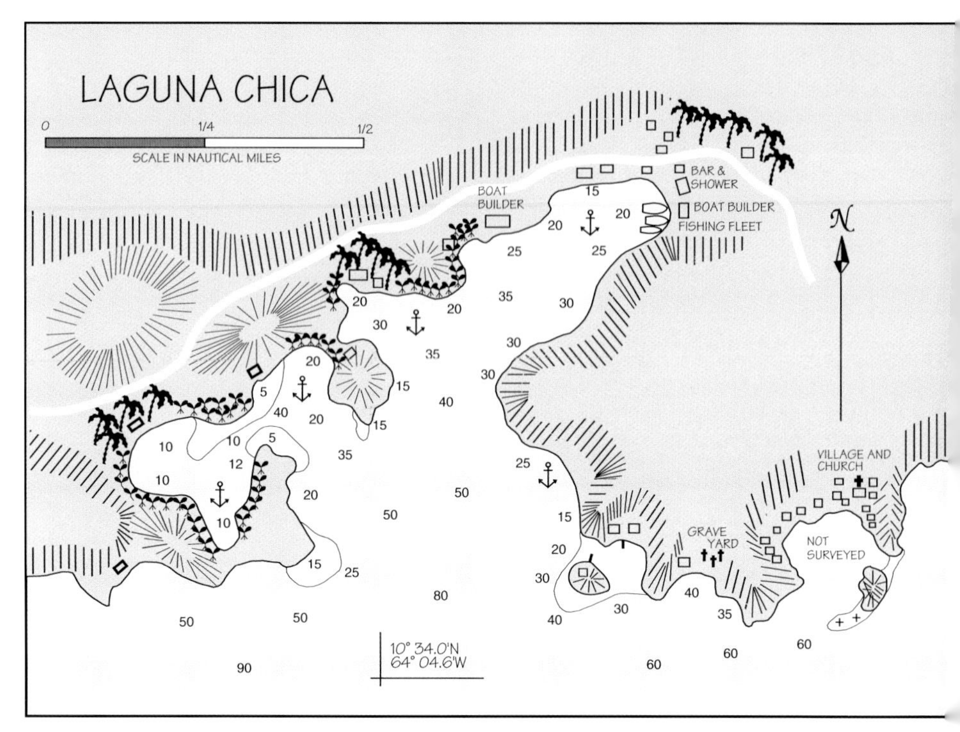

lagoon in the western corner of the bay. Enter carefully in good light as there are shoals on both sides. There is a perfect place to anchor in the southern corner of the bay where you can look across the low sand spit to the gulf outside. Turning room is very tight in here, so if a following wind is blowing hard, you may want to drop hook while you are still moving and let the anchor swing the boat round.

PUERTO REAL

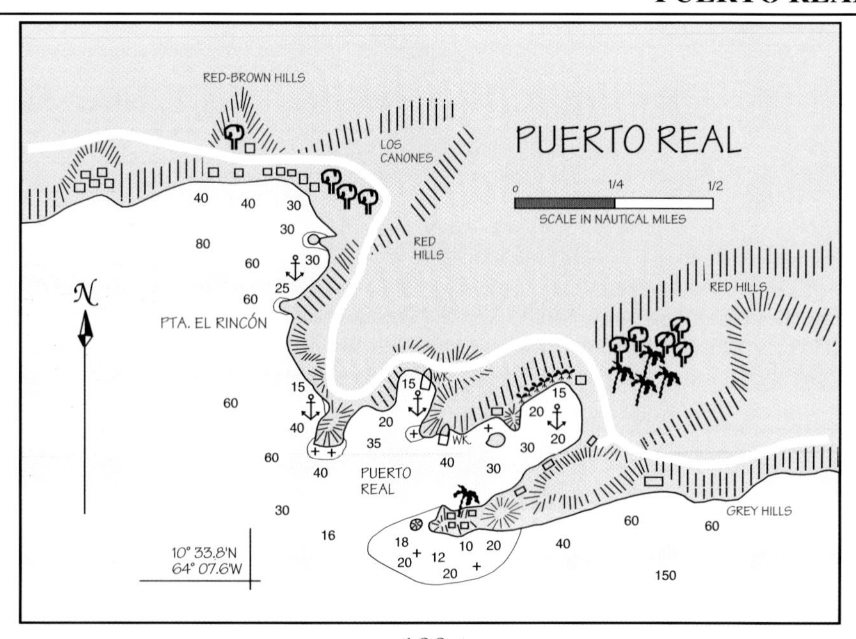

You can find good anchorage off Los Cañónes or Puerto Real. Of the two, Puerto Real is far more scenic, and the most appealing anchorage is right up in the eastern corner. This is a delightful and very protected anchorage. Over the bow the green valley makes a pleasing contrast with the red hills and off the stern the little fishing village built out on the point is picturesque. There is easy access to the beach for walking ashore.

When entering Puerto Real give good clearance to the eastern headland as a rocky shoal extends almost half a mile out. The depths over this shoal are mainly 10-16 feet, but there are shallower spots. (See our aerial photo.)

.aguna Grande

FROM CUMANÁ TO PUNTA PARGO

(See also our previous sketch chart of the ;olfo de Cariaco which includes the 'enínsula de Araya.)

For those heading east to Trinidad, fol- owing the coast along Península de Araya nd Paria is the easiest and shortest way to o. For those sailing to the Windwards this ; considered the soft option, though it is robably a bit faster to motor sail directly) the Windwards from Margarita.

The prevailing wind in this area is east- rly; somewhat north of east from Cumaná) Chacopata then northeasterly to south- asterly from Chacopata to Punta Pargo. The winds often calm down after nightfall and stay light till mid-morning. There is not usually much current within a mile or two of land. Farther out the prevailing current is west setting. Winds are typically calmer in the summer and stronger in the winter.

There are exceptions to this rule and those that attract the demons of adverse winds and seas can occasionally fight a knot of current close to the coast and the winds blowing hard all night.

From Araya to Chacopata there is a degree of protection from ocean swells

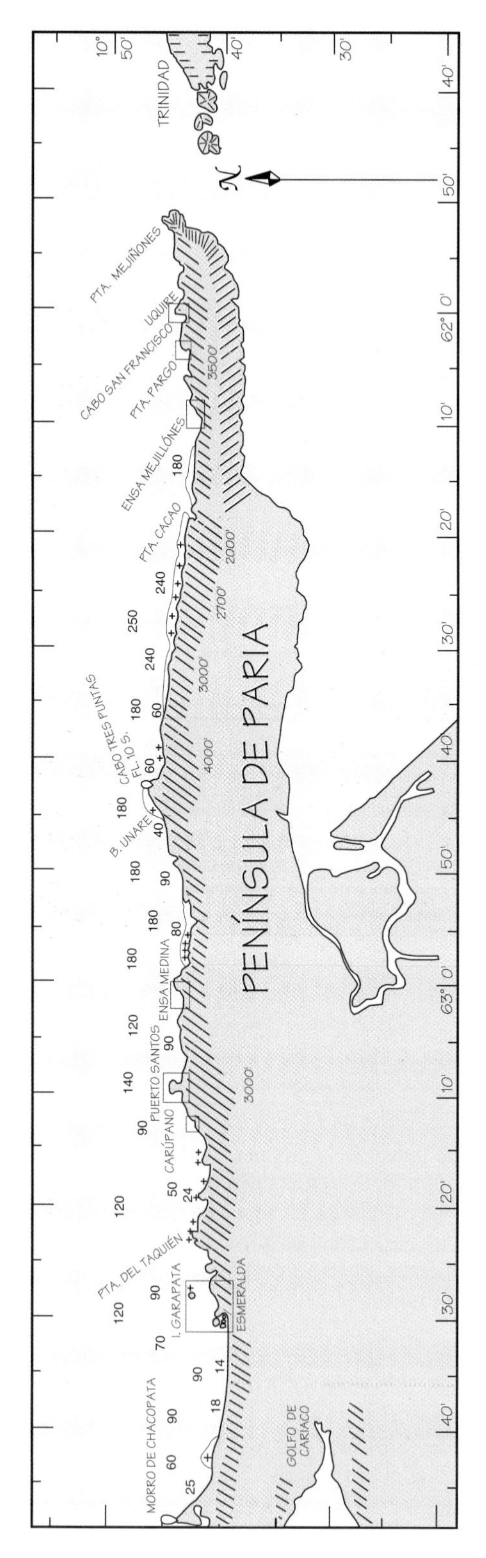

because of Margarita, Coche and Cubagua. The trip from Chacopata to Punta Pargo is in open ocean. This part of the coast can be placid or it can be stirred up and rough.

Those heading east can break the trip into manageably short runs. If you get up at first light you can motor until the wind starts blowing hard, then beat or motor sail the rest of the way to the next anchorage.

There is just one long stretch between Puerto Santos (or Ensenada Medina) and the next reliable harbor which is Punta Pargo. This is 50-60 miles depending on where you start and it is probably best done as an overnight trip.

The westward passage along these shores is no problem, though if winds are light the sailing will be improved by taking a swing out to Testigos to get the wind on the quarter.

WEST COAST OF PENÍNSULA DE ARAYA

The west coast of the Península de Araya is an appealing area of light sand beaches soft red-brown cliffs and dry scrubby plants. It is well known for its salt produc tion from the naturally occurring salt flats At peak production the salt factory ca produce 120,000 tons of salt a year.

In the old days, when salt was the onl means of preserving many foods, Aray was an especially important possessior The Spanish who owned it became in creasingly frustrated because the Dutc kept sneaking in on them and stealin boatloads of salt. In response they built th largest fort in Venezuela, the Castillo d Santiago de Araya. It was started in 161 and completed in 1665. It held a comple ment of 300 men and 45 cannons. Thi effectively stopped the pilfering and ev erything went well until 1726 when hurricane passed by and winds and wave not only damaged the fort but rendered th salt ponds useless and the fort unnece sary. The Spanish didn't fancy leaving there for someone else, so they blew a larg part of it up. The salt lagoon later reforme and is still productive. This is an are where several thefts have been reported.

Navigation

If approaching from the east, give Punta Arenas a wide berth as a shoal extends southeastwards about two thirds of a mile.

There are four good places to anchor along this coast. All of them offer wide areas in which to anchor and they are fine for a one night stop. For longer stays they suffer the disadvantage of being on a very busy seaway of ferries and fishing boats. Always leave a good light on at night and be prepared to rock with the wash of passing craft.

The southernmost anchorage is just west of Punta Arenas where there is an attractive, inhabited beach. About two miles up the coast there is another long and mainly deserted beach with a perfect anchoring shelf. Perhaps the most interesting spot is between Punta Barrigón and the old fort. There is a long stretch of beach here with little cliffs and you can choose your spot. This also positions you to explore the old fort ruins. The other anchorage is off the town of Araya itself which is perfect for those who like to check out the local bars. You can also anchor much further north.

When you leave Araya to head east (or if you are approaching from that direction) beware of the shoal that extends a couple of miles northwest of Punta de Araya. A buoy that marks the extent of the shoal is sometimes there, sometimes missing. On our

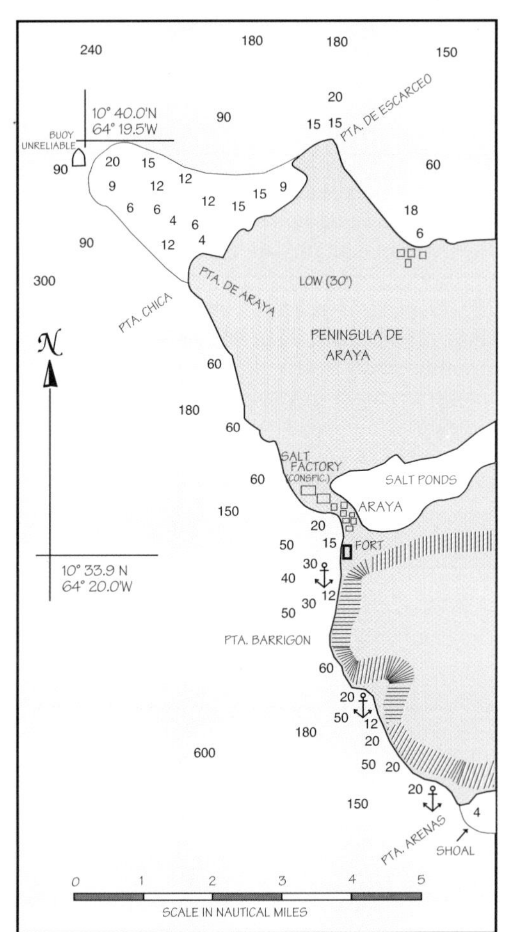

sketch chart we have given GPS coordinates which might be helpful. Otherwise, just give a good wide berth. The water is deep outside it, so if you have an echo sounder with an alarm and set it on 40 feet, it should give you enough warning.

Just off the north coast of the Península de Araya are three rocks called Islotes La Tuna. (See our Golfo de Cariaco chart which includes the western end of Península de Araya.) These are too small to give any shelter and you need to treat them with caution as submerged rocks extend for several hundred yards around them. There is plenty of room and water to pass midway between the two northern ones.

The next anchorages eastwards are Isla Lobos and Isla Caribe. Some people heading east prefer to visit El Saco in Coche which we dealt with in an earlier chapter.

ISLA LOBOS

Isla Lobos are two small hilly islands which are joined by a rocky shallow. This breaks up the sea and gives good protection. The islands have some ruins on them but today the main inhabitants are hundreds of cormorants who line up in ranks on the flat parts of the shore like a small, dark, avian army. There is even a thimble-sized beach. In all a great spot for a night or two.

Approach from the west and anchor between the two islands. To get the best protection from the seas, edge up as close as you dare to the rocks.

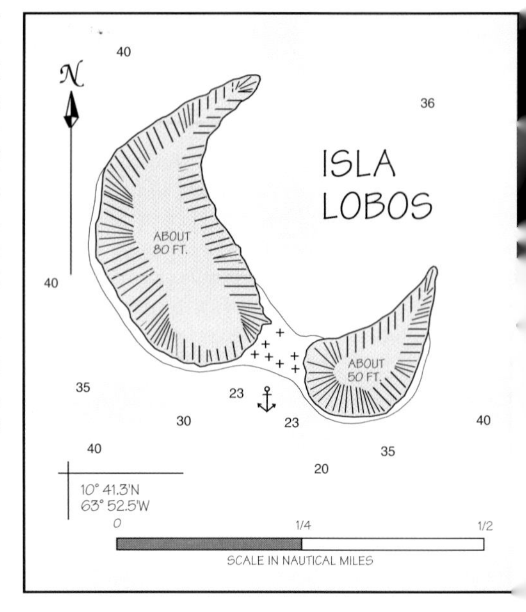

ISLA CARIBE

Isla Caribe also makes a pleasant overnight stop. It has a fair beach with a couple of fishermen's huts. Approach the island from the west or northwest and anchor off the beach in about 16 feet of water.

Do not attempt to pass round the south side of Isla Caribe, between it and th mainland. A long shallow bank extend from the mainland to the eastern end c Isla Caribe. This is marked as mainly 9-1 feet on the charts but many places seer much shallower. A good place to avoid.

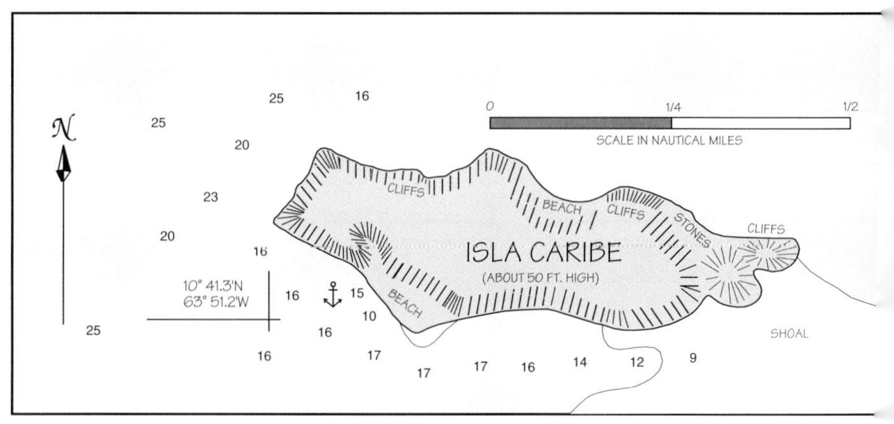

PUNTA ESMERALDA

Just 22 miles from Isla Caribe, Esmeralda makes a very easy step to the east. The island is high (325 feet) as is the headland off which it lies. Farther south are three smaller islands. Unlit oyster rafts are often anchored in this area. Their positions vary, so keep a good watch. The bottom shelves gradually from 12 feet into the shallows. The water is generally murky and the bottom sticky mud. Occasionally enough swell enters the bay to create a bit of a roll. Despite the cloudy water the anchorage is scenic and for those who wish to explore ashore there is a poor but picturesque fishing village. Tie your dinghy to the stone wall to the north of the village. Elsewhere thick, gooey, black silt lies close to shore.

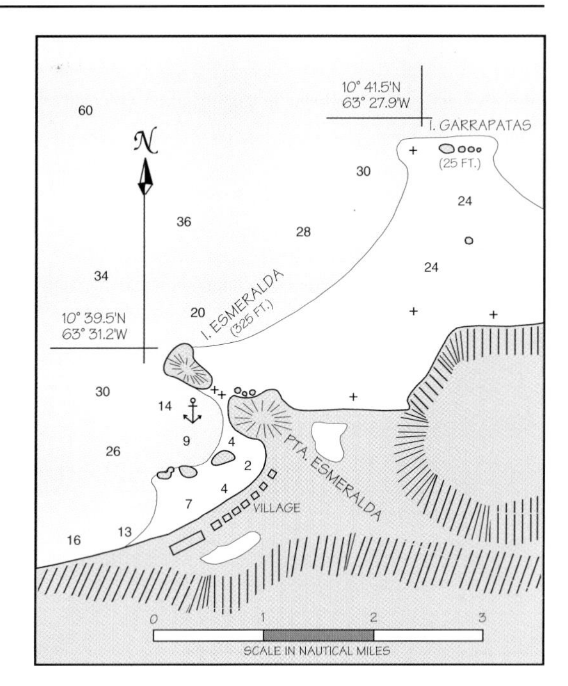

CARÚPANO

(15 miles from Esmeralda)

The coastline from Esmeralda to ;arúpano is indented and interesting with umerous rocks. It is also poorly charted, nd the water is often too murky to be eadable. In completely calm conditions vhen the water is clear, this is a great area or those who want to explore uncharted vaters off the beaten track. For anyone lse, it is best to give this coast a wide erth. Sail outside Islas Garrapatas and ;ive a good clearance to Punta del Taquién nd all its attendant rocks. If you look at ur sketch chart of Carúpano, you will otice that there are several frightening hoals dotted up to a mile out to sea west of ne town. To avoid these stay over a mile ffshore (head more for Puerto Santos ian Carúpano) until the conspicuous new partment blocks to the east of the town ear 45° mangnetic. You can then head oward these buildings. Lights around arúpano are unreliable.

As you approach from the west, the city is hidden away. The first thing you see is a huge block of apartment buildings that lies just to the east of the harbor wall. The finished ones are painted white and the rest are still concrete grey. Shortly afterwards more apartment buildings come into sight. These are colored and they are a couple of miles to the west of Carúpano.

Carúpano Harbor is small and somewhat exposed to the swells. You can tuck in between the harbor walls or anchor in the bigger bay inside them both. When you have finished in town there is a pleasant anchorage which is just as protected as Carúpano inside Punta Hernán Vásquez. Puerto Santos is a much better anchorage, fuel and water are more easily available and it is only a few miles farther up the coast. Some people prefer to leave their boats in Puerto Santos and take a por puesto back to Carúpano.

Regulations

Carúpano is a port of clearance for entering or leaving the country. If you need to clear in or out you should anchor your yacht in town. Customs and immigration are quite close to the head of the dock, the port captain is farther west along the waterfront near the bus station.

Services

Water is available on the inner side of the harbor wall, but diesel has to be trucked in. Telephone calls can be made from CANTV.

Ashore

Carúpano is attractive and green with public squares and parks. There is a pleasant, though as yet uncompleted, walk all along the water front. CADA is good enough for a major provisioning and near the local market there are several wholesale stores. Most are willing to deliver to the docks.

Just to the left of customs you will find a fisherman's shop with some marine hardware and a pleasant little seafood restaurant ($D).

We are told that Carúpano has a spectacular carnival, though small compared to Trinidad. It attracts People from all over Venezuela.

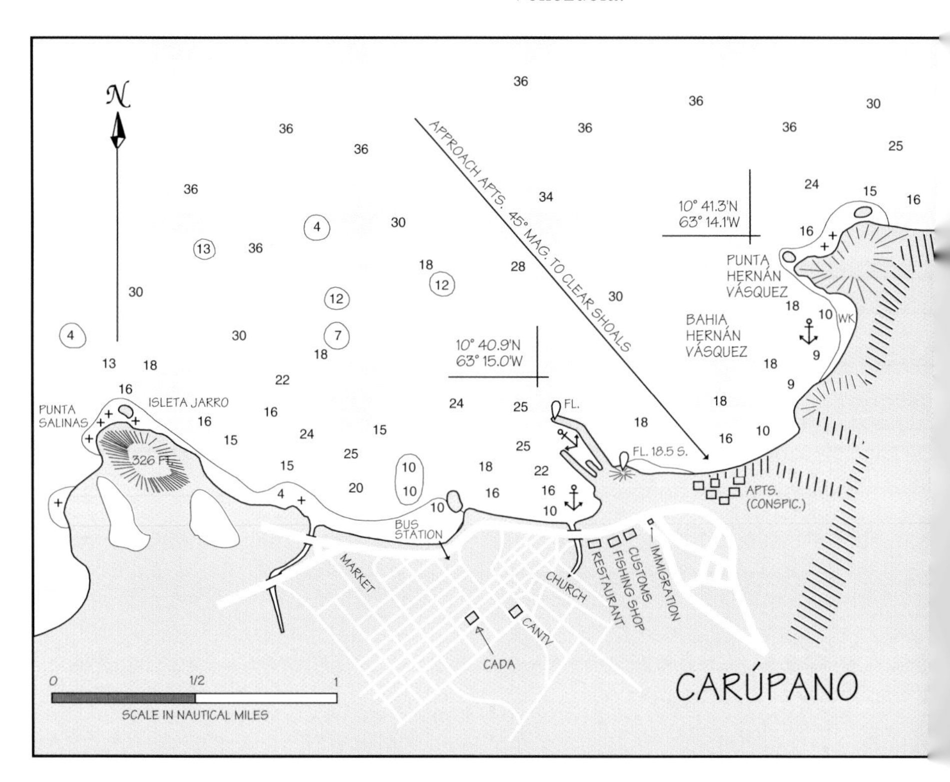

PUERTO SANTOS

Puerto Santos is the best protected harbor between Esmeralda and Punta Pargo. The bay is picturesque, though the water frequently has brown scum across the surface, possibly effluent from the fishing industry. A little diesel fuel and engine o are usually added to this. All in all, not th best place to give granny her first swin ming lesson. The cleanest and most plea ant anchorage is tucked up close to th island, in the northern part of the bay.

Services

Water and fuel are available at the fuel dock. There is a good 12 feet of water at the head of the dock and about nine feet of water a third of the way down. It is easy to get water and fuel in jerry jugs here. Bringing the yacht in presents a problem because the dock is one mass of fishing boats most of the time. An incoming swell does not help. Water comes out of a one inch water pipe and for alongside filling you need your own hose and connection. Check it out by dinghy first, then come in and join the fray. Block ice is available from the fish factory.

Ashore

There are a few bars and small shops where you will find essentials. Otherwise, Carúpano is easily reached by por puesto. There is a pleasant walk over on the windward beach.

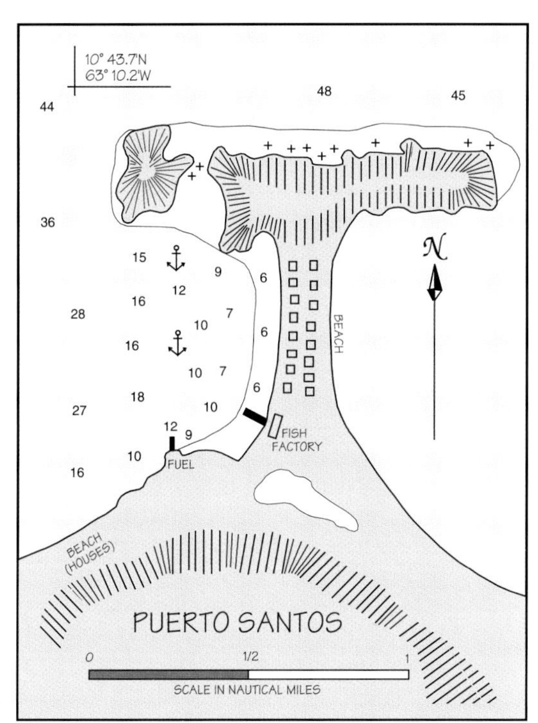

ENSENADA MEDINA

There are no really well protected nchorages between Puerto Santos nd Punta Pargo. This is best done by notor-sailing overnight. Still, if you ave spent the night in Puerto Santos nd have a whole day to use before eading out, consider heading nine niles east to Ensenada Medina. It has gorgeous beach and you can take nteresting walks. However, it is not ll that well protected and frequently oo rolly for comfortable overighting. If you are lucky enough to et it in a calm mood you could spend day or two here.

The best anchorage is tucked right p in the northern part of the bay in the e of Punta Medina and its small off-ing island. You can use bow and ern anchors to cut the swell.

There is small hotel facility on the outh end of the beach. A snack bar pens on weekends and holidays and henever there are enough people

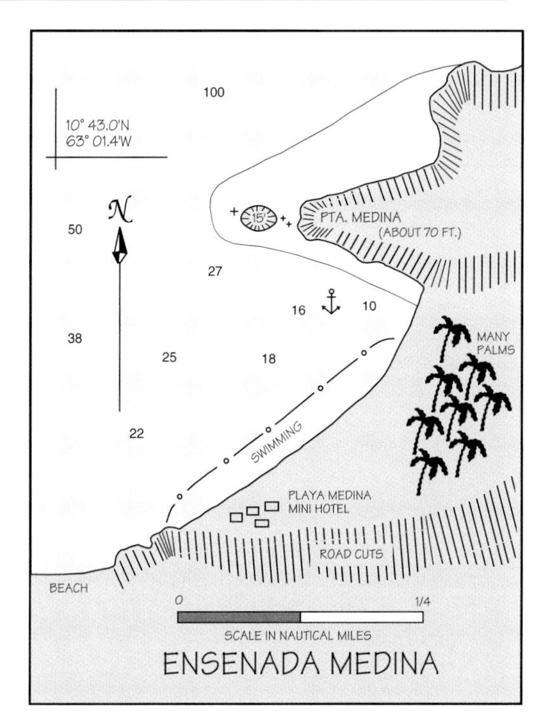

around. We had one report they were no longer serving yachtspeople, but check it out for yourself. If you do get here in a period of calms, talk to the management about their inland hotel in a wild ranching area. You could visit it and return in a day.

ENSENADA MEJILLÓNES TO UQUIRE

Some people prefer this part of Venezuela over all others. Certainly, you could not wish for wilder terrain farther away from civilization. Tall mountains of rainforest rise abruptly from the sea. Fast mountain rivers create pools and waterfalls. Ashore you are in the wild. There are monkeys, parrots and jungle cats. But before you rush up in shorts and flip-flops, remember there are also poisonous snakes and giant centipedes among the lesser biting bugs.

While this area can be as calm as a lake, all too often there are huge sloppy swells along the coast which make the anchorages rolly, though they are normally tenable. Since you never know when a swell may arrive, it makes sense to anchor a few hundred feet offshore rather than go stern to the rocks.

The overnight run from Puerto Santos or Ensenada Medina to Ensenada de Mejillónes, Punta Pargo or Cabo San Francisco is not usually too bad, though you can get an uncomfortable swell. There are quite a few villages with lights as far as Cabo Tres Puntas, after which it is black. The Cabo tres Puntas light sometimes works.

For those without a GPS the problem at daylight is to know where you are. Ensenada Mejillónes makes a good landmark. Five distinctive looking rocks lie in line out to sea from the eastern end of this bay. Península de Paria is at its narrowest point here, and in the middle of the bay the mountains are a little lower than most of the rest of the coast.

ENSENADA DE MEJILLÓNES

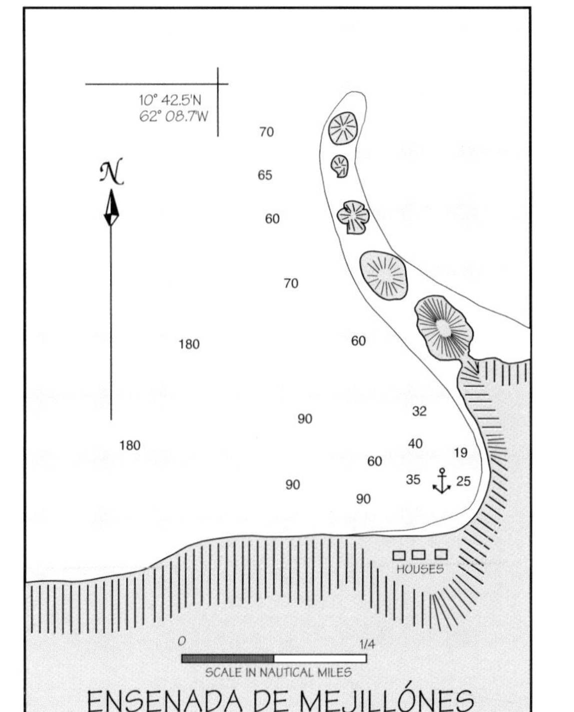

You can find a passable anchorage tucked right up in the eastern corner of Ensenada de Mejillónes where you get some protection both from the head land and the off lying islands. There is a large anchoring shelf with 19-40 feet on it. Bow and stern anchoring is advisable with your bow into the swells.

Ashore there are a few houses and lots of wild terrain to explore.

PUNTA PARGO

Punta Pargo is five miles from Ensenada Mejillónes. Once you have passed Ensenada Mejillónes you can follow the coast a few hundred yards offshore. About two miles farther on you will notice a large rock with a hole right through it. Punta Pargo is inside the next major headland you see from this rock.

Punta Pargo and the next door bay, San Francisco, are the two best protected bays along this coast. Punta Pargo is the more open of the two with a delightful palm-backed beach and fair sized village. Anchor right in the east of the bay under the headland. I would advise bow and stern anchoring away from the rocky shore with your stern a couple of hundred feet out, in case a swell comes up.

It is a good idea to introduce yourself to the villagers in whose territory you are anchoring. They are generally helpful and friendly and will direct you to the best hikes. Follow the river for some great natural swimming pools.

Snorkeling and dinghy exploration are outstanding all along the eastern shore. Just inside the small island with a hole through it is a long tunnel that goes way back into the cliff. There are several other intriguing holes and little beaches tucked in the rocks.

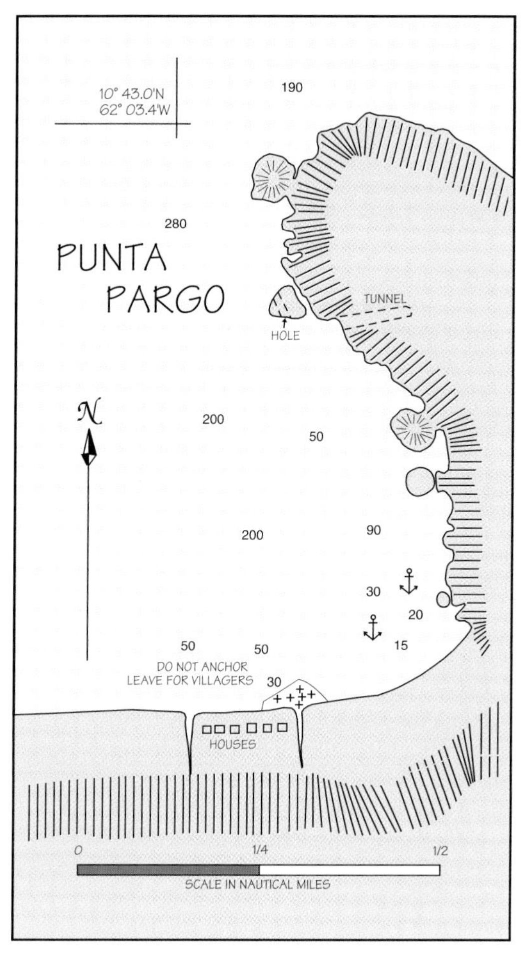

Approaching Punta Pargo from the west

Cabo San Francisco is the most dramatic anchorage along this coast. Towering jungly mountains drop straight into the sea. Red splashes from bright tropical flowers peek through the green. Clouds hang off the land, rising like steam. There are two small fishing shacks, one on a stony beach and the other hidden up a hill. Fishermen sometimes use this bay as base. There is a large anchoring shelf in the southeast corner of the bay with depths of 15 to 34 feet. Anchoring bow and stern with your bow to the swells is advised.

Ashore there are just a few small trails to fishing lookouts but the adventurous can explore up the river.

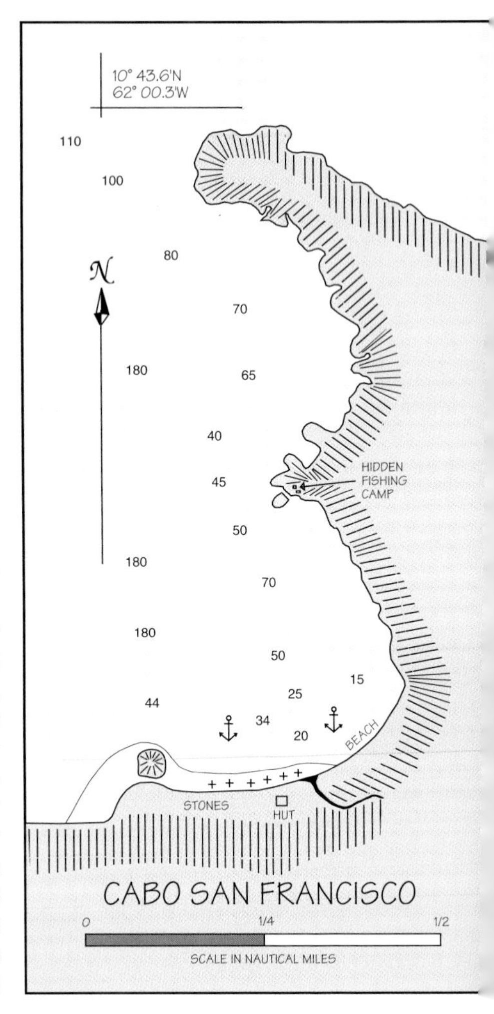

UQUIRE

Uquire (Providencia on some charts) is one bay after Cabo San Francisco. It makes a good landmark as there is a distinctive island that looks like three huge boulders leaning into each other on the eastern headland. So if you pass this bay from the west when looking for Punta Pargo or San Francisco you know you have come too far. There is also a beach and sizeable village which boasts lamp posts. The water is very deep in the bay, making anchoring tricky, but some yachts like to visit Uquire because you can sometimes get cold beers and fuel.

PASSAGES TO TRINIDAD AND GRENADA

From Cabo San Francisco to Trinidad is only 25 miles and easily accomplished in a day's sail.

From Punta Pargo to Prickly Bay in Grenada is about 80 miles and the course is about 13° true or 26° magnetic. Remember to allow for current. The light flashing every ten seconds on Trinidad's Chacachacare Island shows up very well as does Grenada's Point Saline (2+1 every 20 second) light with its 18-mile range. A you get closer to Grenada you will see tw quick flashing lights, one on the end o Point Saline and the other on Glove Island. It is impossible to predict the win direction from observations alon Venezuela's coast. The wind ofte changes after the first 10 to 20 miles. It ca be a wonderful trip with sheets eased in southeasterly wind or it can be a re struggle to windward in a northeaster. If you can lay Grenada easily do not be tempted to ease off too soon as the current is often strongest just south of Grenada. Plan to arrive in daylight so you can avoid the Porpoises Rocks. If you have to come in at night, then entering in St. George's is easier.

BUEN VIAJE!

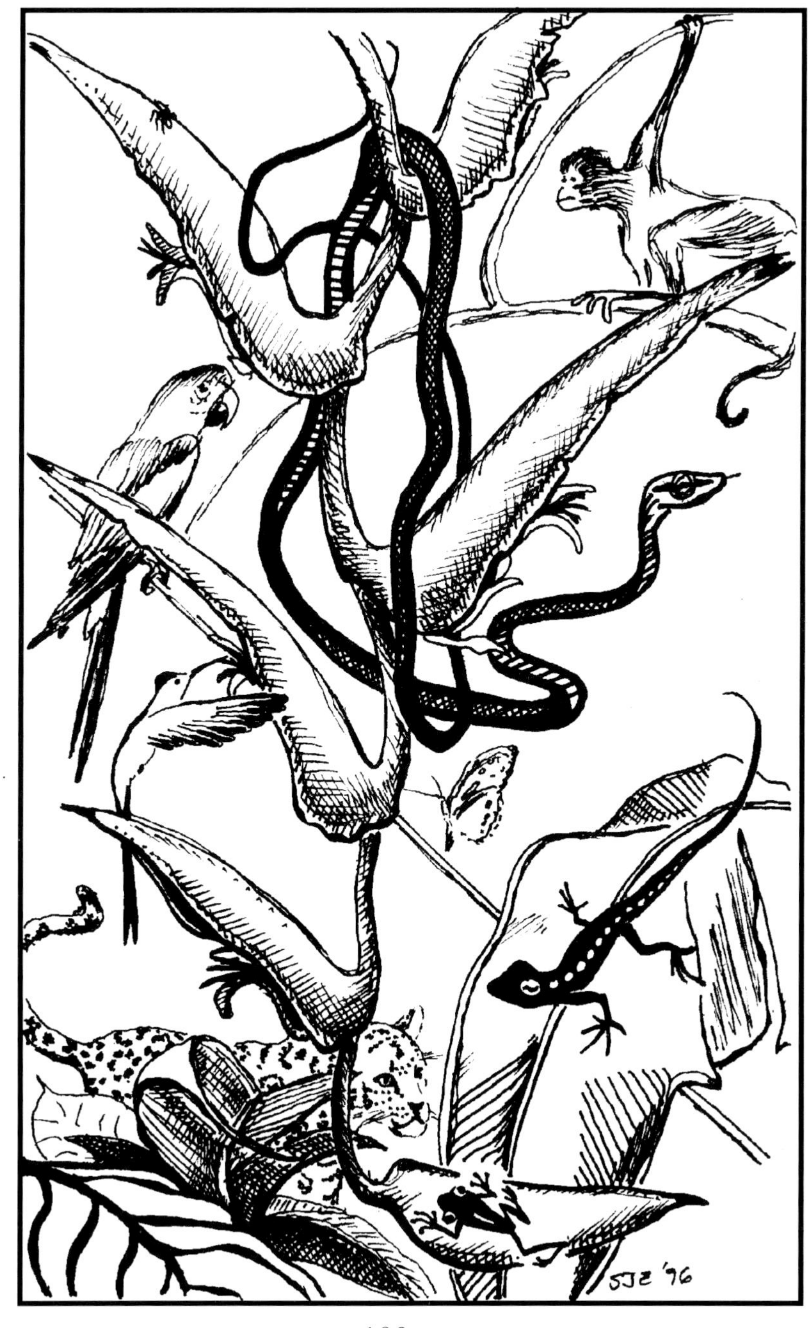

Regulations

You need to clear with customs when you arrive in Bonaire. See "Regulations" under Kralendijk.

The whole of Bonaire is a marine park and anchoring is limited to the shallow strip of water in Kralendijk between North Pier and the marina. You can also pick up a yacht mooring here. Dive moorings have been put all around Klein Bonaire and there are also many along the coast. These are primarily for dive boats, but yachts up to 38 feet may use them for up to two hours. Yachts must be fastened to the buoys with a long line or they will endanger the mooring. There are also three dive moorings for larger yachts, up to 55 feet. You have to call the park officials to get permission to use them. Everything on the reef is protected, and spearguns are not allowed. If you have spearguns on board you have to surrender them to customs for the duration of your stay. Divers must buy a valid admission ticket to the park (currently $10US). To get this, you must listen to a short orientation on diving in the park. Further details are given under water sports.

Holidays

New Year's Day
Carnival Monday (last Monday before Ash Wednesday)
Good Friday
Easter Monday
April 30th (Queens birthday and Rincon's day)
May 1st (Labor Day)
Ascension Day
September 6th (Bonaire Day)
Annual Sailing regatta, sometime in mid October
December 25th (Christmas day)
December 26th

Shopping hours

Shopping hours are 0800-1200 and 1400-1800. About half the stores close Saturday afternoon and nearly everything is closed Sundays and holidays. Banks are normally open weekdays from 0800 to 1530.

Local Radio

Trans World Radio, on about 800 kHz AM is a powerful religious station which has news on the hour daily and marine forecasts are given at 20 minutes past the hour. For other local news and views, try Radio Netherlands on 6020, 6165, 15135 or 11720 kHz, or Ritmo on FM97.1. Try also Mega Super FM at 101.1. Good music and daily news at noon.

Telephones

The telephone office is in town and it is open daily, including Sundays from 0700 to 2325. You can get a USA direct operator by picking up the phone in booth #1. (If this doesn't work, ask at the desk.) You can make and pay for calls at the desk or buy phone cards for use in any public phone. There is also a USA direct phone at the airport. If calling into Bonaire, the code is 5997.

Currency

The Netherlands Antilles' florin is the local currency. It fluctuates with the US dollar. At last count it was 1.78 NAf to 1 US.

Transport

There is a large airport and KLM flies direct to Europe. ALM and Air Aruba fly to the USA and Avensa flies to Venezuela.

Inexpensive minibuses run between

Kralendijk, Rincon and other inhabited areas. The buses are private and set their own schedules, so before you go make sure you can get back the same day. The minibuses usually wait outside Cultimara Supermarket.

Taxis are sometimes available at the town stand (T:5330). Otherwise you have to call the airport (T:8100). Typical taxi rates in $US are:

Kralendijk to Marina	*5*
Supermarket to Marina	*6*
Kralendijk to Plaza Resort	*6*
Kralendijk to Lac Bay	*15*
Northern tour	*30*
Southern tour	*30*

Each tour is about 2 hours and taxis take a maximum of 4 people.

Tours are also available through many hotels.

You can rent a car and use your own license. It is hard to get lost. Drive on the right.

Bonaire is a charming, quiet and clean island with a population of around 14,000. The main town is attractive, with ochre walls and red roofs. It comes with a wonderful selection of waterfront restaurants. This alone would rate it as a great port to visit, but when you throw in the attraction of some of the Caribbean's clearest and best diving, you have an unbeatable combination.

Bonaire is part of the Dutch Caribbean with its sister islands, Curacao and Aruba, a little to the west. Other islands under Dutch influence include Saint Maarten, Saba and Statia in the what we call the Leeward Islands. But to the Dutch who had to try to sail from Bonaire to Saint Maarten, those northern islands were very much to Windward and they called Bonaire, Curacao and Aruba the Leewards.

Bonaire's two main industries are salt and tourism. The attractions for tourists are scuba diving, windsurfing and bird watching (about 200 species have been sighted). The windsurfing takes place on a large lagoon that is open to strong winds but protected from high seas. Those that want waves can sail outside the lagoon. Much of the island is a nature preserve to help conserve these attractions.

The Bonaire regatta is held sometime early October and runs for a week. It is the major Bonaire yachting event. There are races for yachts, catamarans, windsurfers, sunfish, lasers and local fishing boats. For information call: T:5555, F:5576.

Navigation

Navigation is very straightforward. If you are approaching from the east, note that the high land is in the north. The southern part of the island barely peeps above sea level, so you don't see it till you are within a few miles. The large framework elevator at the saltworks usually shows before the 70-foot high lighthouse at the south end.

Sailing to Kralendijk along the coast from the south is very pleasant, with lots of wind and no sea.

It is deep all around the island, often dropping to a couple of hundred feet close to shore and then to over a thousand. In many places there is a narrow coastal ledge of shallow water up to 300 feet wide.

Kralendijk is the capital of Bonaire and is the only place yachts are allowed to anchor. The permitted area is on a ledge between North Pier and the marina. This ledge is 10-16 feet deep and ample enough to anchor on, though holding is variable with a thin layer of sand over a bank of hard dead coral. The Marine park has placed some 40 moorings in this area which you are free to use (no charge at the moment). You have to tie to the mooring with your own line (do not use chain) and you should use at least 30 feet of line to give the mooring enough scope. You can also anchor. If you have a choice of anchors, this is a place where a plough is more likely to hold than a Danforth-style anchor. You need to put down two anchors and make sure they are well set. You cannot anchor too close to shore as the currents sweep you north and south rather than holding you constantly to the west. Do not anchor in front of the Club Nautico Dock, keep the access free. The park would prefer it if you did not drop an anchor over the ledge into the deep water, as they are hoping that coral will reestablish itself there.

There are two good marinas which usually have space: Harbour Village Marina is about 15 feet deep. Call them on VHF:17. Plaza Resort Marina can handle yachts up to 7.5 foot draft on a high tide, call them on VHF:18.

About four times a year the wind comes out of the southwest and blows hard. The results have occasionally been disastrous, with many boats landing on shore and some being wrecked. This most often happens during the hurricane season, but has been known to happen as early as May. Often people try to get out, but get anchor ropes fouled in their propellers.

Since the last bad southwesterly, the park tries to get warnings from Curacao on the approach of such a wind. When they do, they attempt to let everyone know. The first people they are likely to tell are the dive operators, so if you see all the dive boats running for shelter it is time to d something. Go into one of the marinas. I that is not possible you could stand to se for a few hours till it is all over. Had yo been planning to head east, this might b an excellent opportunity to gain a fe miles.

Regulation

Formalities are simple and straightfor ward. First get yourself anchored or pic up a mooring or go to a marina. Check firs with customs then with immigration When you clear in make sure custom gives you the marine park informatio which includes regulations and a map o all the dive sites. Customs is in a gree

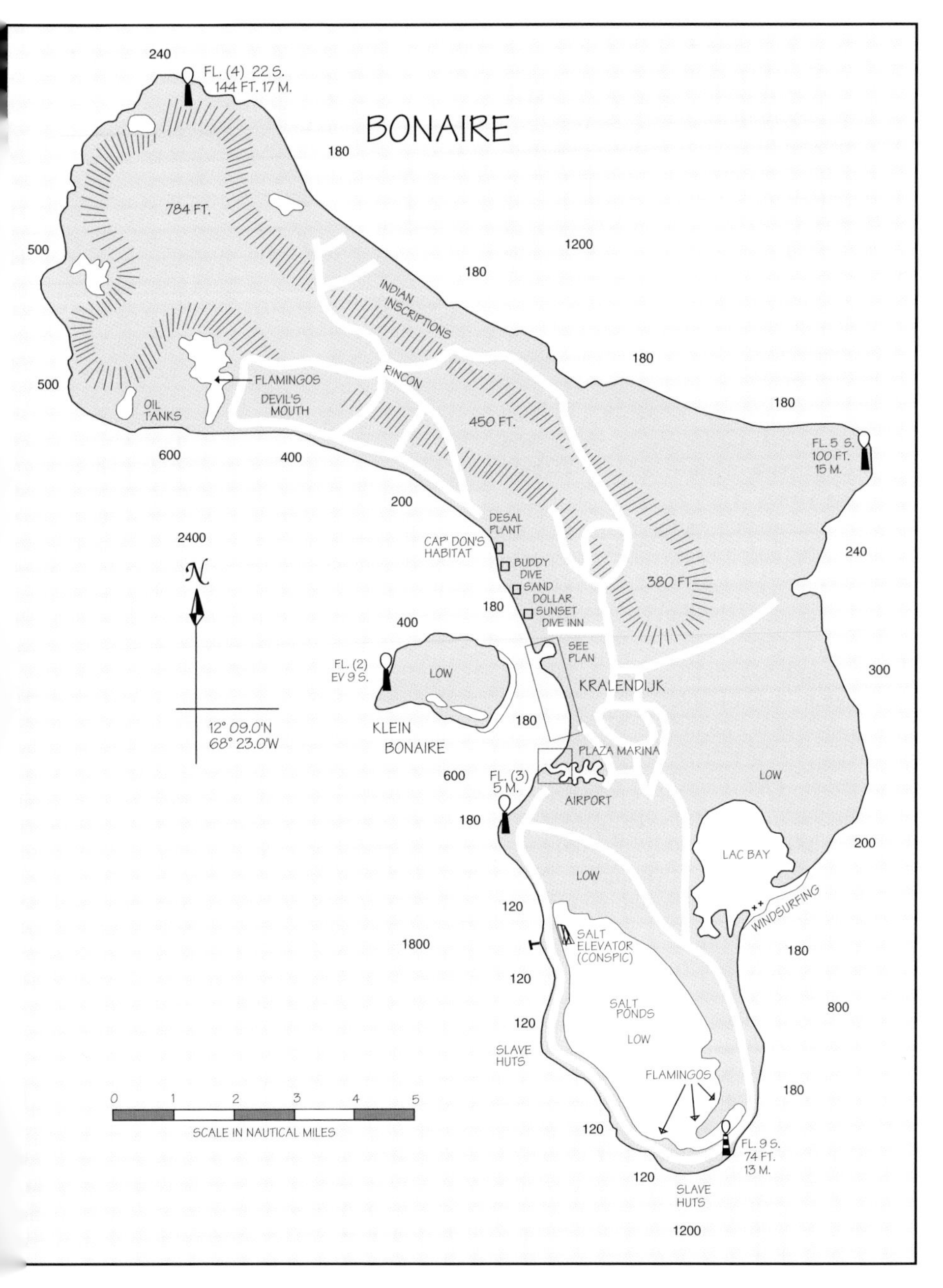

BONAIRE
FL. (4) 22 S.
144 FT. 17 M.
240
180
784 FT.
500
500
1200
180
INDIAN INSCRIPTIONS
RINCON
FLAMINGOS
DEVIL'S MOUTH
OIL TANKS
450 FT.
180
180
FL. 5 S.
100 FT.
15 M.
600
400
200
2400
DESAL PLANT
CAP' DON'S HABITAT
BUDDY DIVE
SAND DOLLAR
SUNSET DIVE INN
180
400
380 FT.
240
SEE PLAN
FL. (2)
EV 9 S.
LOW
KRALENDIJK
300
KLEIN BONAIRE
180
12° 09.0'N
68° 23.0'W
PLAZA MARINA
600
FL. (3)
5 M.
AIRPORT
LOW
180
LAC BAY
200
LOW
120
WINDSURFING
SALT ELEVATOR (CONSPIC)
1800
180
120
SALT PONDS
800
120
LOW
SLAVE HUTS
FLAMINGOS
180
SCALE IN NAUTICAL MILES
120
FL. 9 S.
74 FT.
13 M.
120
SLAVE HUTS
1200

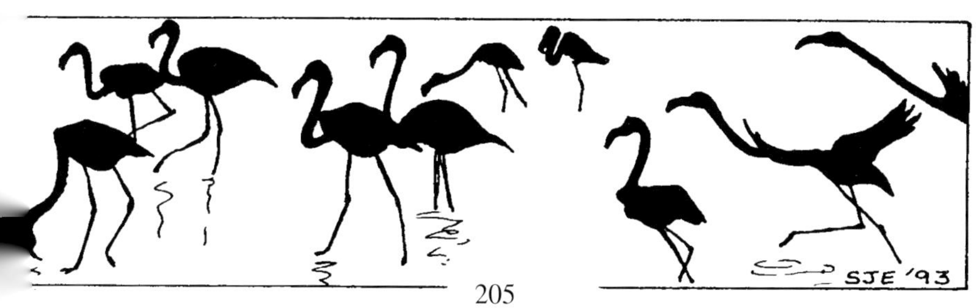
SJE '93

waterfront building, Immigration is at the police station.

You are not allowed to leave your yacht unattended in the anchorage while you go abroad. You can arrange to do so with either of the marinas. You have to make arrangements with both the marina and customs. Ask for details in the marinas.

Services

You can take on fuel at the Harbour Village Marina. You can get water in both marinas.

Harbour Village Marina (T:7419 F:5028, VHF:17, cc:V) is small and peaceful, part of the Harbour Village Marina Hotel. They have 90 slips and can accommodate yachts up to 180 feet, maximum draft 14 feet. They have water and electricity on the dock (220/120 volt, 50 cycle). The fuel dock sells both diesel and gasoline. There are showers, toilets and a laundry and ice can be arranged. They offer telephone, fax and mail or courier receiving services and will help you get gas, arrange rental cars and most other things you may need.

The marina office is open weekdays 0800-1200 and 1300 to 1700, Saturdays from 0900-1500 and Sundays 0900-1300. When they are closed, you can go to the hotel front desk.

There is a new chandlery in the marina offering everything from nuts and bolts to watermakers, refrigerators and inverters. They can bring in anything you need that is not in stock.

Plaza Resort Marina has 30 slips with a maximum draft of 7 feet (7.5 feet at high tide) and can take yachts up to 170 feet long. They plan to expand to 70 slips and be dredging the marina to 15 feet (call for the latest information). Contact them on VHF:18 T:2500, F: 7133. If you are over 7 foot draft call for tide information. They are also willing to come out and pilot you in. The docks have water and electricity (110/220V, 50 cycle) and some slips have cable TV. There are showers and toilets. Repairs and maintenance can be arranged. They have full communications including

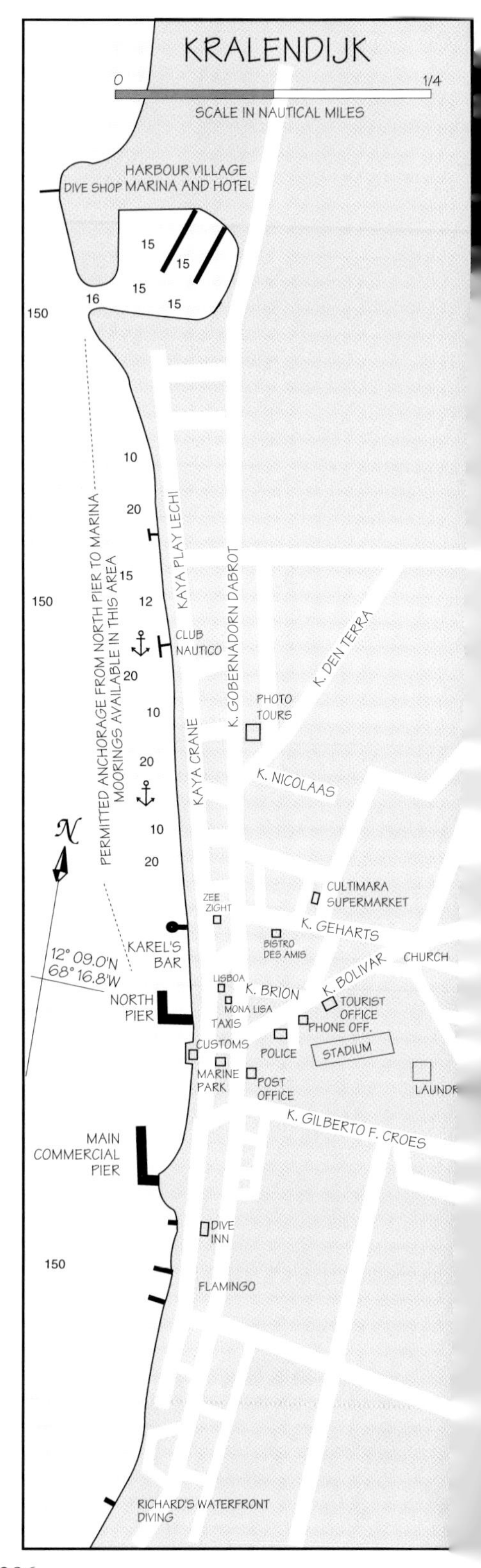

Fedex courier service. All the facilities of the 5-star hotel are open to marina guests, room service is available on your boat and all services can be put on one account. Car rentals can be arranged. They are open seven days a week.

Club Nautico is less than half a mile north of Karel's Bar. They have 10 slips and a maximum draft of 10 feet. Water and electricity are available. Surge does affect these docks which are untenable in the case of wind reversal. Use nylon docking lines. Club Nautico stand by on VHF:68, T:5800.

Marlis Sail and Canvas Shop (T:7741) is on Kaya Gobernor Debrot one block from the fishermen's Pier. Marlis will mend your sail, make you new cushions, or replace that rotting bimini. She also makes designer bags and other items. When she is not sewing or gardening, she is tending to the sick birds of the island which makes the yard an interesting place to visit.

Caribbean Laundry Services (T:5220) is near the stadium (see our town map). Here they have a big laundrette operation with dryers. You can do it yourself or they will do it for you. They are open weekdays from 0800-1800 and Saturday from 0800-1700.

Boto Blanco Marine Services is run by John Merrick (T:5050, F:4309, VHF:65 USA). John is the authorized Yamaha dealer, and duty free prices are available to yachts in transit. He also services engines.

Caribbean Fasteners (T:5560) at Kaya Noord Nikiboko not only have an excellent supply of stainless nuts, bolts and screws but they also carry some good tools. Another hardware store worth a visit is General Store Bonaire.

If you need a marine surveyor contact Robert St. Jago at the harbor masters office (VHF:11 or 16).

There are garbage dumpsters near Karel's dinghy dock and Hotshot Scooter and bike rentals may be found nearby.

Ashore

Pay an early visit to the tourist office to get the latest visitors' newsletter which will tell you about free slide shows and other entertainment. It also contains good island and town maps. There are several stores for developing film.

A good reason to come to Bonaire is to provision at the Cultimara Supermarket (T:8278). It is large, modern, clean and well stocked with an excellent selection of fresh produce, meats, seafood and staples. It is open weekdays 0800-1300 and 1400-1830 and Saturdays from 0800 to 1830. They also sell ice. You can alternatively provision through Gonsales Wholesale (T:8468) on #29 Kaya Industria. They deliver aboard.

Karel's Bar, beside having the most convenient town dinghy dock, is a great place

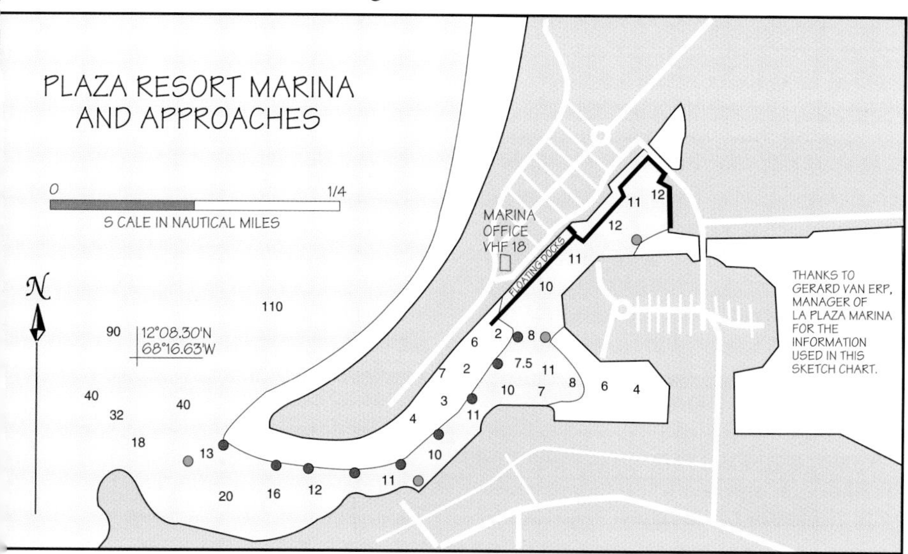

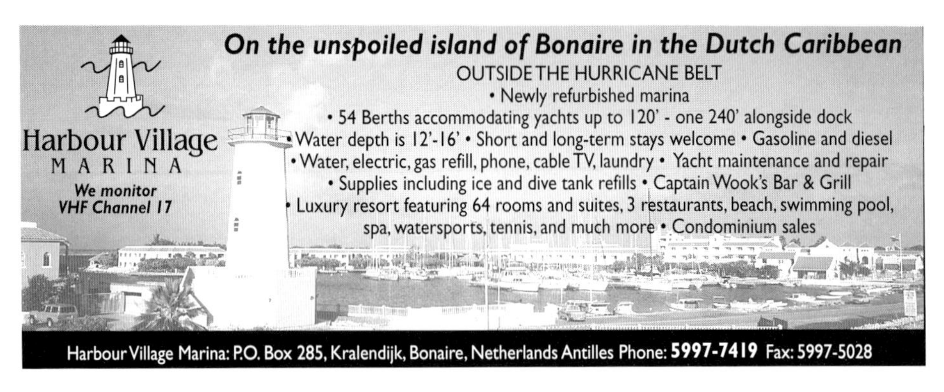

to start your evening. Wednesday sailors' happy hour (1700-1900) has cheap drinks and great free snacks. They become a local hot spot on Fridays and Saturdays with a live band till 0200, a consideration when you choose your anchoring spot. Owned by the same people, the restaurant Twins which is under the Papaimento Restaurant (T:4433, $C, cc:V) offers fast food and a salad bar with special night barbecues.

Zee Zicht (T:8434, $C, cc:A,V) right behind Karel's Bar, is in the same family and makes a good lunch spot and you can eat there when you emerge from happy hour without enough energy to cook.

One of the best and most pleasant restaurants is Richard's (T:5263, $B, cc:V, closed Monday, evenings only). Richard Beady was on his way round the world on his Cal 40 and stopped in Bonaire for a crew change. He loved the island and before his new crew arrived he was offered a job as food and beverages manager at the Flamingo. He took it for some years. Now he runs his own restaurant right on the waterfront. He has worked for some eight years with his chef Benito LaRosa and the combination is unbeatable. They have a romantic dining room leaning out over the water, good service and excellently prepared and presented food. To get there, dinghy south to one of the last small docks where a few boats are moored. Richard's has no sign facing the sea but it has a good dock and is very obviously a restaurant.

Mona Lisa (T: 8718, $B, cc:V,A, closed Sunday) is a well decorated restaurant with a pleasant bar. They serve modern French cuisine and are open lunch and dinner.

Lisboa (T:8286, $B), overlooking the waterfront, is open daily for breakfast, lunch and dinner. The food is good, especially the chateaubriand steak.

With a dinghy it is no hardship to head south past the marina where there are several more restaurants.

Den Laman (T:8955, $B-C, cc:V, dinner only, closed Tuesdays) is worth a visit at least for a drink to see their incredible six thousand gallon aquarium with its actively swimming turtles, barracudas, school of big jacks and much more. Den Laman offers fresh seafood. They are right on the waterfront and have their own rickety dinghy dock. There is no sign facing the sea but they are just south of Sand Dollar.

The Green Parrot Restaurant at the Sand Dollar (T:5454, $B-C, cc:V,A,D) is in the open air on the dock and very congenial. They open 0800-2200 daily to serve breakfast, light lunches, steak and seafood.

The Flamingo has two restaurants, entertainment most nights, and is the place to go gambling as they have the casino. They have two docks and ask those with dinghies to use the northern one.

Are you dying for Italian food? Try the Croccantino (T:5025, $C) opposite Interbank's parking lot, Kaya Grande 48.

Three restaurants at the Plaza Resort should stop you going hungry. The most luxurious for a special night out is Caribbean Point ($B, CC:A,V). The Banana Tree ($C, CC: A,V) is a more inform-

moderately priced restaurant, while Tipsy Seagull ($C) is the popular yachty hangout with a beautiful view over the bay. They offer fast type food and their Brandaris Hamburger is said to be quite special. Their Friday happy hour (1730-1930) with live music and low prices is one of the most popular on the island.

Near the Plaza Resort Marina, The Old Manor Inn (T:7776, $C) offers excellent Indonesian food and good service.

Other new restaurants worth checking out include the Beefeater (T:7776, $C) with live music on Sundays and Mondays, Het Ankertje, ($C) with good vegetarian dishes. Chez Truus and Rendez-Vous (T:8454, $C)

Bonaire is a wild dry island covered in cactus, scrub and hardy gumbo limbo trees. Much of the island is flat and the maximum elevation is under 800 feet. Nevertheless, it is not without interest. From a sightseeing point of view the island can be divided in two halves, the northern and the southern, which are very different though they do share an abundance of birds. In either direction you will see Bonaire's famous pink flamingos and the small green and yellow parrots called prikitchi. It is fun to walk from the car. Bug repellent is advisable, and binoculars invaluable.

The southern half is dominated by salt flats, wetlands and mangroves. Much of the land area is used for the solar evaporation of water to get salt. Both the monster mounds of salt and the salt pens are striking. The salt pens are laid out in giant squares in pastel shades from pale green to pink depending on the drying stage. Some old slave quarters have been restored on the west coast road heading south as a historical monument. You get a good view of flamingos around the southern end of the island from the car. The road behind Lac Bay is most interesting for bird watching with mangroves and wet areas that are home to ducks, egrets, and herons. Take a break at the southern end of Lac Bay to watch the windsurfing. There is a shallow entrance to Lac Bay, but yachts are not given permission to go there any more.

Karel's dinghy dock

The northern half of Bonaire is a wild-west desert landscape. As you drive north plan to take a walk at Devil's Mouth. This is a most beautiful part of the interior with strangely sculpted cliffs, jagged rocks, caves and arches. The bird watching here is excellent, with many small parrots and doves. There is a flamingo observation road where you can often get close to the flamingos. If you wish to see the Lora (larger parrot), you may have to spend time roaming on the dirt roads in the northern mountainous area. If you are taking slides and want them in a hurry, check Paradise Photo or go talk with Photo Tours (T:4089) who also rent underwater camera equipment, develop film and are a bookshop. There are several places for one-hour prints.

For waterfront news, tide tables and more get your free copy of Port Call edited by ex-charter yacht owners George and Laura Desalvo.

Sailing onto the other ABC's, Need more information on Bonaire? Get your copy of the Yachting Guide to the ABC Islands. It is written by Gerard van Erp with help from Arnoud Vernimmem a hydrographic surveyor. Gerard supplied most of the update information of Bonaire for this guide and judging by this, his new guide should be excellent. Gerard is manager of Plaza Marina and he lived for 6 years in the ABC's. The new guide will be out in June 1997 and will have aerial photos, good sketch charts and lots of shoreside detail.

Water Sports

The diving in Bonaire is exceptional. It is not that any one dive site will be better than those on other islands, but the water here is clear and calm, with deep coral-encrusted slopes that surround the island. You can dive almost anywhere. The whole area is run by the Bonaire Marine Park (T:8444, VHF:11). The office is open from 0830-1200 and 1330-1730, Monday through Friday. To dive in Bonaire you must get an admission ticket which costs $10US per year and comes with an orientation talk on the park. There are a few places where diving is forbidden so park officials can see how diving affects the reef. The park is so well organized that nearly everyone dives on their own. A large number of sites are carefully marked for access by car, or if the access is by boat, there are moorings. There are several guide books on the park, describing each dive. If your boat is over 38 feet, either take your dinghy or call the park and use the special larger boat moorings.

You can rent gear or get your tanks filled practically anywhere, as the dive shops have docks all along the water front.

When leaving your dinghy on a dive shop dock, make sure it is clear of the dive boats as they load and unload. Your tanks will have to be in date and you will need a valid dive certificate to rent gear or get air.

If you have never dived before, I cannot think of a better place to give it a go. It would be a shame to miss the opportunity. All the dive shops offer resort and certification courses. If price is an important consideration, check around as prices do vary.

Dive Inn (T:8761, F:8513 cc:A,V, VHF:69) is a pleasant, small, friendly operation. They have two locations so you can choose the most convenient. Dive Inn is just north of the commercial pier. Tie to their dock and walk over the road. If it is more convenient their second shop, Sunset Beach Hotel Dive Inn, is just north of the Marina. Owners Anton and Babs own a yacht and came here from Holland 11 years ago. They often have yachting people working for them, and they offer pleasant, personal service. Their 10-refill package is a bargain.

Buddy Dive Resort (T:5080, F:8647, cc:V) is a big new operation catering to Europeans who are here on long vacations. Their prices are very competitive and operations manager Pascal de Meyer is helpful. You can dinghy right to their dock.

Sand Dollar (T:5252, F:8760, cc:A,V) is one of the bigger dive operations. They have big VCR's, all the modern equipment and they offer free slide shows. This is a good option for those who like the feeling of a large establishment and don't mind following back-to-school systems you always find in such places. However, Sand Dollar only fills European tanks if they are stamped with a date sometime in the future. I have never seen such a tank, but the man in charge has very definite ideas. They fill in-date US tanks without a problem.

Toucan Diving (T:2500, F:7133) at the Plaza Resort is a full service dive operator. They teach in English, Dutch, German and Spanish and have three 30-foot dive boats. In the same area Blue Band Water sports offers day sailing, snorkeling, charter trips and more.

Captain Don's Habitat (T:8290, F:8240, cc:A,V) is another big operation. They also offer free instructive slide shows, and they work with Photo Tours (T4089) for underwater photo instruction.

Carib Inn (T:8819, F:5295, cc:A,V) offers good package rates.

There are also Patrick's Dive shop (T:4080), Dive Bonaire (T:8285, 8238) and Great Adventures, (T:7500, 7507).

Venezuela and Bonaire Directory

To call into Bonaire dial (011) 5997, to call into Venezuela dial:(011) 58 where the area code starts with a 0, leave off the 0.

BONAIRE

ABC RACE INFORMATION
Gerared van Erp, 2500, F:7133

AIRLINES
Avensa, 5415
ALM, KLM, and Air Aruba, 8300/8500

AUTO RENTALS/TAXIS
Avis, 8033
Budget, 8300
Camel Car Rental, 5120
Good Wheels Car Rental, 8724
Island Car Rental, 5111
Sun and Sand Car Rental, 8677
Taxis, town stand, 5330
Taxis, airport 8100

CHANDLERIES
Caribbean Fasteners, 5560
Harbour Village Marina, 7419, F:5028, VHF:17, cc:V

CRUISING GUIDES
Yachting Guide to the ABC's, 2500, F:7133, (P210)

FUEL
Harbour Village Marina, 7419, F:5028, VHF:17, (206)

LAUNDRY SERVICES
Caribbean Laundry Services, 5220

MAIL DROP
Harbour Village Marina, P.O. Box 285, Kralendijk, Bonaire, Netherland Antilles
Plaza Resort Marina, J.A. Abraham Blvd 80, Bonaire, Dutch Caribbean

MARINE PARK
Bonaire Marine Park, 8444, VHF:11

MECHANICS
Boto Blanco Marine Services, 5220

MARINA
Club Nautico, 5800, VHF:68
Harbour Village Marina, 7419, F:5028, VHF:17, In USA: 800-424 0004, cc:V, (P206)
Plaza Resort Marina, 2500, F:7133, VHF:18, cc:A,V, (P206)

OUTBOARDS
Boto Blanco Marine Services, 5050, F:4309, VHF:65

PHOTOS
Photo Tours, 4089, F:4089

PROVISIONING
Cultimara Supermarket, 8278
Gonsales Wholesale, 8468

RESTAURANTS
Banana Tree, 2500, cc:A,V
Beefeater, 7776
Bistro des Amis, 4191, cc:A,V,D,Dc
Caribbean Point, 2500, cc:A,V
Croccantino, 5025
Den Laman, 8955, cc:V
Green Parrot Restaurant, 5454, cc:V,A,D
Lisboa, 8286
Mona Lisa, 8718, cc:V,A
Old Manor Inn, 7776
Rendez-Vous, 8454
Richard's, 5263, cc:V
Tipsy Seagull, 2500, cc:A,V
Twins, 4433, cc:V
Zee Zicht, 8434, cc:A,V

SAIL REPAIR, CANVAS WORK
Marlis Sail and Canvas Shop, 7741

SCUBA DIVING
Black Durgeon Dive, 8978/8846
Bonaire Marine Park, 8444
Buddy Dive Resort, 5080, F:8647, cc:V
Captain Don's Habitat, 8290, F:8240, cc:A,V
Carib Inn, 8819, F:5295, cc:A,V
Dive Bonaire, 8285/8238
Dive Inn, 8761, F:8513 VHF:69, cc:A,V
Great Adventures, 7500/7507
Patrick's Dive shop, 4080
Photo Tours, 4089
Sand Dollar, 5252, F:8760, cc:A,V
Toucan Diving, 2500, F:7133
Zen Divers, T&F:5425

SURVEYS
Robert St.Jargo, VHF:11,16 (Port office)

TOURIST INFORMATION
Tourist Corperation Bonaire, 8322

VENEZUELA

ACCOMODATION

Hato Nuevo, Puerto La Cruz, 082 23 57 2/ 016 81 75 71, 016 81 75 71, 71,

Hotel Bella Vista, 095 61 72 22

Hotel Colibrí, Porlamar. T/F 095 61 63

Hotel Gaeta, Puerto La Cruz 081 65 04 11 F: 081 65 00 65

Intmar, Pampatar T/F 095 62 35 27

AIRLINES

Aerotuy, Porlamar, 095 63 03 67/61 04 32 F: 61 45 89, 095 61 44 62 V.A

Aerotuy, Puerto La Cruz, 081 76 27 10/67 80 72, V,.A

Avior, Barcelona, 081 76 27 05/76 14 65/77 02 31, 081 76 02 66, cc:V, A

Avior, Margarita, 095 69 13 14/69 10 14, 095 69 11 14 cc:V, A

Servicios Aereos, Puerto La Cruz, 081 65 33 71, 014 80 01 15 (P.139)

BANKING

American Express, Porlamar, 095 61 43 23/61 89 86

American Express, Puerto La Cruz, 081 66 88 06/ 66 89 52

Asecambio, Puerto La Cruz, 081 67 33 02/68 78 51

Oficambio, Cumana, 093 66 16 26/31 16 27/66 16 28

Oficambio, Puerto La Cruz, 081 67 56 71/67 59 87, F:081 67 44 98

BOAT BUILDING

Astilleros Mansanillo, Margarita, 095 49 17 62/ 014 95 21 97, F:095 64 02 65

Marine Tech, 095 61 12 24

CMO, Puerto La Cruz, 081 69 22 54/67 70 11 F: 081 69 20 21/ 67 85 50 VHF: 80, SSB: 6250

CAR RENTAL

Amigo, Puerto La Cruz, 081 67 27 59, cc:A, V

Avis Rentacar, Porlamar, 095 61 89 20/61 82 64, cc:V, A

Budget Car Rental, Puerto La Cruz,081 65 81 70 / 65 36 55

Hertz, Margarita, 095 62 33 33

CHANDLERY

Budget Marine (see ad page 7)

Caribbean Sport, Puerto La Cruz, 081 66 84 30/66 72 64, F:081 67 24 86, VHF:77, cc:A (P143)

La Casa del Pescador, Porlamar, 095 63 93 05

Casamar , Cumaná, 093 31 38 51, (P60)

La Cruz Nautic Shop 081 63 04 19 , F:081 63 17 36, e-mail:omcca@telcel.net.ve (P.134)

Marine Store, Tucacas, 042 83 21 20

Nauti Hogar, Cumaná, 093 66 38 04, F:093 66 35 18, 18, cc:V

CHANDLERY (cont)

Nautic Center Puerto La Cruz 081 86 19 11 11, F:081 86 38 29, VHF:71, cc:V, (P.139)

Off Shore Marine, Porlamar, 095 63 43 22 63 15 82, F:095 61 65 64, VHF:11, 12, cc:V,A, (P59)

Rich Marine Center, Puerto La Cruz, 081 81 16 30/ 81 15 64, F:081 81 16 30/81 15 64, VHF:71, cc:V

Servi Fibra, P. Cabello, T:042 61 53 83

The Marine Collection, Puerto La Cruz, 081 86 50 34/86 42 69/016 81 17 50, cc:V

Vemasca, (Venezuelan Marine Supply),Porlamar, 095 63 16 46/64 25 29, F:095 64 25 29, VHF:72, (P57)

Xanadu Marine, Puerto La Cruz, 081 65 38 44/ 016 81 88 21, F:081 65 24 48, VHF:77 e-mail:xanadu@telcel.net.ve (P.141)

CHARTS AND GUIDES see also chandleries

Comercial Stop, Puerto La Cruz, 081 66 82 08, F:081 66 82 08

COMMISSION AGENTS

MBS, Puerto La Cruz, 081 65 00 12, F:081 68 82 43, VHF:77 e-mail: mdeb@telcel.net.ve (P.145)

COMMUNICATION

CANTV, Porlamar, 095 63 83 10/63 86 21

CANTV, Puerto La Cruz, 081 66 33 33,

Communications Center, Puerto La Cruz, 081 63 05 51/63 06 66/014 80 73 24, F:081 63 05 51/63 06 66, VHF:77

MBS, Puerto La Cruz, 081 65 00 12, F:081 68 82 43, VHF:77 compuserve102213, 1634, e-mail: :mdeb@telcel.net.ve

CONSULS (see also embassies)

Canada, Margarita, 095 64 14 04/64 00 86, F:095 63 48 18

Chile, Margarita, 095 63 29 52/63 72 24, F:095 63 72 24

Denmark, Margarita, 095 63 71 43/63 30 02/63 56 75/63 43 55, F:095 61 83 46/61 12 91

France, Margarita, 095 61 84 31, F:095 64 14 25

Germany, Margarita, 095 61 52 12/61 53 31, F:095 61 51 34

Great Britain, Margarita, 095 62 46 65/014 95 12 67,

Holland, Puerto La Cruz, 081 81 42 62, F:081 81 47 86

Italy, Margarita, 095 61 02 13, F:095 61 02 13

Italy, Puerto La Cruz, 081 65 28 47, F:081 65 28 47

Spain, Margarita, 095 61 54 35/61 54 46/61 99 79/ 61 52 35, F:095 61 54 46

Switzerland, Margarita, 095 62 86 82/62 56 72,

COURIER

DHL P. La Cruz, 081 67 36 69 F:081 86 67 64

DHL, Porlamar, 095 61 38 80 F:095 61 38 80

Federal Express, Polamar, 095 63 35 78

MBS P. La Cruz, 081 65 00 12, F: 68 82 43, (P.145)

CUSTOMS BROKERS
Carlos Alverez, P. Cabello, 042 61 08 68, 014, 43 25 45, VHF:71
Dockside, 081 67 76 92, F:081 67 76 92, VHF:77, (P.134)
Intmar, Pampatar, 095 62 80 17/62 35 27/014 95 35 27, F:095 62 35 27, VHF:72, e-mail: hart@enlared.net
Marianella, P.Cabello T/F 042 64 60 97
Marina Cumanagoto, Cumaná, 093 31 08 04/31 08 37/ 31 09 08/36 63 56, VHF:13, (P169)
Vemasca, (Venezuelan Marine Supply), Porlamar, 095 63 16 46/64 25 29, F:095 64 25 29, VHF:72, (P57)
Winds, Gestoria Maritima, Puerto La Cruz, 081 67 16 07/016 81 96 57, F:081 68 66 98, VHF:77, (P.139)

DIVING
Explosub, Puerto La Cruz, 081 65 36 11/65 05 74, F:081 67 32 56, VHF:77,
Horisub, Puerto La Cruz, 081 81 48 78/81 67 55/016 80 38 00, F:081 81 48 29, VHF:77,
Lolos Diving Center, Puerto La Cruz, 081 68 30 52/014 80 15 93, F:081 68 28 85, VHF:71
Scuba Divers Club, Puerto La Cruz, 081 81 10 11 ext. 1629/65 57 03/014 80 03 70 VHF: 71
Sest Continte Dive Resort, Los Roques, T:014 24 18 53, 02 731 1507, VHF:16
Venaquarium, Porlamar, 095 63 93 96/63 11 60

ELECTRICS
Electromar, Puerto La Cruz, 081 81 58 61, F:081 81 61 96, VHF:77
Electrotecnico, P. Cabello, T:042 63 861/779
Lilo's, Porlamar, 016 95 10 55/64 55 6572
Radio Marine, P. Cabello, 042 61 57 96

ERRANDS
Armando Cordova, 081 86 36 69, VHF:77
Jose, Peurto la Cruz, VHF:77
Miguel c/o Marina Cumanagoto

EMBASSIES (see also consuls)
Argentina, Caracas, 02 731 3311/731 3058/731 2145,
Australia, Caracas, 02 263 4033, F:02 261 3448
Austria, Caracas, 02 993 9844/8923/9923/ 9932, F:02 993 9935
Belgium, Caracas, 02 262 0421/1445, F:02 261 1333
Brasil, Caracas, 02 261 0513,
Bulgaria, Caracas, 02 993 2714/4852, F:02 993 4839
Canada, Caracas, 02 951 6166, F:02 951 4950
Denmark, Caracas, 02 951 6618/4618/5606, F:02 951 5278
France, Caracas, 02 993 6666, F:02 993 3984
Germany, Caracas, 02 261 3253/0181/2229, F:02 261 0641
Great Britain, Caracas, 02 993 4111/5280/ 4224, F:02 993 9989

EMBASSIES (continued)
Holland, Caracas, 02 263 3622/3387/3476, F:02 263 0462
Ireland, Caracas, 02 985 2286/4144, F:02 985 1545
Italy, Caracas, 02 261 0755/264 0833/0334, F:02 262 1420
Japan, Caracas, 02 261 0581
Portugal, Caracas, 02 263 6670
Spain, Caracas, 02 266 0222/0377/1241, F:02 266 5745
Sweden, Caracas, 02 952 2111/2058/2070, F:02 952 2057
Switzerland, Caracas, 02 951 4064/4166, F:02 951 4866
U.S.A., Caracas, 02 977 2011

FIBERGLASS REPAIRS (see also haul out)
Servi Fibra, P. Cabello, T:042 61 71 23

FUEL
Bahia Redonda, Puerto La Cruz, 081 67 80 47/67 74 12, 081 67 78 10, VHF:71, (P.133)
Los Manglares, Morrocoy, T:014 430030, F:042 84821, VHF:77.
Marina Cumanagoto, Cumaná, 093 31 08 04/31 08 37/ 31 09 08/36 63 56, VHF:13 (P169)
Marina de Caraballeda, 031 88 27 12, F:031 99 88 77, VHF:16
Marina El Morro, (Nauti Norca) Puerto La Cruz, T:081 81 88 80, F:81 71 17, VHF:23, cc:V.
Marina Paseo Colón, (Servinauti), Puerto La Cruz, T:081 65 25 63/65 16 45/ F:081 68 63 16, VHF:71, SSB:2738
Marina Puerto Cabello, 042 61 72 77, VHF:71
Polarmar Fuel Dock, Porlamar
Puerto Azul, 031 72 24 15, VHF:16, SSB: 28.37
Puerto Calera, 031 51 50 11, VHF:69/71, SSB:2738
Puerto Viejo, 031 52 40 44

FREE LEGAL ADVICE
Consultoria Juridica Gratuita, Puerto La Cruz, 081 68 81 70

GALVANIZING
King's Service, 081 67 83 54, 016 80 25 98, VHF:77

HAUL OUT
Astillero de Higuerote, Carenero, 034 21 293, 02-92 06 38, F:02 64 11 06.
Astilleros de Oriente, Cumaná, 093 32 10 59 /32 41 19, F:093 66 49 29
Centro Marino de Oriente, Puerto La Cruz 081 69 22 54/67 70 11/69 20 21, F:081 69 20 21/ 67 85 50, VHF:80 (USA) SSB:6250, (P.135)
Mi Calichar, Carenero, T:02-81 40 81/81 35 65, VHF:16
Navimca, 93-31 90 64, F:93 31 71 62, VHF:16 (P175)

HAUL OUT (cont)
The Navy Yard, Cabello, T:042 61 01 11, F:042 61 58 86, VHF:07 in Spanish only.
Varadero Caribe, Cumaná, 093 31 08 04/31 08 37/31 09 08/66 31 56, F:093 66 25 64, VHF:13 compuserve:102213, 3340, (P172)
Varamar, Puerto La Cruz, 081 81 50 32/014 80 28 29, F:081 81 50 32, VHF:77, (P.137)

INFLATABLES AND LIFERAFTS (see also chandleries and commission agents)
AB Inflatables, 02-97 9-0031/979-7179/ 9794544, F:02-9794722 (see Xanadu)
Carlos Gonzales (liferafts), Barcelona, 081 77 21 21, F:081 77 81 83

LANGUAGE TEACHERS
Grupo Centeno, T/F: 081 68 55 74

LAUNDRY
Altagracia, Puerto la Cruz, 081 65 22 01
Bahia Redonda, 014 80 60 30/80 61 32
Lavanderia Altagracia, P. La Cruz, 081 65 22 01

MARINAS
Ancla Marina, Morrocoy, VHF:74
Bahia Redonda, Puerto La Cruz, 08167 74 12, F:081 67 78 10, VHF:71, (P.133)
Centro Marino de Oriente, Puerto La Cruz, 081 69 22 54/67 70 11/69 20 21, F:081 69 20 21/ 67 85 50, VHF:80 (USA) SSB:6250, (P.135)
Guanta Marina, T:081 68 28 34, VHF:71
Marina Americo Vespucio, (Varamar) 081 81 48 78/ 81 67 55, F:081 81 48 29, 016 80 38 00, VHF:71
Marina Cumanagoto, Cumaná T/F 093 31 14 23 VHF:16/71, (P169)
Marina de Carabelleda, 031 88 27 12, F:031 99 88 77, VHF:16
Marina Deportes Nautico (Concorde Marina), Porlamar, VHF:16
Marina El Morro, T:081 81 88 80, F:81 71 17, VHF:23, cc:V
Marina la Cuevita, Morrocoy, VHF:72
Marina Maremares, 081 81 30 22/81 10 11, F:081 81 44 94/81 30 28, (P.136)
Marina Margarita Yachting, 016 95 33 38/95 33 36, T/F:095 61 02 13
Marina Nauti Norca, (Marina el Morros) Puerto La Cruz, 081 81 88 80/81 71 17/016 21 19 26 VHF:71
Marina Paseo Colón, (Servinauti) T:081 65 25 63/ 65 16 45/ F:081 68 63 16, VHF:71, SSB:2738
Marina Puerto Cabello, 042 61 72 77, VHF:71
Puerto Azul, 031 72 24 15, VHF:16, SSB: 28.37
Puerto Calera, 031 51 50 11, VHF:69/71, SSB:2738
Puerto Viejo, 031 52 40 44

MECHANICS, MACHINE SHOPS
Lilo's Marine Services, Porlamar, 016 95 10 55/64 55 65 VHF:72
Marine Mechanics, Puerto la Cruz, 014 81 11 58, VHF:77
Servi-Boat, Puerto la Cruz, 081 68 62 84, 014 80 3331, F:081 65 64 05, VHF:77, (P143)

MEDICAL-DENTAL
Taller Ind. Meesca, P. Cabello, T:042 61 36 51
Claudia Sambrano,Puerto La Cruz, 081 68 67 47
Ernesto Suarez, Puerto La Cruz, 081 86 23 03
Claudia Cifuentes B. de Leotaud (Dentist), Puerto La Cruz, 081 68 67 47/014 80 68 55

MEDICAL EMERGENCIES
Aeroambulancias, Puerto La Cruz, 014 21 49 42
C. Medico Anzoategui, P. La Cruz 081 86 39 11
Hospital Razetti, Puerto La Cruz, 081 67 63 63

MEDICAL-EYES
Konrad Schargel, P.L.C, 081 65 03 31/65 26 98
MEDICAL G.P
Pedro Garroni Hernandez, P.L.C, 081 65 23 60
MEDICAL GYNECOLOGY
Dr. Rafael Pinto C., P.L.C, 081 65 17 10

OUTBOARDS AND REPAIRS (for new outboards see also chandleries)
Lilo's Marine Services, Porlamar, 016 95 10 55/64 55 65, VHF:72
Yamapuerto, Puerto La Cruz, 081 66 43 85, F:081 65 76 08

PAINTS (see also chandleries and haul out)
Distribuidora Colorama, P.L.C. F:081 66 48 04
International Paints, P.Cabello, 042 63 670/763
Pintacasa, P.L.C., T/F 081 68 79 95/68 70 45

PHOTO SUPPLIES/DEVELOPING
Foto Piva, Puerto La Cruz, 081 67 54 31
Fotolisto, Puerto La Cruz, 081 65 21 73

PROVISIONING
Automercado Veracruz, P.L.C., 081 65 24 98 F:081 68 78 80, VHF:77
CADA (2), Puerto La Cruz, 081 65 13 61,
CADA, Puerto Cabello, T:042 61 29 09
CADA, Porlamar, 095 61 87 13
CADA, Puerto La Cruz, 081 65 69 11/66 37 71
Comercial Las Flores, Puerto la cruz, 081 65 13 63/ 65 78 94, cc:V
El Bogedón de Jose, 095 55 386/55 714
Ratan, Porlamar, 095 61 79 11, cc:A,V
Villa Marina, Cumaná, 093 32 03 11, F:093 31 50 23

REFRIGERATION
Sea Frost , USA, (see ad page 35)
Thomas Winfield, Puerto la Cruz, 016 81 24 12

RESTAURANTS
Biseño Ven, P. Cabello, T:042 63 569/707
Cheers, Porlamar, 095 61 09 57
Christopher's, Puerto La Cruz, 081 65 39 95 VHF:77
Club Bahía de Los Piratas, Carenero, T: 034-21 448, VHF:70, cc:A,V,D
Cocody, Margarita, 095 61 84 31, cc:V
El Bohio de Doña Carmen, Coche, 095 99 1 77
El Buho, Juangriego, T:095 55 879, cc:A,V,D
El Chipi, Porlamar, 095 63 61 01

El Parador del Puerto, P. La Cruz 081 65 03 91
RESTAURANTS (cont)
El Rancho del Tío, P. La Cruz, 081 65 36 77, cc:V, D
El Rincón Del Bucanero, P.L.C., 081 67 07 65/68 82 05, cc:V, A
El Viejo Muelle, Juan Griego, 095 53 00 73, cc:V
El Viejo Muelle, Juangriego, T:55 073
Hotel El Fortín, Juangriego, T:095 55 092, cc:A,V,D
Isla de Coche Hotel, Coche, 095 99 118, cc:A,V
L'Oasis, 095 91 53 39
La Italiana, T:61 27 56, cc:A,V,D
Lanceros, P. Cabello, T:042 63 634
Mandinga, Porlamar, 095 64 30 03, cc:V
Milano, P. Cabello, 042 61 58 59, cc:A,V
Mosquito Coast, Porlamar, 095 64 14 04/64 00 86, F:095 63 48 18
Restaurant Yacht Club de Guanta, Puerto La Cruz, 081 68 30 30
Riccardo's, Puerto La Cruz, 081 65 06 29, cc:V
Trimar Restaurant, Pampatar, 095 62 33 32

SAILMAKERS
Doyle Sails, Barbados, (see ad on page 1)
Kostan Sails, Puerto La Cruz, 081 68 82 66 F:081 68 82 66, VHF 77, e-mail:mckostan@telcel.net.ve, (P.143)

SECURITY
ASONAUTICA, Puerto La Cruz, 081 67 70 11 63 13 63, F:081 67 85 59
Capitania de Puerto (Port Captain), Puerto La Cruz, 081 66 59 95
Coast Guard, Puerto La Cruz, 081 68 38 44/68 21 88
Cuerpo de Bomberos (Fire Station), Puerto La Cruz, 081 66 21 13/77 46 10
Guardia Nacional, Puerto La Cruz, 081 66 72 62
Policia Metropolitana, Puerto La Cruz, 081 66 14 14/66 72 86

TAXIS AND TOURS
Aeroexpresos Ejecutivos (Bus), Puerto La Cruz, 081 67 88 55
Aerotuy, Porlamar 095 63 22 11 F: 61 77 46
Chaser Tours, 016 80 20 79, F:081 68 45 82/74 49 03, VHF:77, (P.139)
Peli Express (Bus), Puerto La Cruz, 081 86 01 44
Servicios Aereos, Puerto La Cruz, 081 65 33 71, 014 80 01 15, (P.139)

TOURIST INFORMATION
Inparques, Morrocoy, 042 83 00 69
Tourist Information, P. La Cruz, 081 68 81 70

TRAVEL AGENTS
Dockside, 081 67 76 92, F:081 67 76 92, (P.134)
Winds, Gestoria Maritima, Puerto La Cruz, 081 67 16 07/016 81 96 57, F:081 68 66 98, VHF:77, (P.134)
Varadero Tours, Tucacas, 042 83 47 45 F: 042 86 754

VETERINARIAN
Clinica Veterinaria, P. La Cruz, 081 66 52 27

EXTRA TELEPHONE NUMBERS:

Index

Directory of Advertisers

SOME USEFUL SPANISH WORDS AND PHRASES

NUMBERS

0 .... cero
1 .... uno
2 .... dos
3 .... tres
4 .... cuatro
5 .... cinco
6 .... seis
7 .... siete
8 .... ocho
9 .... nueve
10 .... diez
11 .... once
12 .... doce
13 .... trece
14 .... catorce
15 .... quince
16 .... dieciséis
17 .... diecisiete
18 .... dieciocho
19 .... diecinueve
20 .... veinte
21 .... veintiuno
22 .... veintidos
30 .... treinta
31 .... treintiuno
32 .... treintidos
40 .... cuarenta
50 .... cincuenta
60 .... sesenta
70 .... setenta
80 .... ochenta
90 .... noventa
100 .... cien
101 .... ciento uno
200 .... doscientos
1000 .... mil
1200 .... mil doscientos
2000 .... dos mil
100,000 .... cien mil
1,000,000 .... millon

How much is? .... ¿Cuánto es?
How much does it cost .... ¿Cuánto cuesta
Where is .... ¿donde esta?
How far? .... ¿Qué distancia?
here .... aqui
I like it .... me gusta
I don't like it .... no me gusta
good morning .... buenos días
write it .... escríbamelo

TRAVEL

Where is the bus stop?	¿Dónde está la parada de autobús?
When does the next bus go to...?	¿A que hora el próximo autobús a...?
How long does it take?	¿Cuanto tiempo dura el trayecto......?
Do I have to change buses?	¿Tengo que cambiar de autobús?
Will you tell me where to get off?	¿Me dirá cuándo tengo que bajarme?
Bus terminal	Terminal de pasajeros

NAVIGATION/GEOGRAPHY

bay	bahía
beach	playa
bottom	fondo
cay	cayo
coast	litoral
depth	fondo
east	este
fathom	braza
gravel	grava
gulf	golfo
headland/cape	cabo
headland/mountain	morro
island	isla
isthmus	istmo
lagoon	laguna
lake	lago
leeward	sotavento
lightouse	faro
mangrove	manglar
mangrove bay	ciénega
mud/swamp	fango
north	norte
ocean	mar
pier	muelle
point	punta
port	puerto
reef	arrecife
rock	piedra
salt flats	salinas
sand	arena
sand dunes	médanos
seaweed	alga
shoal	bajo
small gulf	golfete
south	sur
tide	marea
west	oeste
wind	viento
windward	barlovento

BOAT

2 stroke oil	aceite de dos tiempos
air	aire
anchor	ancla
boat	barco
boatyard	varadero
bow	proa
brass	latón
bronze	bronce
canoe	canoa
captain	capitán
copper	cobre
crew	tripulación
customs	aduana
danger	peligroso
diesel	gas-oil/diesel
dinghy	barquito
fisherman	pescador
flag	bandera
galvanized	galvanizado
garbage	basura
gasoline	gasolina
gas station	bomba de gasolina
hull	casco
hydraulic fluid	aceite hidraulico
ice	hielo
immigration	inmigración
mast	mástil
oil	aceite
outboard	fuera-bordo
port	babor
power yacht	yate
propane	gas propano
propeller	hélice, propela
rope	cabo
rudder	timón
sail	vela
sailboat	velero
spark plug	bujía
stainless steel	acero inoxidable
starboard	estribor
steel	acero
stern	popa
water	agua

FOOD\RESTAURANT

the bill please .... La cuenta por favor
menu please .... carta por favor
I'd like .... quiero
may I have some? .... ¿puerde darme?
have you any vegetarian dishes .... ¿tiene platos vegetarianos?
I'd like some more .... quiero más
no more, thanks .... nada más gracias
where are the toilets? .... ¿donde están los baños?
do you have? .... ¿tiene?
a little more .... un poco más
Do you accept credit cards .... ¿acepta tarjeta de credito?

FOOD:ENGLISH-SPANISH

apple .... manzana
bakery .... panaderia
pasteleria
barracuda .... picua
beef steak .... beefstec
beer .... cerveza
black coffe .... café negro
bread .... pan
butcher .... carniceria/
charcuteria
cashew .... merey
change .... cambio
chicken .... pollo
cheese .... queso
clams .... almejas
coconut custard .... bienmesabe
coffee with milk .... café maron
corn .... maíz
custard .... flan
eat .... comer
egg .... huevo
filet mignon .... filet mignon
fish .... pescado
garlic .... ajo
goat .... cabrito
grilled .... a la parrilla
grocery .... bodega
grouper .... mero
juice .... jugo
ketchup .... salsa de
tomate
kingfish .... sierra
lobster .... langosta
luncheonette .... lunchería
mackerel .... carite
meat .... carne
milk .... leche
(with milk) .... (con leche)
milk shake .... merengada
mustard .... mostaza
octopus .... pulpo
oil .... aceite
orange .... naranja
oven .... horno
oysters .... ostras
papaya .... lechosa
peach .... melocotón
pineapple .... piña
pork chop .... chuleta de
cerdo
potatoes .... papas
quail .... codorniz
rabbit .... conejo
red snapper .... pargo
red wine .... vino tinto
restaurant .... restaurante
rice .... arroz
salad .... ensalada
shellfish .... mariscos
shop,store .... tienda
shrimp .... camarón
sirloin .... solomo
soda fountain .... fuente de soda
soursop .... guanábana
squid .... calamar
steak .... lomo/lomito
supplies .... abastos
t-bone .... tibón
tea .... té
trout .... trucha
vegetables .... verduras
vinagre .... vinagre
water .... agua
white wine .... vino blanco

GENERAL

a little	un poco
big	grande
bus	autobús
cold/hot	frio/caliente
copy	fotocopia
corner	esquina
do you have?	¿tiene?
empty/full	vacio/lleno
good afternoon	buenas tardes
good day	buenos días
good night	buenas noches
one minute please	un momento por favor
more/less	más/menos
no	no
open/closed	abierto/cerrado
pharmacy	farmacia
please	por favor
public phone	teléfono público
shared-taxi	por puesto
shopping center	centro comercial
small	pequeño
sorry	perdone
street	calle
taxi	taxi
thank you	gracias
where is there?	¿dónde hay?
where is?	¿dónde esta?
with	con
yes	si

RESTAURANT SPANISH-ENGLISH

a la parrilla	grilled
aceite	oil
ajo	garlic
almejas	clams
arroz	rice
azúcar	sugar
beefstec	beef steak
bienmesabe	coconut custard
cabrito	goat
café negro	black coffee
café con leche	white coffee
calamar	squid
camarón	shrimp
carite	mackerel
carne	meat
cerveza	beer
chuleta de cerdo	pork chop
codorniz	quail
conejo	rabbit
ensalada	salad
filet mignon	filet mignon
flan	custard
guanábana	soursop
huevo	egg
horno	oven
jamon	ham
jugo	juice
langosta	lobster
leche	milk
lechosa	papaya
lomo/lomito	steak
maíz	corn
manzana	apple
mariscos	shellfish
melocotón	peach
merengada	milk shake
merey	cashew
mero	grouper
mostaza	mustard
naranja	orange
ostras	oysters
pan	bread
papas	potatoes
pargo	red snapper
pescado	fish
picua	barracuda
piña	pineapple
pimienta	pepper
pollo	chicken
pulpo	octopus
queso	cheese
salsa de tomate	ketchup
sal	salt
sierra	kingfish
solomo	sirloin
té	tea
tibón	t-bone
tocino	cheese
trucha	trout
verduras	vegetables
vinagre	vinegar
vino blanco	white wine
vino tinto	red wine

ORDER FORM

To order, please fill out coupon on back and send check or money order to:
Cruising Guide Publications, P.O. Box 1017, Dunedin, Florida 34697-1017.
For credit card orders only, call 1-800-330-9542 • Fax 813-734-8179
E-mail: cgp@earthlink.net

- ❑ $19.95 CRUISING GUIDE TO THE VIRGIN ISLANDS (8th Edition) by Simon and Nancy Scott. New color charts and photos.
- ❑ $24.95 VIRGIN ANCHORAGES (Color aerial photos of the Virgin Islands with sailing directions)
- ❑ $24.95 CRUISING GUIDE TO THE LEEWARD ISLANDS-- (5th Edition) by Chris Doyle. With new color charts and GPS coordinates.
- ❑ $19.95 SAILOR'S GUIDE TO THE WINDWARD ISLANDS (8th Edition)-- with color charts & GPS by Chris Doyle.
- ❑ $14.95 CRUISING GUIDE TO TRINIDAD AND TOBAGO with color charts &GPS by Chris Doyle & Jeff Fisher
- ❑ $26.95 CRUISING GUIDE TO VENEZUELA & BONAIRE -- by Chris Doyle & Jeff Fisher. With new color charts & GPS coordinates.
- ❑ $24.95 CRUISING GUIDE TO CUBA--With GPS Coordinates and Charts (2nd Edition) by Simon Charles.
- ❑ $24.95 GENTLEMAN'S GUIDE TO PASSAGES SOUTH-- With GPS Coordinates--The "Thornless Path to Windward," by Bruce Van Sant.
- ❑ $15.95 CRUISING GUIDE TO THE SPANISH VIRGIN ISLANDS AND THE PUERTO RICO --by Bruce Van Sant-- an all new guide.
- ❑ $15.95 CRUISING GUIDE TO THE SEA OF CORTEZ (from Mulege to La Paz)
- ❑ $19.95 CRUISING GUIDE TO THE FLORIDA KEYS by Capt. Frank Papy. With Florida West Coast supplement.
- ❑ $29.95 YACHTSMAN'S GUIDE TO JAMAICA by John Lethridge -- 1st edition.
- ❑ $12.00 CRUISING MANUAL TO THE KINGDOM OF TONGA IN THE VAVA'U GROUP (Chart included) The Moorings.
- ❑ $9.95 CRUSING GUIDE TO ABACO BAHAMAS -- by Steve Dodge. Covers the popular Abacos.
- ❑ $99.00 CARIBBEAN YACHTING CHARTS -- The Windward Islands and the Lower Leeward Islands -- 2 seperate sets. These charts are coordinated with Chris Doyle's Guides. 6 charts per set (printed both sides). price per set.
- ❑ $29.95 VIDEOS FROM CHRIS DOYLE -- CRUISING THE NORTHERN LEEWARDS -- SAILING THE WINDWARD ISLANDS -- ISLAND PORTRAITS: ST. VINCENT AND THE GRENADINES -- TRINIDAD AND TOBAGO -- Four separate videos featuring these popular cruising spots (price per video)
- ❑ $14.95 THE NATURE OF THE ISLANDS: PLANTS & ANIMALS OF THE EASTERN CARIBBEAN by Virginia Barlow (a Chris Doyle guide).
- ❑ $22.50 AT ANY COST: LOVE, LIFE AND DEATH AT SEA (hardcover). By Peter Tangvald:thrilling autobiography of a cruising sailor whose primary home for 50 years was a 49' handcrafted wooden sailboat.

- ❑ $14.95 RESTAURANT AND RECIPE BOOKS -- Fo... separate books to the Leewards, the Virgin islands, Puerto Rico and Chesapeake Bay. Color photographs and easy to follow recipes. (Price per book)
- ❑ $12.95 BAHAMA MAMA COOKBOOK. Authentic Bahamian recipes
- ❑ $14.95 SHIP TO SHORE (680 recipes and cooking hints from Caribbean charter yacht chefs.) compiled by Cpt. Jan Robinson.
- ❑ $14.95 SEA TO SHORE (280 seafood recipes and cooking hints.)
- ❑ $14.95 SWEET TO SHORE (Robinson's ultimate dessert collection).
- ❑ $10.95 SIP TO SHORE (Robinson's cocktails and hors d'oeuvres collection).
- ❑ $11.95 CARIBBEAN ADVENTURES -- Classic Cajun cooking and tales from the reign of pirates. More than 100 Cajun style recipes.
- ❑ $12.00 CALENDAR: THE BRITISH VIRGIN ISLANDS. Photography by Dougal Thornton (New year available in October of preceding year).
- ❑ $4.50 CLEAR, WATERPROOF, HEAVY DUTY PLASTIC ZIPLOCK CRUISING GUIDE COVER Holds cruising guides open and dry leaving hands free for sailing. Grease pencil included.

WATERPROOF CHARTS

- ❑ $18.95 CARIBBEAN SEA AND GULF OF MEXICO
- ❑ $18.95 U.S. & BRITISH VIRGIN ISLANDS
- ❑ $18.95 BRITISH VIRGIN ISLANDS
- ❑ $18.95 UPPER FLORIDA KEYS
- ❑ $18.95 LOWER FLORIDA KEYS
- ❑ $ 8.50 CLEAR, WATERPROOF, REUSABLE PLASTIC STORAGE TUBE

CALL FOR A COMPLETE CATALOG

(For orders only, call 1-800-330-95... or 1-888-330-9542).

ORDER FORM VISA MasterCard DISCOVER

To order, check the appropriate box(es), fill out coupon and send check or money order to: Cruising Guide Publications, P.O. Box 1017, Dunedin, FL 34697-1017. Florida residents add 7% sales tax. See schedule for shipping charges. All books are shipped via UPS within 10 days of receipt of order.

SHIPPING & HANDLING:

	U.S./Terr.	Canada	Other
Up to $15.00	$3.50	$5.50	$7.00
15.01-30.00	4.95	6.95	9.90
30.01-40.00	6.75	8.75	13.50
40.01-50.00	7.75	9.75	15.50
50.01-75.00	8.75	10.75	17.50
Over 75.00	9.75	11.75	19.50

Additional Address Add $3.25.

$ ________ Total Merchandise

$ ________ Sales Tax 7% (Florida residents only)

$ ________ Shipping & Handling

$ ________ Total Enclosed

Name ________________________

Address ________________________

City ____________ State ________ Zip ________

Daytime telephone (______) ________________________

(Prices subject to change without no...